AF531073

ART OF THE OKLAHOMA STATE CAPITOL

THE SENATE COLLECTION

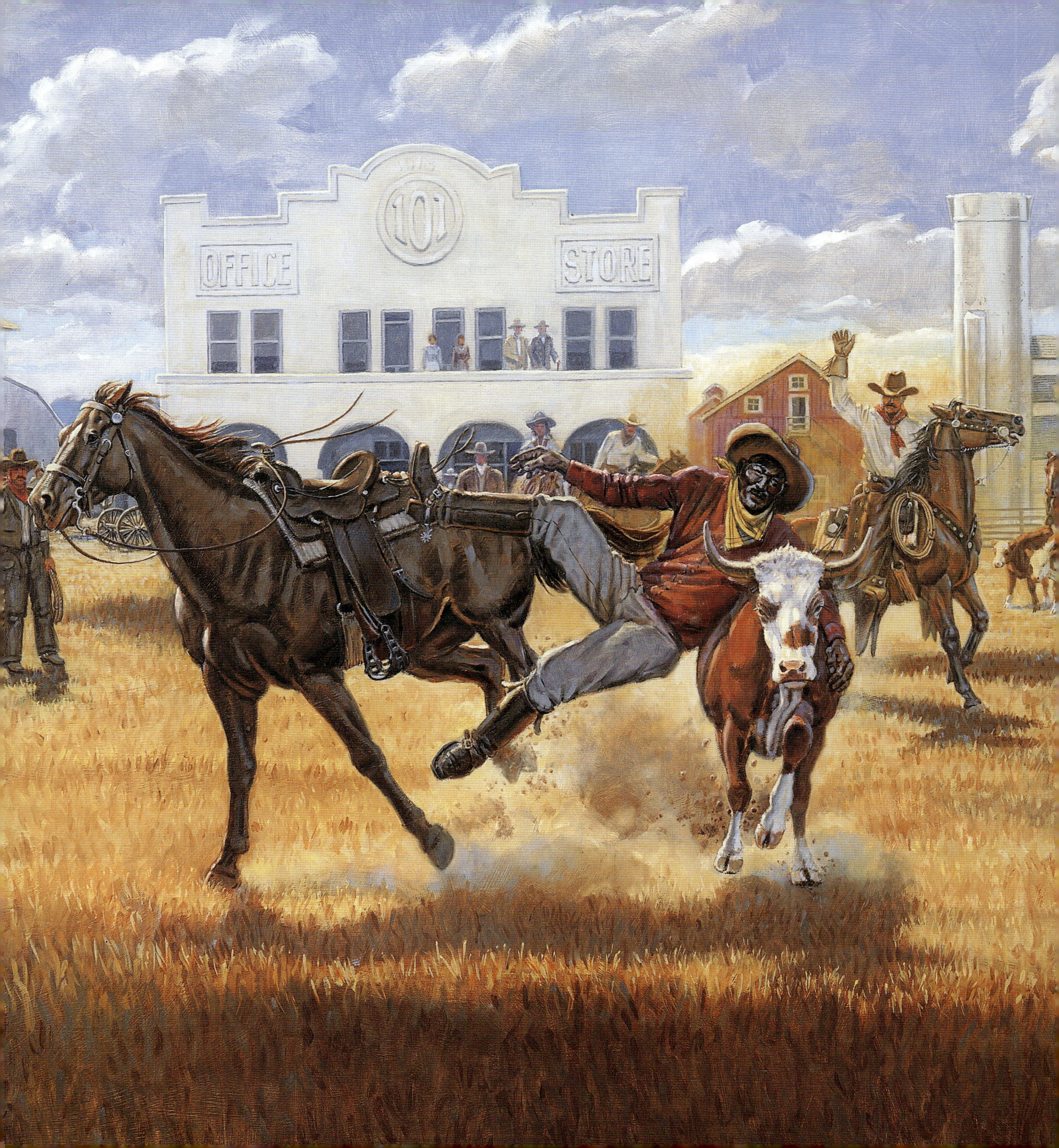
101
OFFICE
STORE

ART OF THE OKLAHOMA STATE CAPITOL

The Senate Collection

BY BOB BURKE

PREFACE BY FRANK KEATING

INTRODUCTION BY DUANE H. KING, PH.D.

THE OKLAHOMA STATE SENATE HISTORICAL PRESERVATION FUND, INC.

IN CONJUNCTION WITH GILCREASE MUSEUM

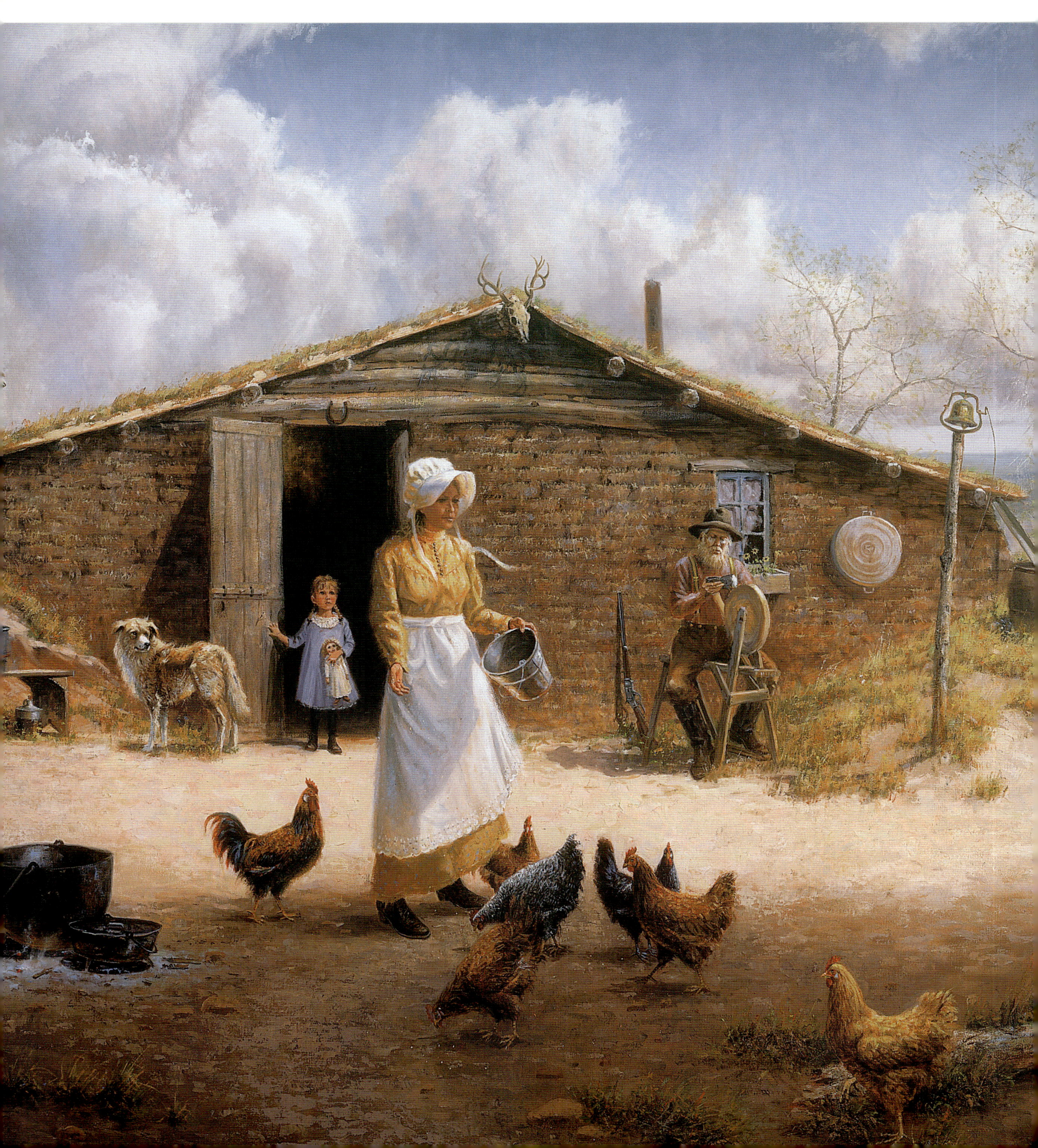

INTRODUCTION: A PERSPECTIVE ON THE ART OF THE OKLAHOMA STATE CAPITOL

IF OKLAHOMA'S IDENTITY could be defined by art, one would only have to look as far as the collection of the Oklahoma State Capitol. Throughout the years, the collection has increased dramatically, beginning in the 1920s with oilman Frank Phillips, who commissioned paintings to memorialize the history of the state. In the 1960s, portraits of Jim Thorpe, Will Rogers, Robert S. Kerr, and Sequoyah were added to the fourth floor rotunda.

The quantum leap forward in creating an artistic legacy for the Oklahoma State Capitol came under the leadership of state legislator Charles R. Ford of Tulsa. When Ford was first elected to the Oklahoma House of Representatives in 1966, he recognized a great need for preserving the character and history of Oklahoma through art. Ford served 14 years in the House before being elected to the Senate in 1980. Over the years, he became increasingly interested in connecting the aesthetic value of art with the progressive goals of education. He wanted visitors to enjoy the state capitol as a significant building, but also to take away from it a greater appreciation of Oklahoma's heritage. By the 1990s there was general agreement that the capitol should not only be a gathering place but an icon of Oklahoma. In 1994, the senate chamber was restored to its original grandeur. Under Ford's guidance, the Senate and House Lounges were also restored.

As both an elected official and a private citizen, Charles R. Ford worked to enhance the public's understanding of art's importance in personal and collective identity. *Art of the Oklahoma State Capitol: The Senate Collection* inspires pride in the rich heritage of the state and tells a story about the history, diversity, and traditions woven into the cultural fabric of Oklahoma.

Portraits of famous Oklahomans such as Will Rogers by Boris Gordon and Sam Walton by Mike Wimmer remind us of the national and international influence that started here. Landscapes such as Wayne Cooper's image of the tallgrass prairie and Barbara Vaupel's scene of elk grazing in the Wichita Mountains illuminate the natural beauty of the state. Depictions such as *Oklahoma City–April 29, 1889* by Wayne Cooper and *The 45th Division at Pork Chop Hill, Korea (1952)* by R. T. Foster capture poignant moments in history impacted by Oklahomans.

More than 100 works of art grace the walls and the grounds of the state capitol. From bronze sculptures to magnificent murals, portraits, and landscapes, the art brings a vibrancy and energy to the capitol, transcending regional and ethnic diversity. Historical references and notable individuals are frozen in time through the art collection. Together they form an invaluable resource for anyone interested in the study of Oklahoma history and character.

Gilcrease Museum is pleased to bring this unique body of work to Tulsa, where the pride and inspiration with which it is suffused can touch a broad and welcoming audience.

DUANE H. KING, PH.D.
Vice President for Museum Affairs, Thomas Gilcrease Chair, The University of Tulsa, and Executive Director, Gilcrease Museum

Preserving History through Art

FOR THE FIRST FEW DECADES AFTER it was occupied in 1917 the Oklahoma State Capitol contained very little fine art. Oklahoma was a poor agrarian state and not committed to spending public money on embellishment. Instead, early Oklahoma history and its leading people were memorialized on capitol walls in photographs and inexpensive prints.

Oilman Frank Phillips funded paintings to be placed in the capitol in the 1920s, and portraits of Sequoyah, Robert S. Kerr, Jim Thorpe, and Will Rogers were added to the fourth floor rotunda in the 1960s. In the following two decades, a few other murals, portraits, and landscapes were added, largely due to the efforts of the Oklahoma Arts and Humanities Council and the Capitol Preservation Commission.

When Charles Ford became a member of the Oklahoma House of Representatives in 1966 he found little interest among members of the legislature in the commissioning of paintings for the capitol. He also discovered that much of the architectural integrity of the capitol had been destroyed by renovations. As he gained seniority, Ford supported efforts by the Arts and Humanities Council and Chief Clerk Richard Huddleston to assist the Oklahoma House of Representatives in renovation of its chamber. The result was the hiring of Paul B. Meyer as capitol architect to help with the endeavor. Four new conference rooms were added to the chambers of the House during the renovation. The Oklahoma State Senate also added four new conference rooms.

Long before Ford was elected to the legislature, he had begun giving back to the community. A native Tulsan and real estate investment broker, he had attended Oklahoma A & M, now Oklahoma State University, served 12 years on the Tulsa State Fair Board and five years on the Tulsa Metropolitan Planning Commission, and had held many offices, including state president, national vice president, and international vice president of the U. S. Junior Chamber of Commerce (Jaycees). Along the way, Ford married Patricia Ojers. They have four children—Christopher, Roger, Karin, and Robyn.

Ford served 14 years in the Oklahoma House of Representatives before being elected to the Oklahoma State Senate in 1980. With his legislative experience, and the hiring of Meyer as capitol architect, there was momentum to change the look of the capitol. Legislative halls saw significant change in 1994 when the Senate Chamber was restored to its original grandeur. Under Ford's supervision, the Senate Lounge and the House Lounge were also restored.

Ford, completely outside his official duties as a state senator, initiated a program in 1997 to replace prints in the Senate Lounge. He personally commissioned Oklahoma artist Wayne Cooper to paint Washington Irving's historic meeting with the Osage in 1832. When the painting was dedicated the following year, the idea of adding original art to the capitol caught on.

Ford, an art and antique collector for most of his adult life, created the Oklahoma State Senate Historical Preservation Fund, Inc., a tax-exempt corporation that could receive tax-deductible contributions to donate art to the state senate. Current members of the governing board of the Historical Preservation Fund include Senator Ford, Oklahoma Centennial Commission director Blake Wade, and Robert Rollins. Former members include Senators Stratton Taylor, Ted Fisher, Jonathan Nichols, and Johnnie Crutchfield.

Senator Charles Ford presides over the State Capitol dedication of portraits of Oklahoma's seven territorial governors.

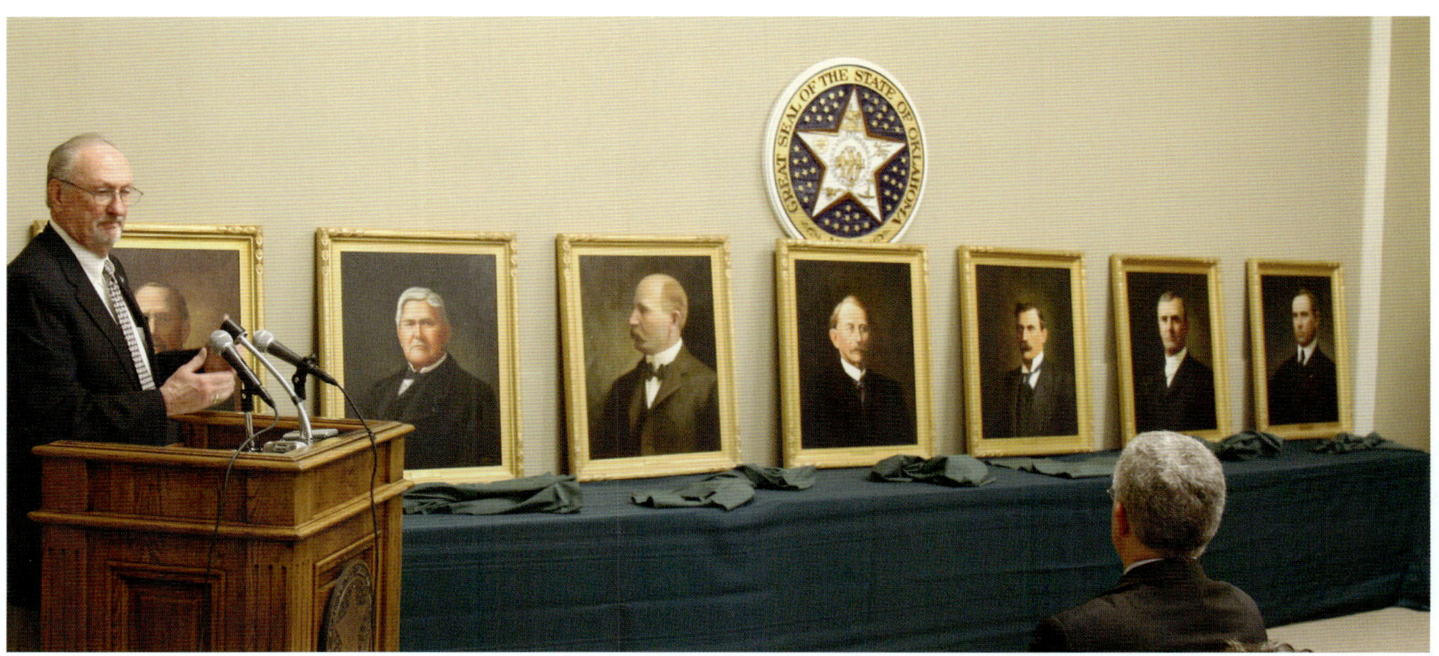

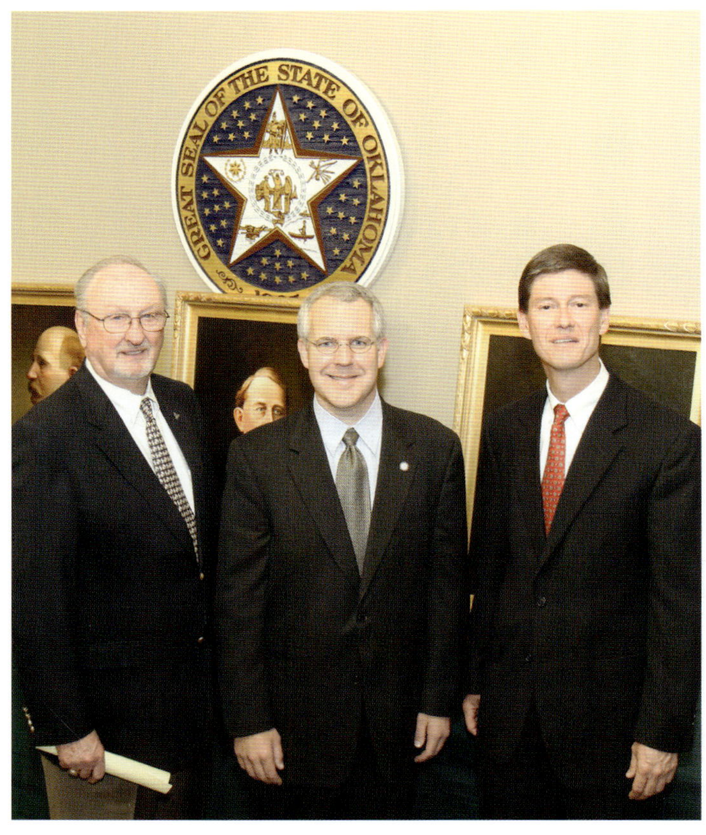

Senator Charles Ford, left, at the dedication of portraits of Oklahoma's seven territorial governors at the Oklahoma state capitol. Governor Brad Henry is at center. At right, Stuart Solomon, CEO of Public Service Company of Oklahoma.

At the beginning of the new century, more works of art were commissioned each year as legislators saw what an important difference they made in the beauty of the capitol. In 2004, Ford was forced to retire from the legislature because of the term-limit amendment to the state constitution. At the time of his retirement, he was the longest-serving member of the state legislature. He is one of two Oklahomans to serve as minority leader in both houses of the legislature. In 1988, he was named Legislator of the Year by the National Republican Legislator's Association. He authored the legislation that created the Oklahoma Centennial Commission to celebrate the state's 100th birthday and is chairman of the tax-exempt fund making the celebration possible. Ford's legislative service of 38 years is the second longest in Oklahoma history.

"The amazing thing," said former Oklahoma governor and University of Oklahoma president David L. Boren, "is that Senator Ford singlehandedly envisioned the Senate Art Collection and literally shaped it by devoting thousands of hours of volunteer time approaching potential donors who also were interested in beautifying the capitol with original art." More than $1.5 million has been raised for more than 90 works of art.

Senator Ford has been honored on many occasions for his work in developing the Senate Collection. He has received the Governor's Arts Award, was named to the Tulsa Central High School Hall of Fame, and was given special recognition by the Oklahoma Museum Association, the Oklahoma chapter of the American Institute of Architects, and the Tulsa Arts and Humanities Council. Perhaps the most significant recognition came when members of both houses of the Oklahoma legislature passed a joint resolution thanking him for adding so much beauty and history to legislative halls.

We are deeply grateful to Dr. Duane King, David Newell, and the entire staff of Gilcrease Museum for giving museum visitors the opportunity to enjoy the State Senate Fine Arts

Right: Members of the House of Representatives welcome the addition of *Arcadia Roundup* by Linda Tuma Robertson to the State Senate Art Collection. Below: Senator Ford with artist Christopher Nick.

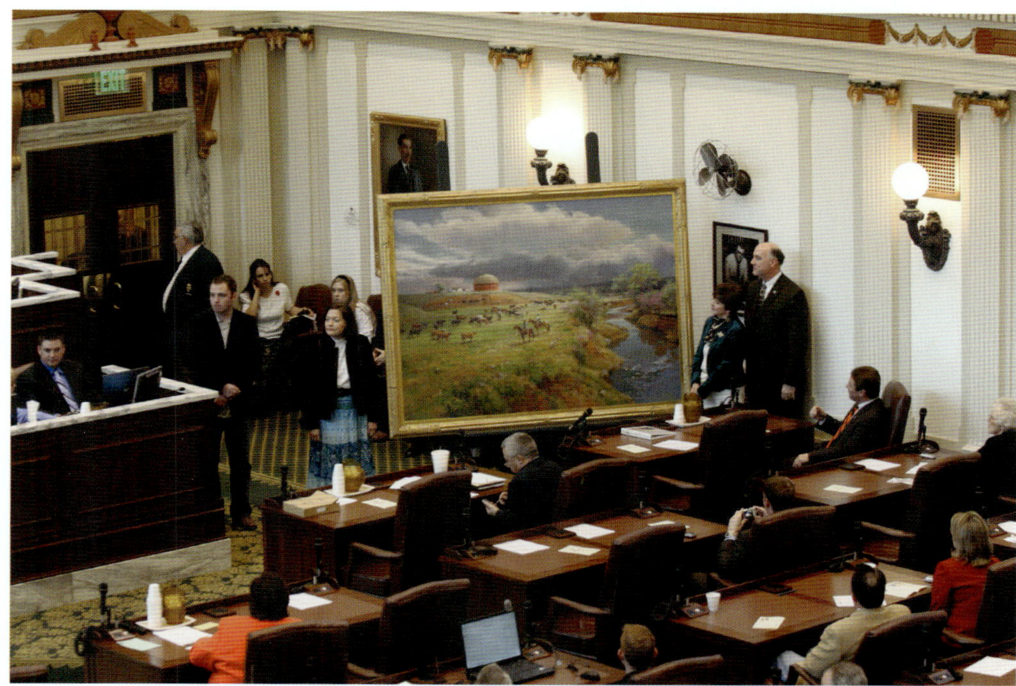

Collection, and to Randy Ramer, Carole Klein, and Kimberly Roblin of the museum's curatorial staff for their comments introducing sections of this book. Thanks to Stuart Ostler for providing photographs and to State Senate Executive Assistants Pam Hodges and Emmalou Ragsdale for editorial support. We also appreciate the creative genius of Oklahoma native Carol Haralson, who I believe is America's finest book producer.

Publication of this book was assisted through a partnership with Gilcrease Museum and through the generosity of Tom and Hillary Clark, Joe and Carol McGraw, the Stuart Family Foundation, Bert Holmes, Rob McCune, and G. T. and Libby Blankenship. Senator Ford and I express our warmest gratitude to each of them.

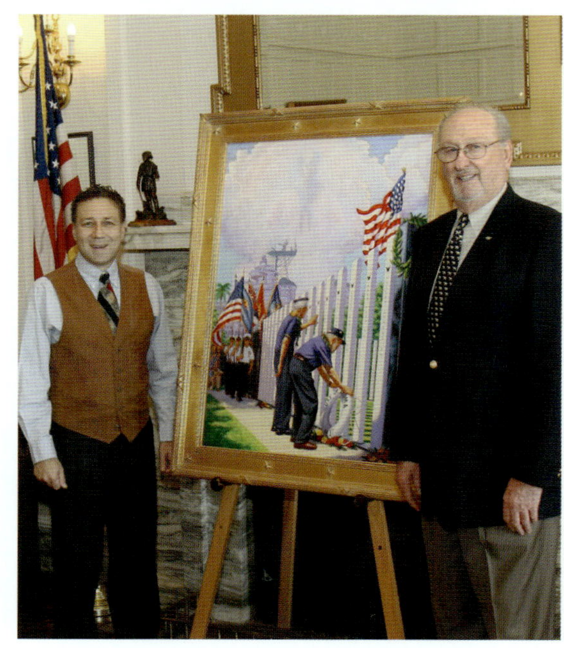

BOB BURKE

Oklahoma City, 2009

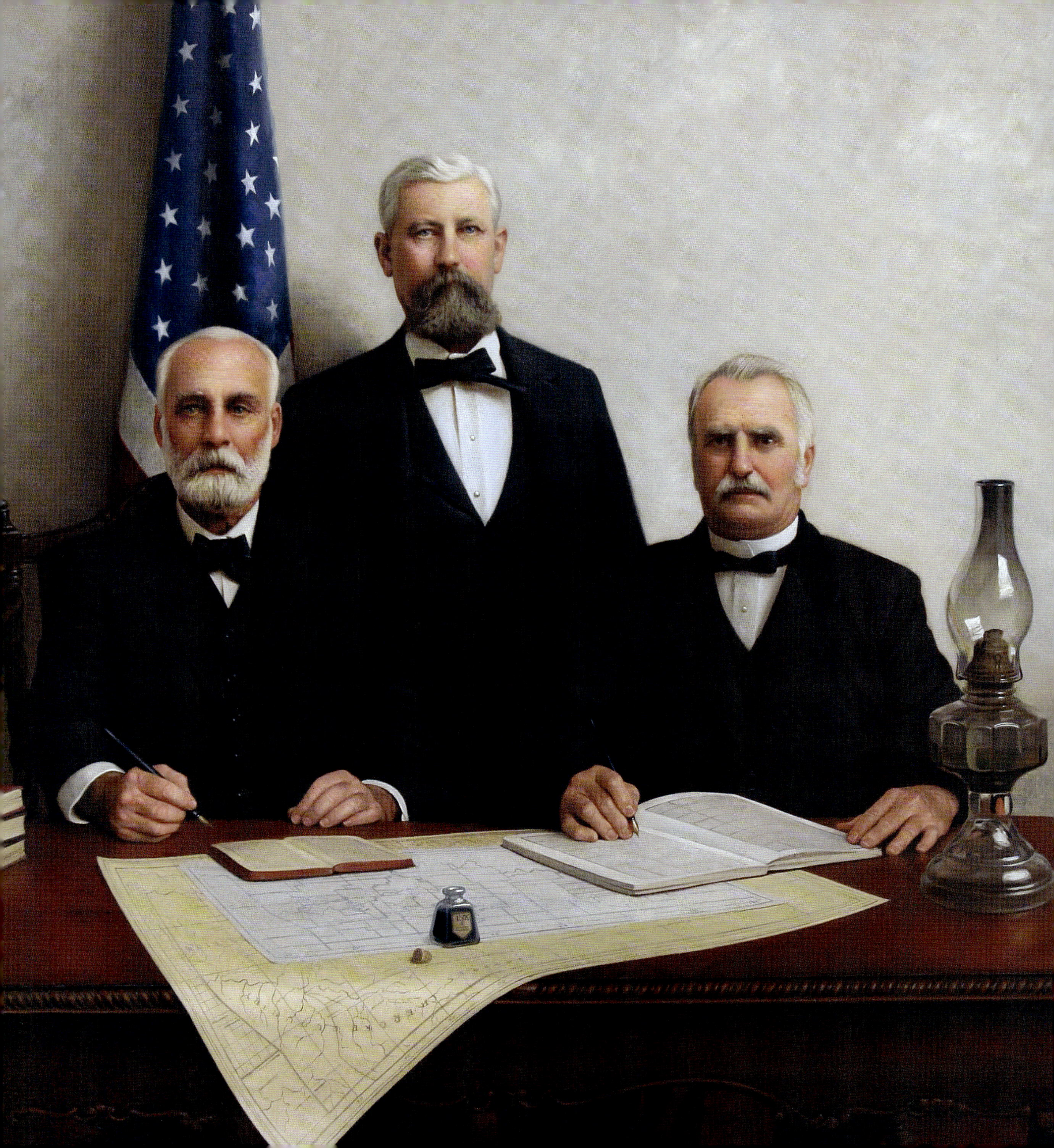

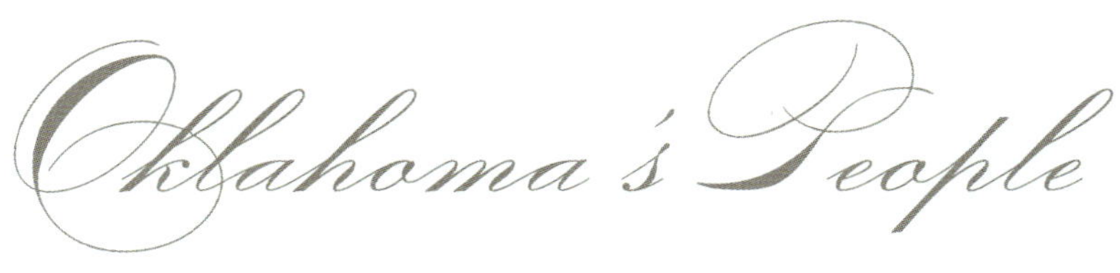

PORTRAITS

CAROLE KLEIN, Associate Curator of Art, Gilcrease Museum

A portrait can be defined as the "likeness" of an individual—that which reveals who he is and distinguishes him from another. Not only are shapes, forms, and colors important, but also aspects of an individual's nature and personality that are beneath surface appearance. A portrait also reveals something about a person's response to his circumstances and the times in which he lives. In this respect it tells of his place in history, while a group of portraits from within a society presents a larger story.

The portraits in the State Senate Fine Arts Collection reveal much about Oklahoma's history through its people. They are ordinary, yet exceptional, people who took opportunities to make contributions to the changing face of Oklahoma and to the world. The individual characters are as diverse as the Oklahoma landscape. There are political leaders, public servants, university presidents, military figures, cowboys, and more. There are those who challenged existing laws, such as segregation, and those who pushed invisible boundaries regarding jobs for women. Some brought down outlaws and others designed buildings. There is a Cherokee banker, a singer/songwriter, and a Creek poet. They are Oklahoma's people. Each made changes to life as it was known for themselves and for others. The portraits not only honor their achievements but are reminders that an individual's contribution can make a difference, creating an awareness of history as a living and continually changing process. Communities, states, countries, and the world can be impacted, influenced, changed and shaped, not only by its heroes, but by citizens from every walk of life.

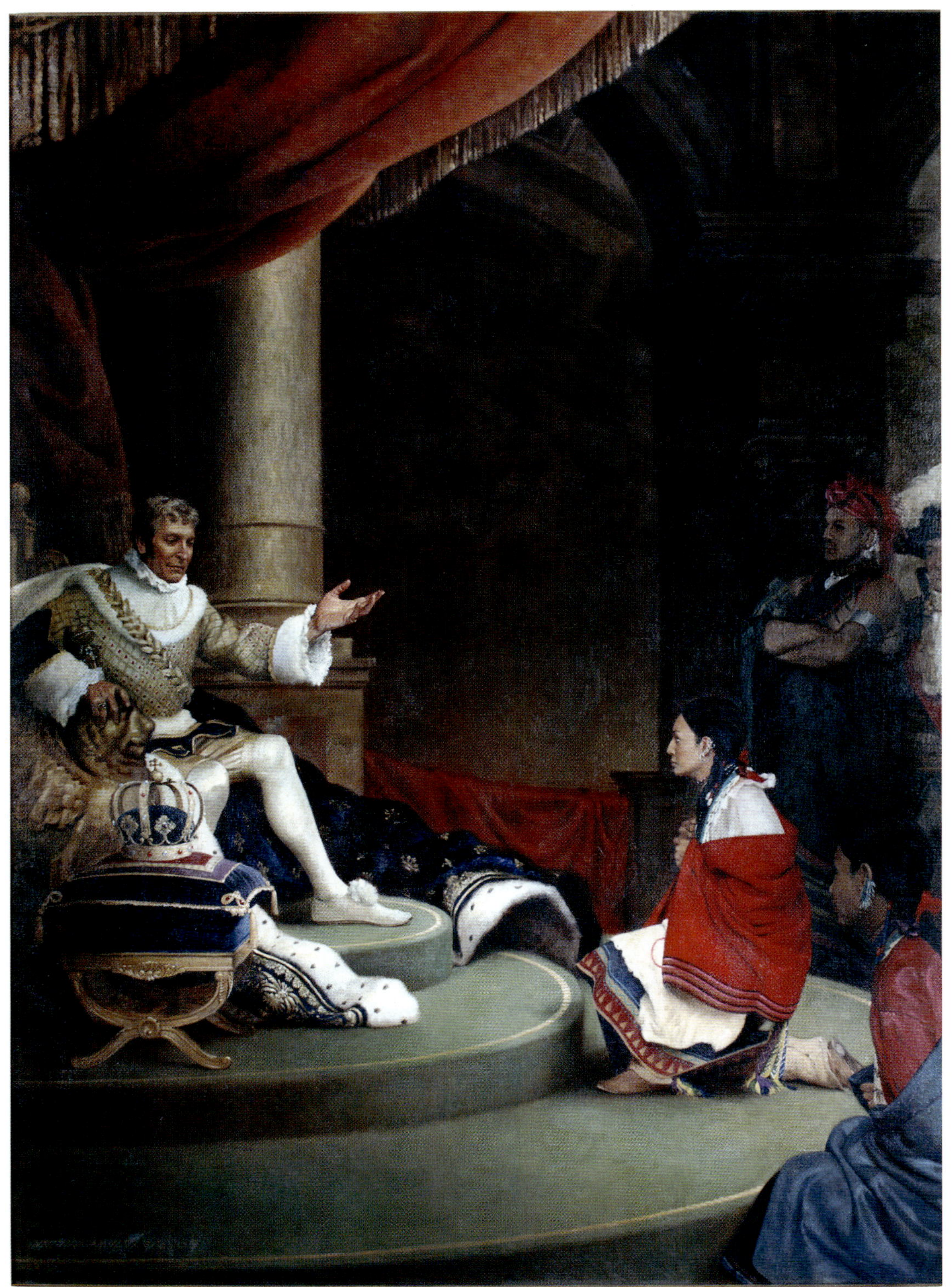

MAHONGO AT THE COURT OF CHARLES X OF FRANCE

BY MIKE WIMMER

36 x 48, oil/canvas

A beautiful Osage woman at the Chouteau camp on the Neosho River in Indian Territory, Mahongo was among a group taken to Europe under false pretenses to perform in a Wild West Show. In this painting, sponsored by State Senator Charles Ford, Mahongo appeared at the royal court of King Charles X of France. Later the Osage were abandoned on the streets of Paris. After being forced to beg for existence, they came to the attention of Marquis de Lafayette, who paid for their passage back to the United States. Mahongo was given the Peace Medal by President Andrew Jackson and was painted by Charles Bird King. King's painting hangs in the National Portrait Gallery in Washington, D. C.

NATHANIEL PRYOR AND SAM HOUSTON AT THREE FORKS

BY MIKE WIMMER

36 x 48, oil/canvas

In this painting, sponsored by State Senator Kevin Easley of Tulsa, Nathaniel Pryor and Sam Houston conduct trade on a flatboat at Three Forks, where the Neosho (Grand), Verdigris, and Arkansas Rivers converge in northeast Oklahoma. Pryor accompanied the Lewis and Clark Expedition and fought at the Battle of New Orleans. He was an explorer and trader who established an early trading post at Three Forks. Houston traded with the Indians in future Oklahoma and built a log house near Fort Gibson. Later Houston helped liberate Texas from Mexico and became the first president of the Republic of Texas. The image is displayed in the form of a giclée print, sponsored by Senator Kevin Easley, at the Mayes County Courthouse.

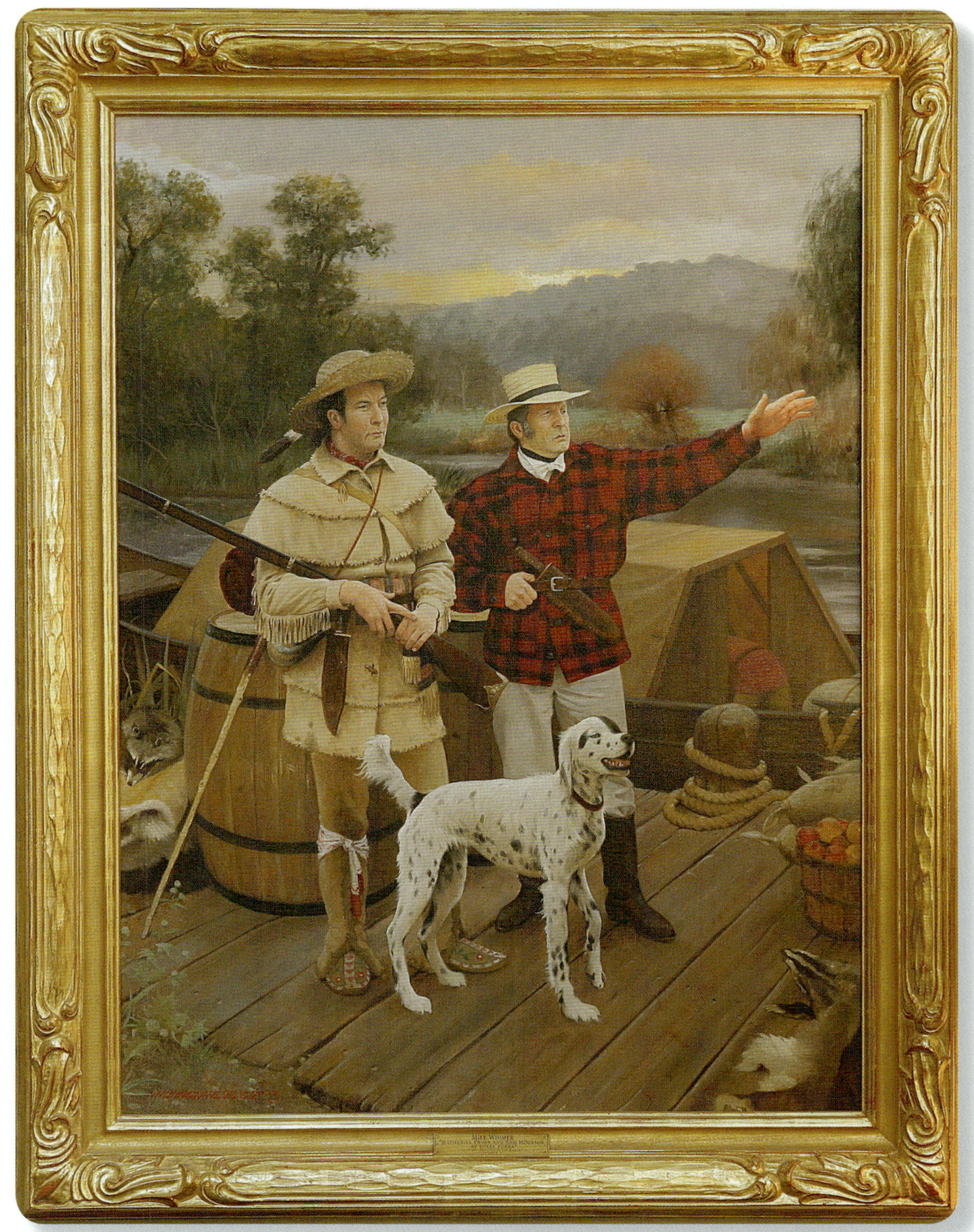

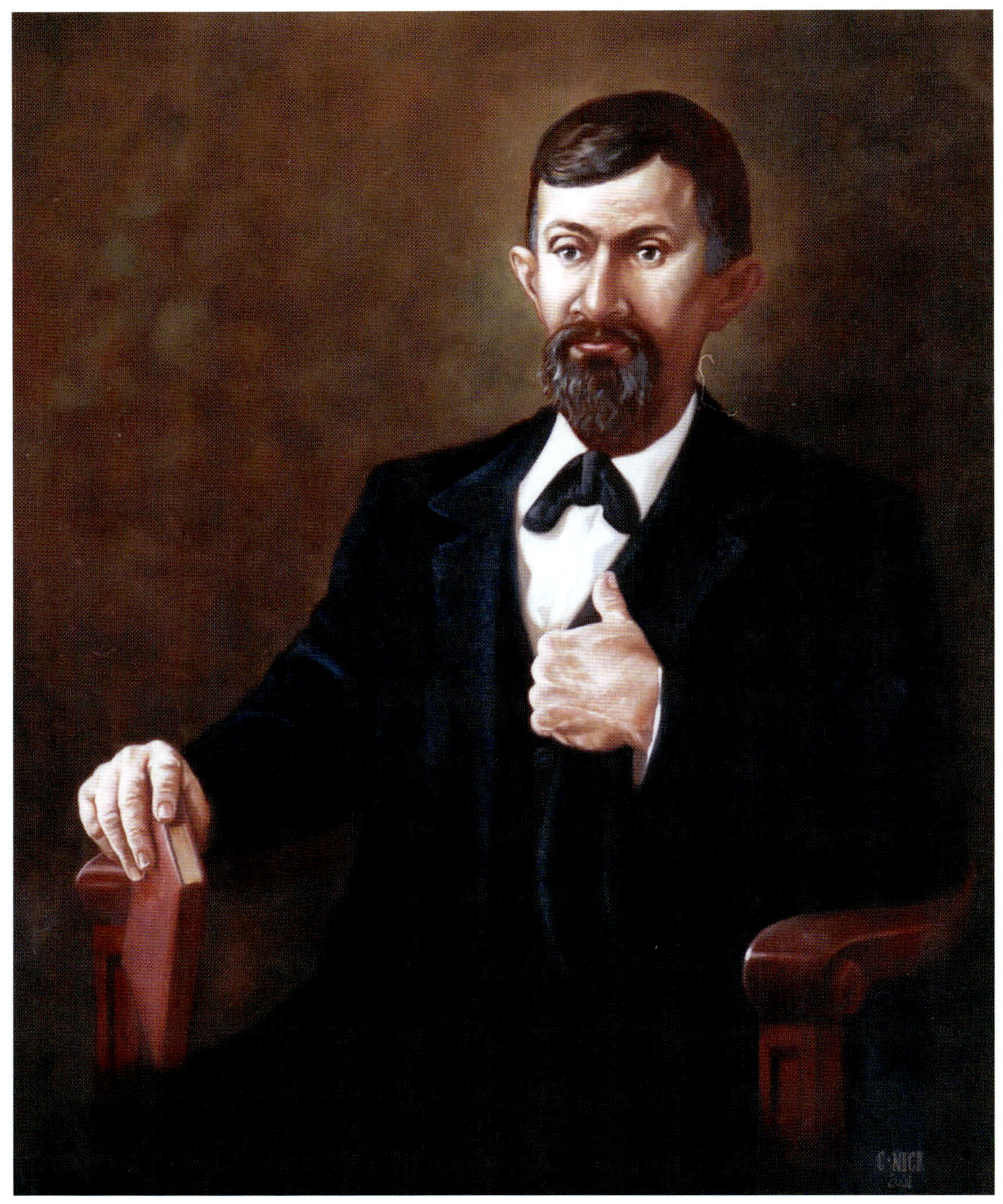

GEORGE W. GARDENHIRE

BY CHRISTOPHER NICK

30 x 36, oil /canvas

Members of the State Senate in 2001 sponsored this portrait of George W. Gardenhire, the first president of the Oklahoma Territorial Council. He was born in Tennessee and settled in Payne County, Oklahoma, in April, 1889. His most notable legislative achievement was the establishment of Oklahoma A & M College at Stillwater, although a political deal had previously been made to build the college elsewhere.

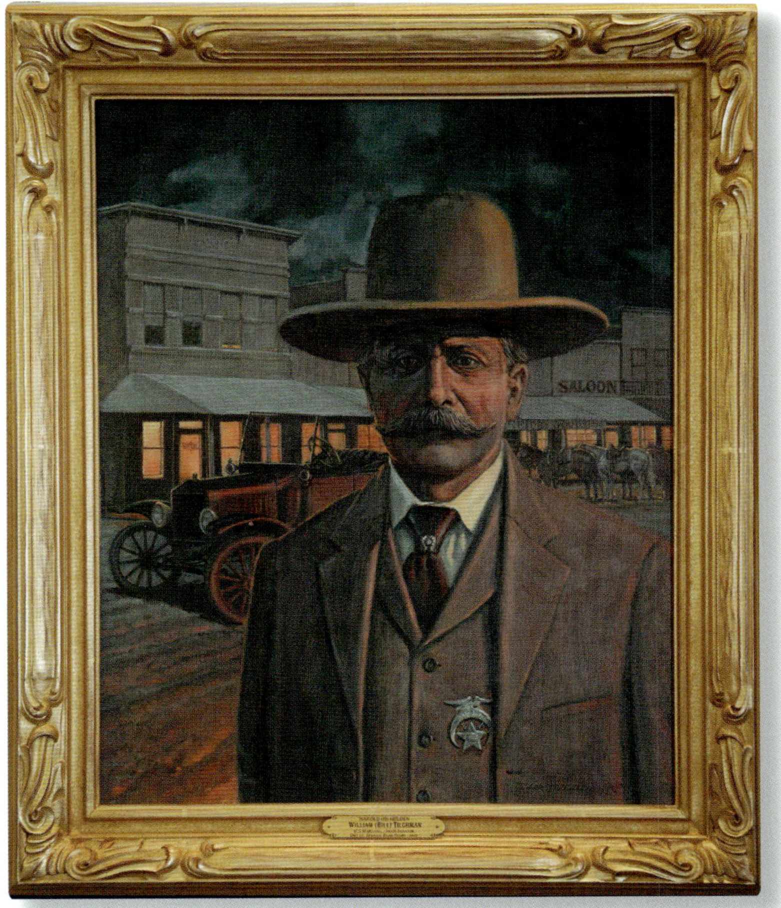

WILLIAM "BILL" TILGHMAN BY HAROLD T. HOLDEN

24 x 30, oil/canvas

A buffalo hunter, frontier scout, and peace officer, William "Bill" Tilghman came to Oklahoma in the Land Run of 1889 and settled at Guthrie. He was a deputy U. S. marshal for 19 years and was described as the "deadliest shot with a six-shooter in the Southwest." He was sheriff of Lincoln County, a member of the state senate, police chief of Oklahoma City, and tracked down members of the infamous Doolin gang. He was killed in the line of duty in 1924. Senator Brad Henry of Shawnee sponsored his portrait.

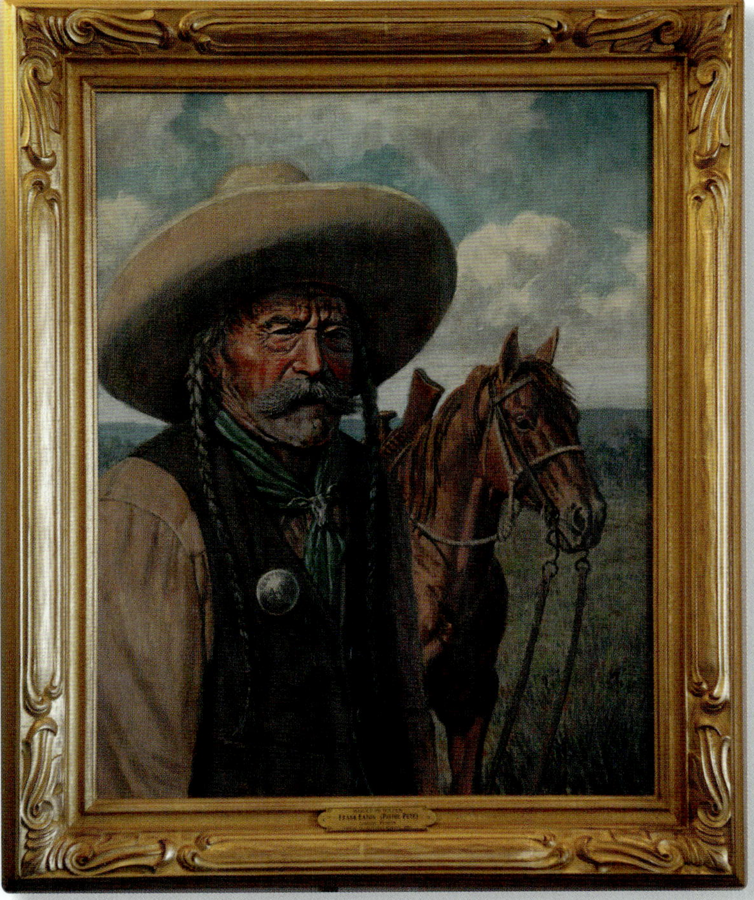

FRANK EATON ("PISTOL PETE") BY HAROLD T. HOLDEN

24 x 30, oil/canvas

Frank Eaton won the nickname "Pistol Pete" as a U. S. Cavalry marksman at Fort Gibson in Indian Territory. At age 17 he became a deputy U. S. marshal. He joined the land rush and settled near Perkins in 1889, serving as sheriff and blacksmith. Establishing a reputation as a real cowboy, Eaton was discovered by students of Oklahoma A & M College in 1923 while appearing in a Stillwater parade. He was asked to serve as the school's mascot, symbolizing the Old West and the frontier spirit of Oklahoma. Senator Mike Morgan sponsored his portrait.

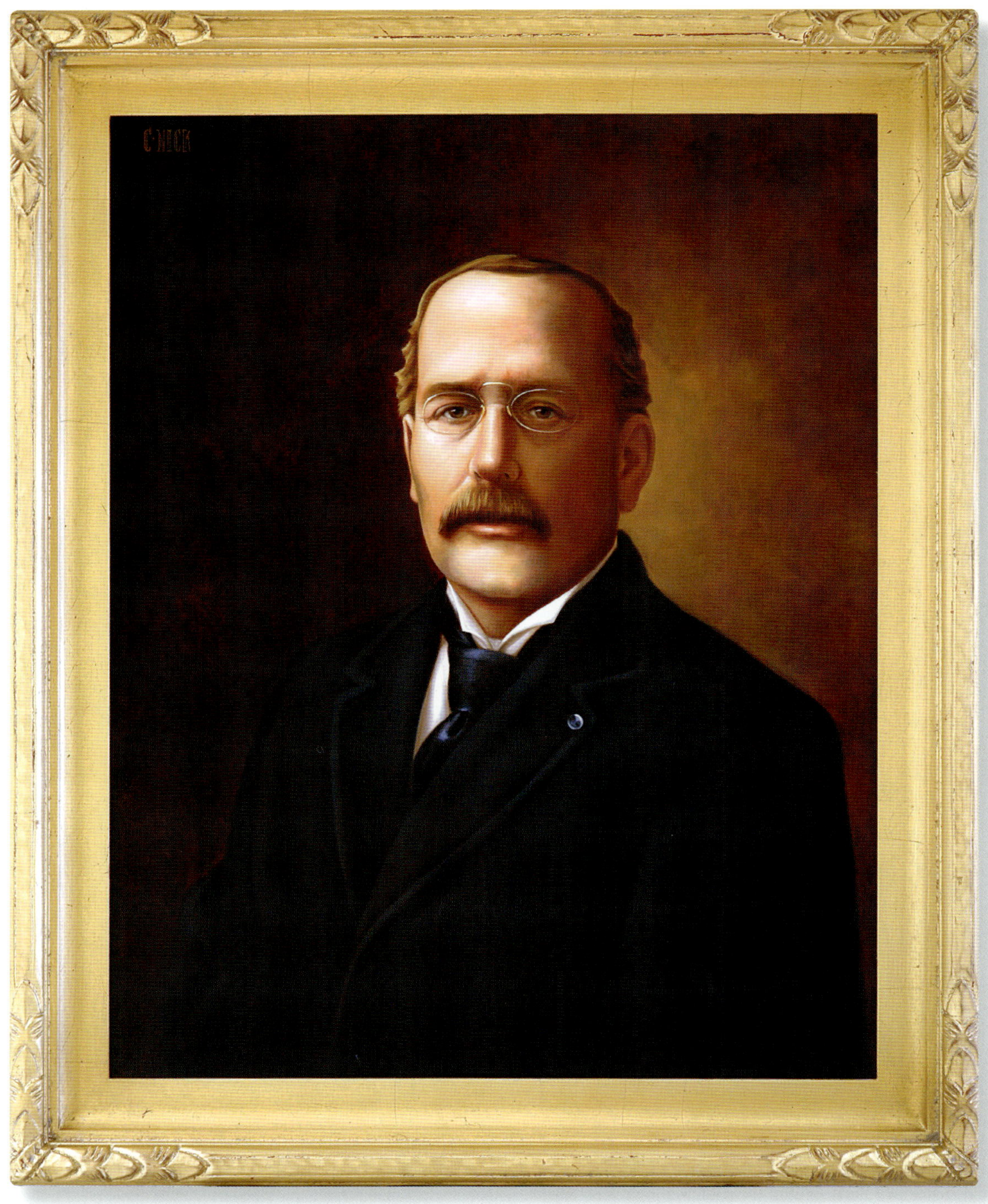

GEORGE W. STEELE

BY CHRISTOPHER NICK

24 x 30, oil/canvas

A native of Indiana, George W. Steele served in the Union Army during the Civil War and in the United States Congress before President Benjamin Harrison appointed him the first governor of Oklahoma Territory in 1890. The educational system, three colleges, and the state library were established during his term, which ended in 1891. Public Service Company of Oklahoma sponsored his portrait.

ABRAHAM J. SEAY

BY CHRISTOPHER NICK

24 x 30, oil/canvas

A colonel in the Union Army during the Civil War, Abraham J. Seay practiced law in Missouri before serving as governor of Oklahoma Territory in 1892 and 1893. He previously served as an associate justice on the Supreme Court of Oklahoma Territory. He died in 1915. His portrait was sponsored by Public Service Company of Oklahoma.

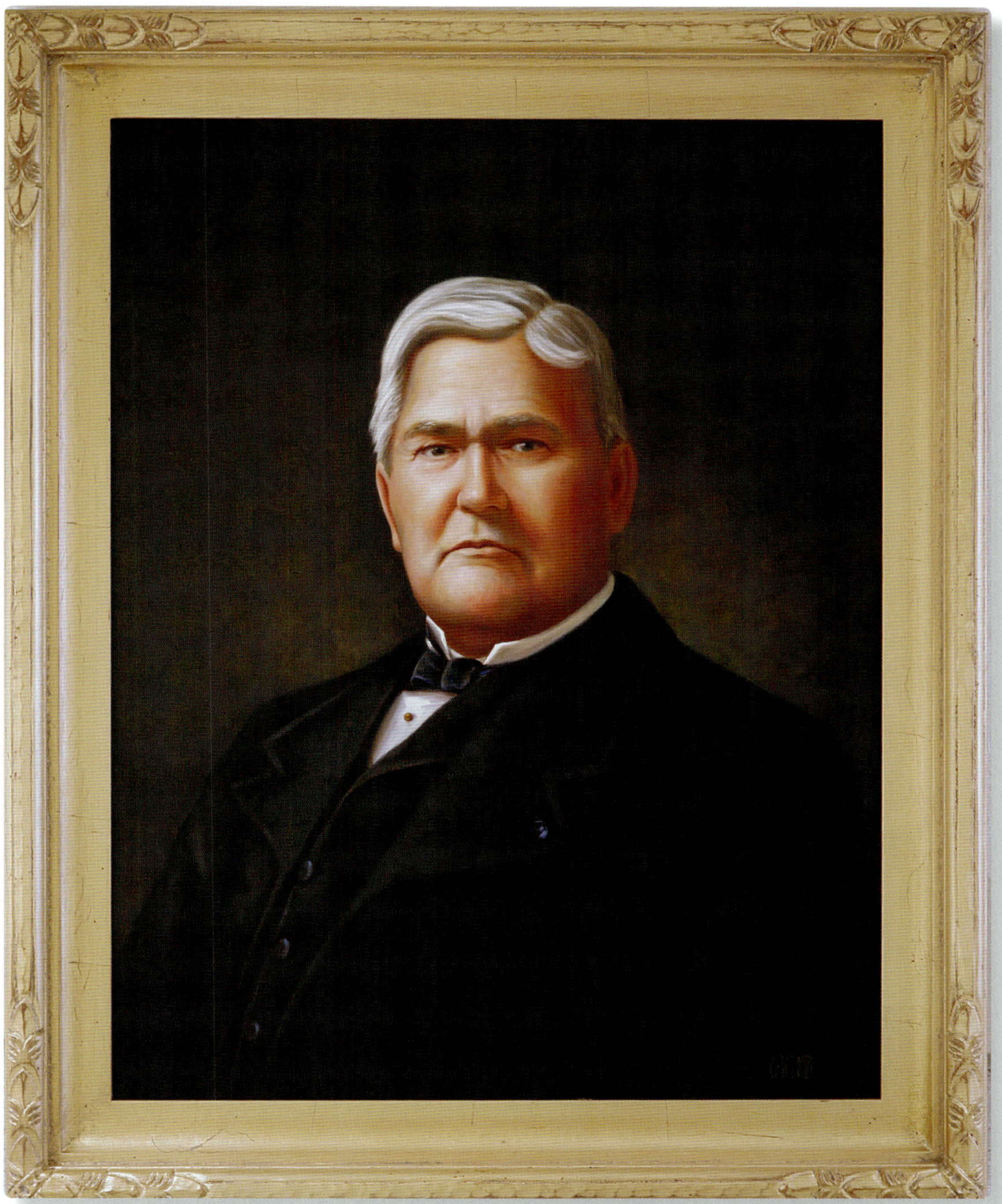

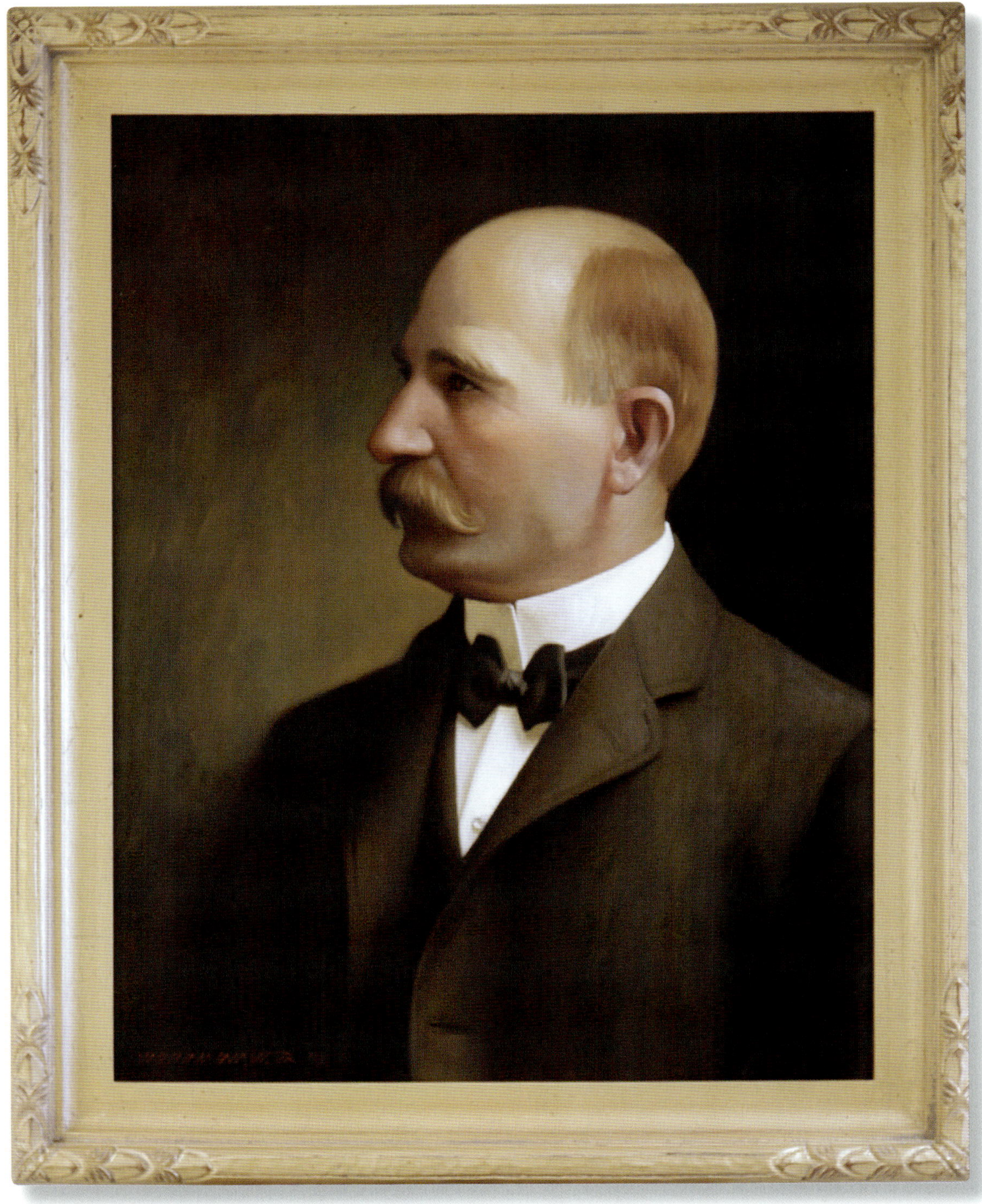

WILLIAM C. RENFROW

BY MIKE WIMMER

24 x 30, oil/canvas

Born in North Carolina, William C. Renfrow left school at age 17 to serve in the Confederate Army. After the Civil War, he was a government official in Arkansas before entering the banking business in Norman, Oklahoma. He became governor of Oklahoma Territory in 1893, the only Democrat to serve in that position. He died in 1922. His portrait was sponsored by Public Service Company of Oklahoma.

CASSIUS M. BARNES

BY TIMOTHY TYLER

24 x 30, oil/canvas

Cassius M. Barnes was born in Michigan and served in the Union Army during the Civil War. He moved to Guthrie in 1890 as receiver of the United States Land Office. He served in the third and fourth territorial legislatures and was appointed governor of Oklahoma Territory on May 24, 1897. Barnes served until 1901 and later was mayor of Guthrie. He died in New Mexico in 1925. His portrait was sponsored by Public Service Company of Oklahoma.

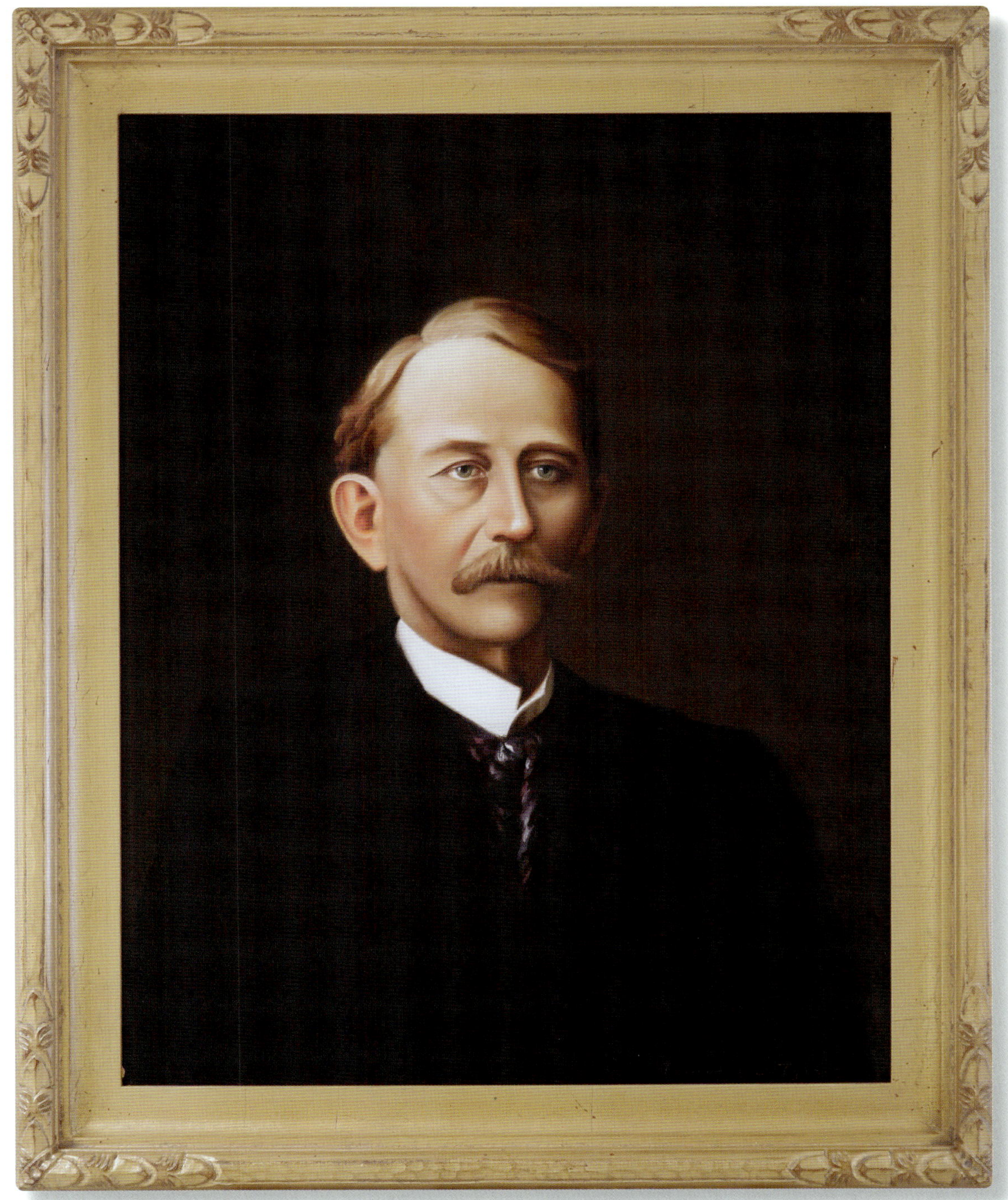

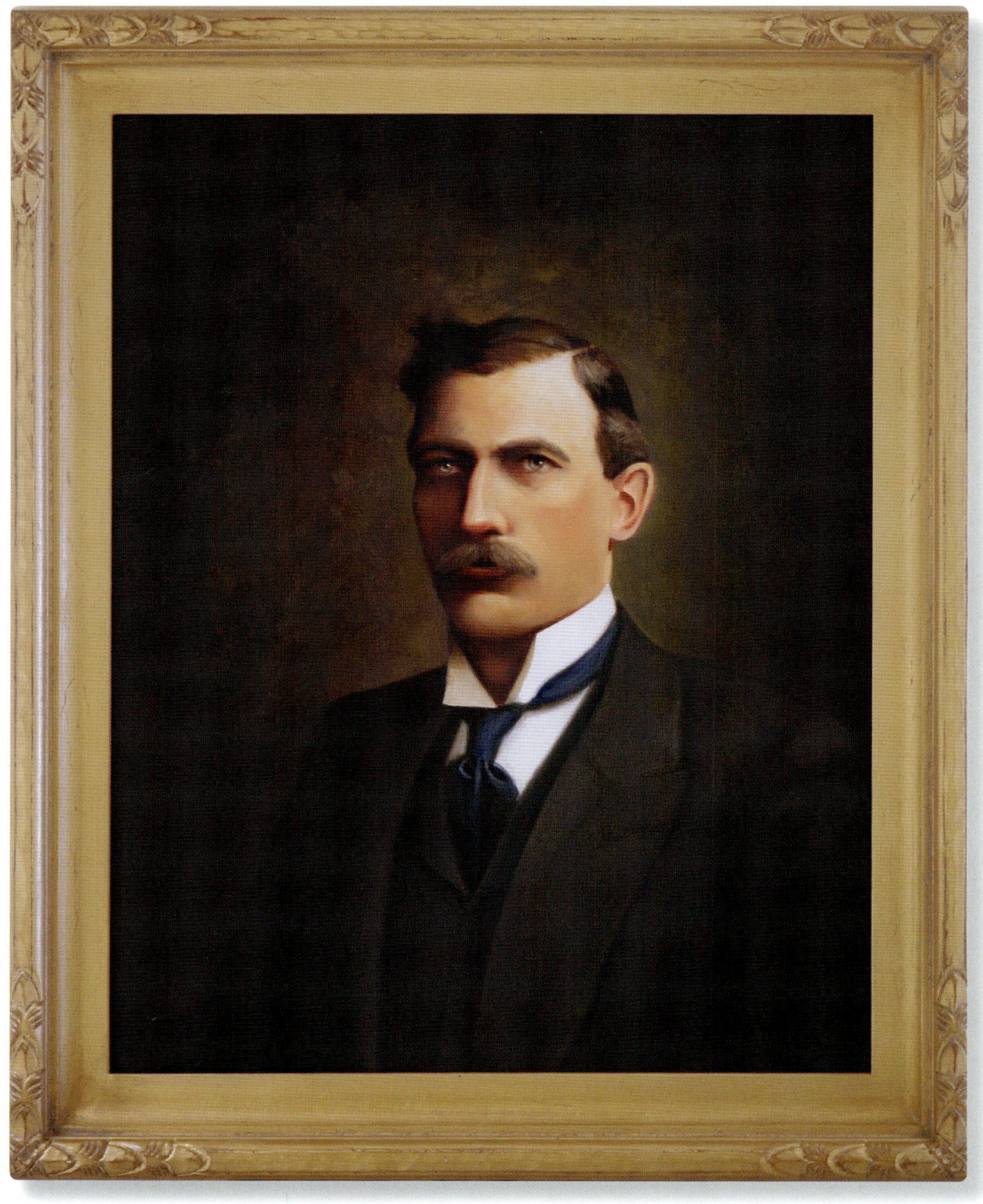

WILLIAM M. JENKINS

BY TIMOTHY TYLER

24 x 30, oil/canvas

Born in Ohio, William M. Jenkins left his law practice in Kansas to homestead in Kay County in the Cherokee Outlet. He was secretary of Oklahoma Territory before serving six months as territorial governor from May to November of 1901. He died in 1941. His portrait was sponsored by Public Service Company of Oklahoma.

THOMSON B. FERGUSON

BY MIKE WIMMER

24 x 30, oil/canvas

Thomson B. Ferguson was born in Iowa and spent his early life in Kansas as a teacher and Methodist minister. He participated in the Land Run of 1889 and secured a claim near Oklahoma City. After establishing a newspaper at Watonga, he was appointed governor of Oklahoma Territory in 1901. He served until 1906 when he returned the newspaper business and died in 1921. His portrait was sponsored by Public Service Company of Oklahoma.

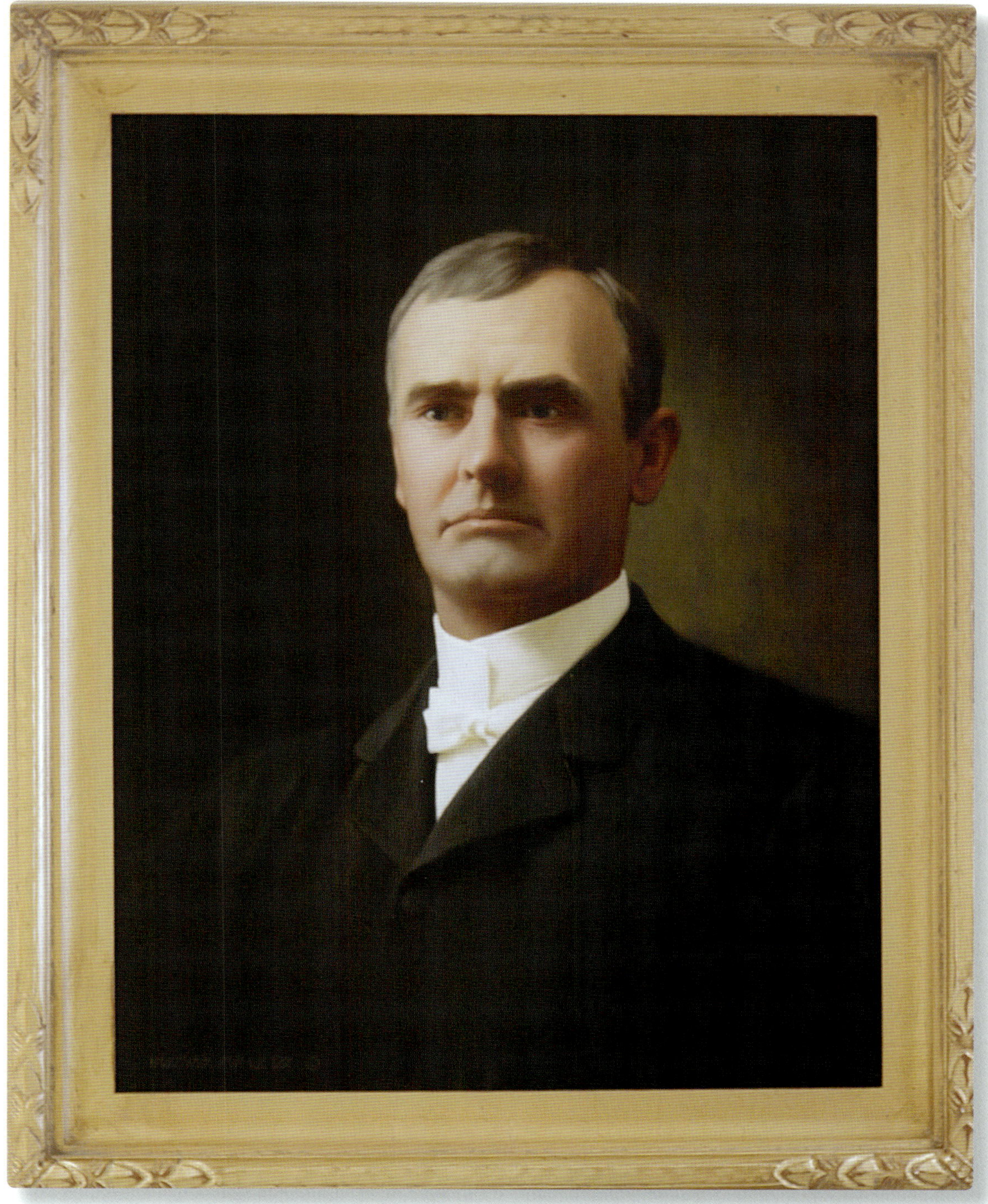

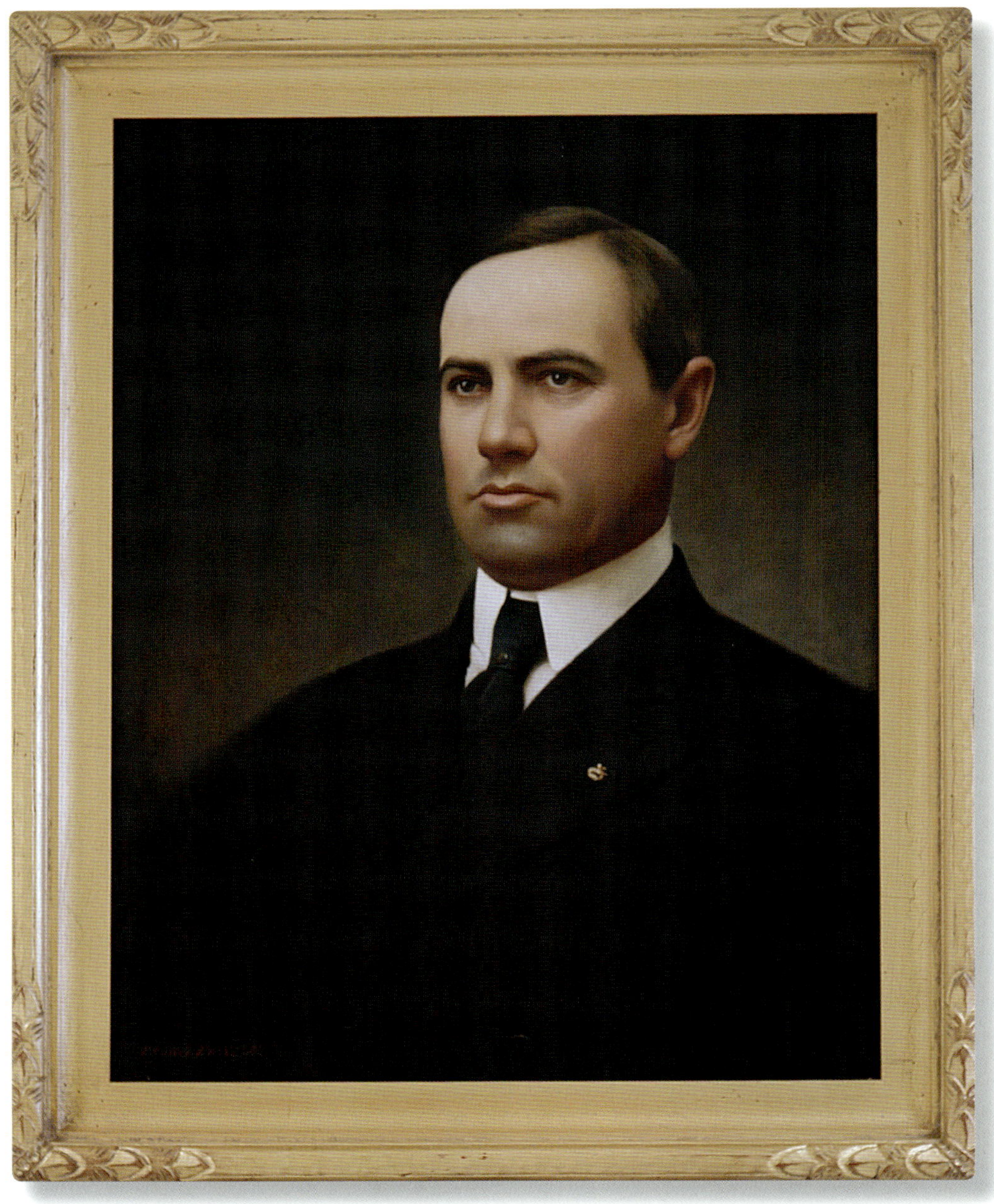

FRANK FRANTZ

BY MIKE WIMMER

24 x 30, oil/canvas

Frank Frantz arrived in the Cherokee Outlet after serving with Theodore Roosevelt's Rough Riders in the Spanish-American War. He was postmaster in Enid from 1901 to 1903 and served as Indian agent of the Osage Agency. He was governor of Oklahoma Territory from 1906 until statehood in 1907. He was an oilman until his death in 1941. Public Service Company of Oklahoma sponsored his portrait.

GREEN I. CURRIN (FACING)

BY TIMOTHY TYLER

24 x 30, oil/canvas

Green I. Currin, a Tennessee native, was the first African American to serve in the Oklahoma Territorial Legislature. He staked a claim in Kingfisher County in the Land Run of 1889. He introduced the first civil rights bill in the territorial legislature, but it was defeated. He later served as a deputy U. S. marshal and as a member of the Board of Regents of Langston University. He died in 1918. Mr. and Mrs. Russell Perry of Oklahoma City sponsored his portrait.

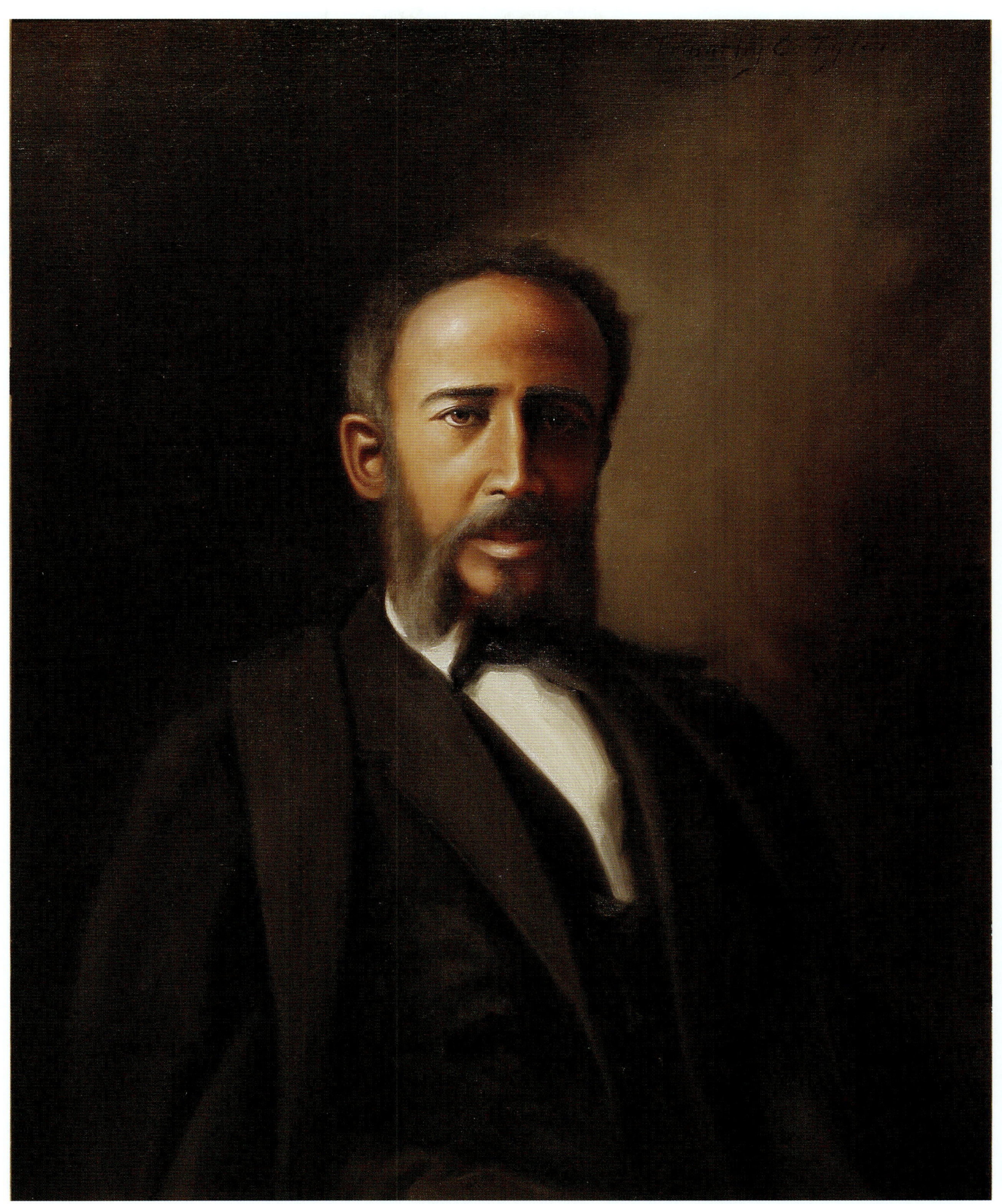

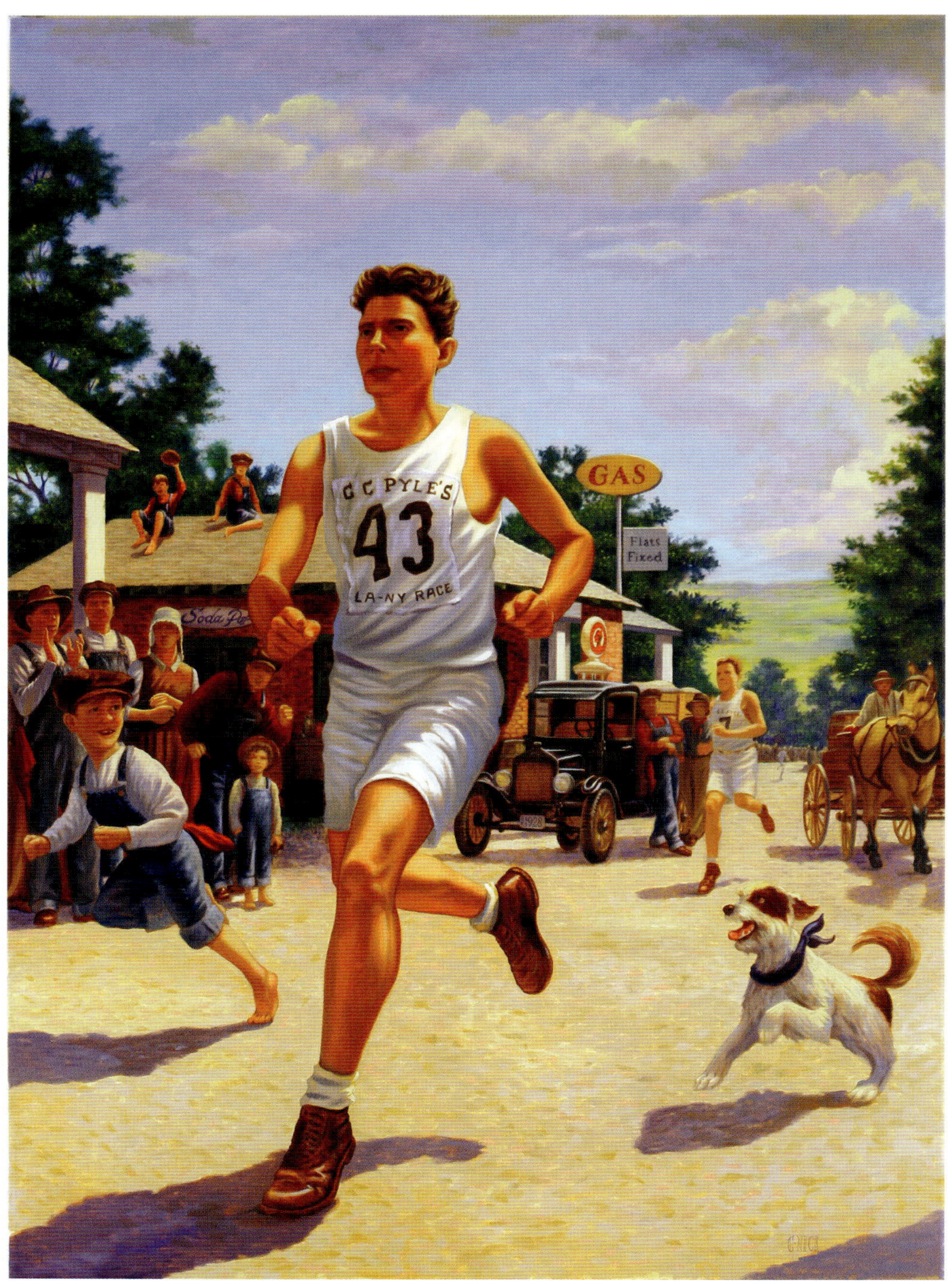

ANDY PAYNE

BY CHRISTOPHER NICK

33 x 42, oil/canvas

In 1928, Andy Payne, a Cherokee from Foyil, Oklahoma, entered the Bunion Derby, a footrace run from California to New York. Payne won the 84-day competition and its $25,000 prize. Later, Payne served many years as clerk of the Oklahoma Supreme Court. His portrait was sponsored by his family.

DAVID ROSS BOYD

BY MIKE WIMMER

30 x 40, oil/canvas

David Ross Boyd arrived in Norman as the first president of the University of Oklahoma in 1892 and was greeted by a campus with no buildings and no trees. The following year, the Ohio native began planting trees and oversaw construction of OU's first building. Boyd was university president until 1908. He later established schools in the Southwest for the Presbyterian Church and was president of the University of New Mexico. He died in 1936. President Boyd's portrait was sponsored by University of Oklahoma President David Boren, First Lady Molly Shi Boren, and Senator Cal Hobson.

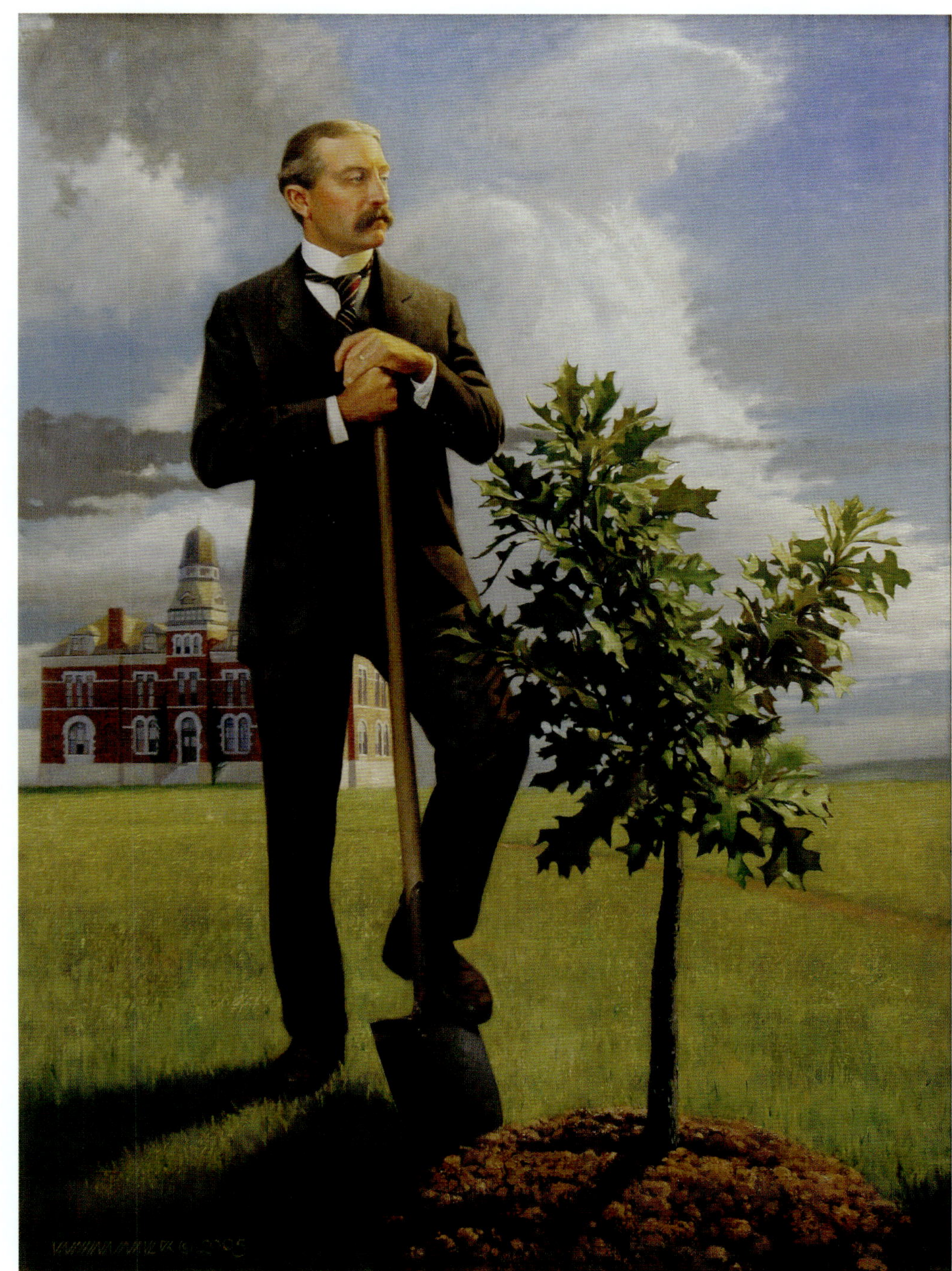

ADA LOIS SIPUEL FISHER

BY MIKE WIMMER

40 x 30, oil/canvas

Ada Lois Sipuel Fisher of Chickasha, Oklahoma, was the plaintiff in historic litigation that challenged Oklahoma's segregation laws. When she was denied admission to the University of Oklahoma College of Law because of race, a lawsuit was filed. The United States Supreme Court swiftly ordered Oklahoma to provide Fisher a legal education as it did for white students. Fisher was represented by attorneys Amos T. Hall of Tulsa and Thurgood Marshall of the NAACP. Marshall later became the first African American appointed to the U. S. Supreme Court. Fisher completed law school. In 1992, 45 years after she was denied admission to the OU law school, she was appointed by Governor David Walters to the OU Board of Regents. The painting was sponsored by Senator Penny Williams of Tulsa.

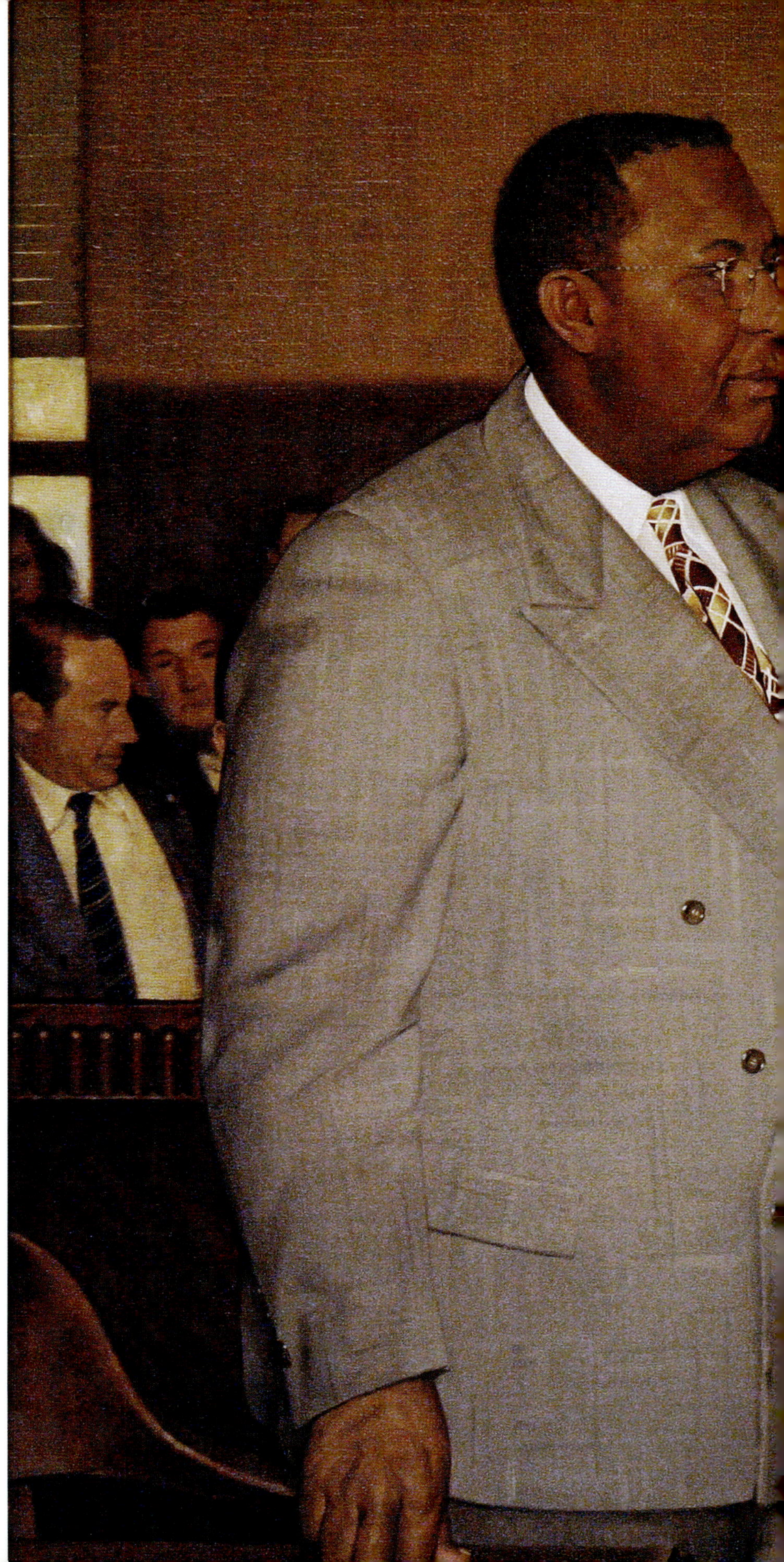

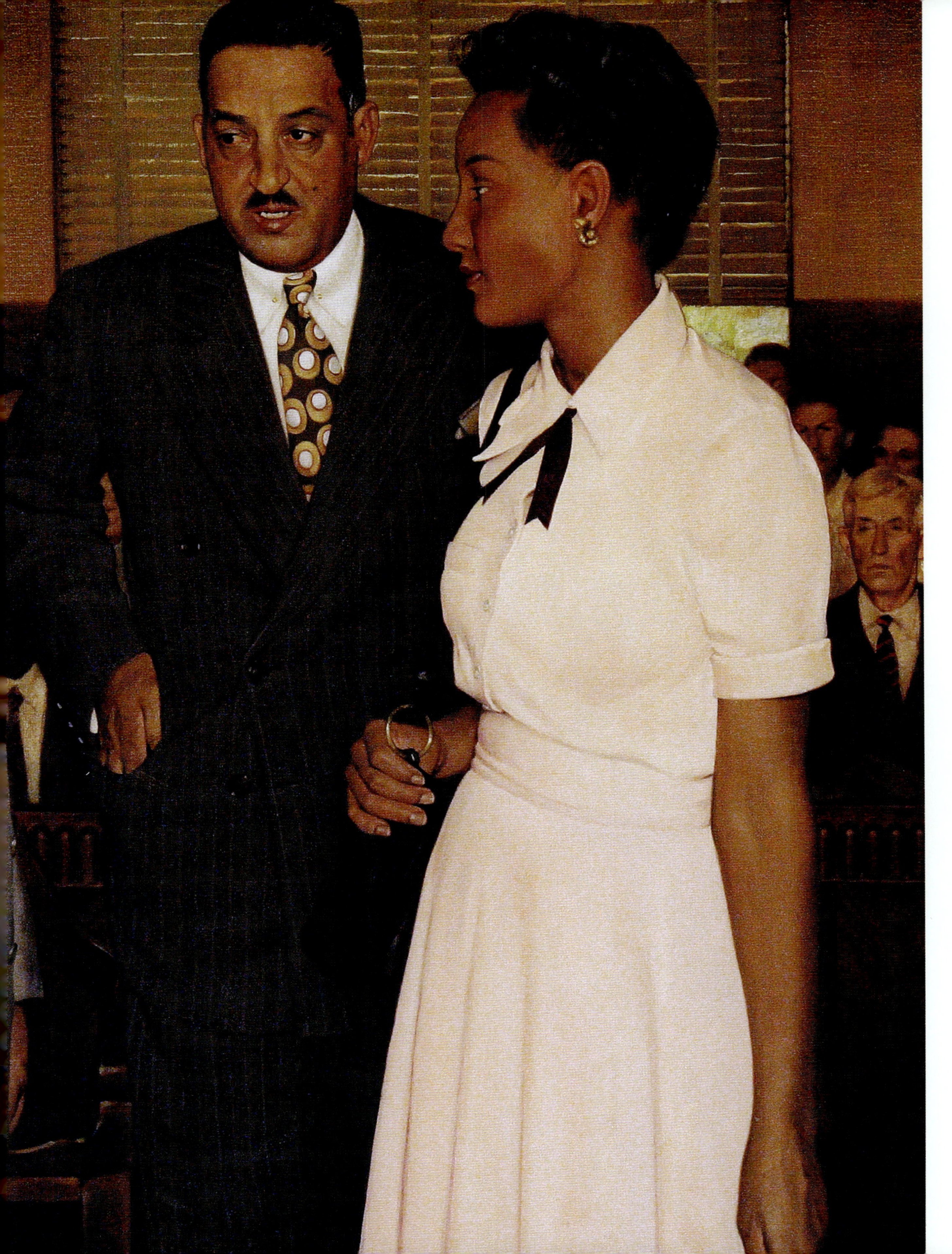

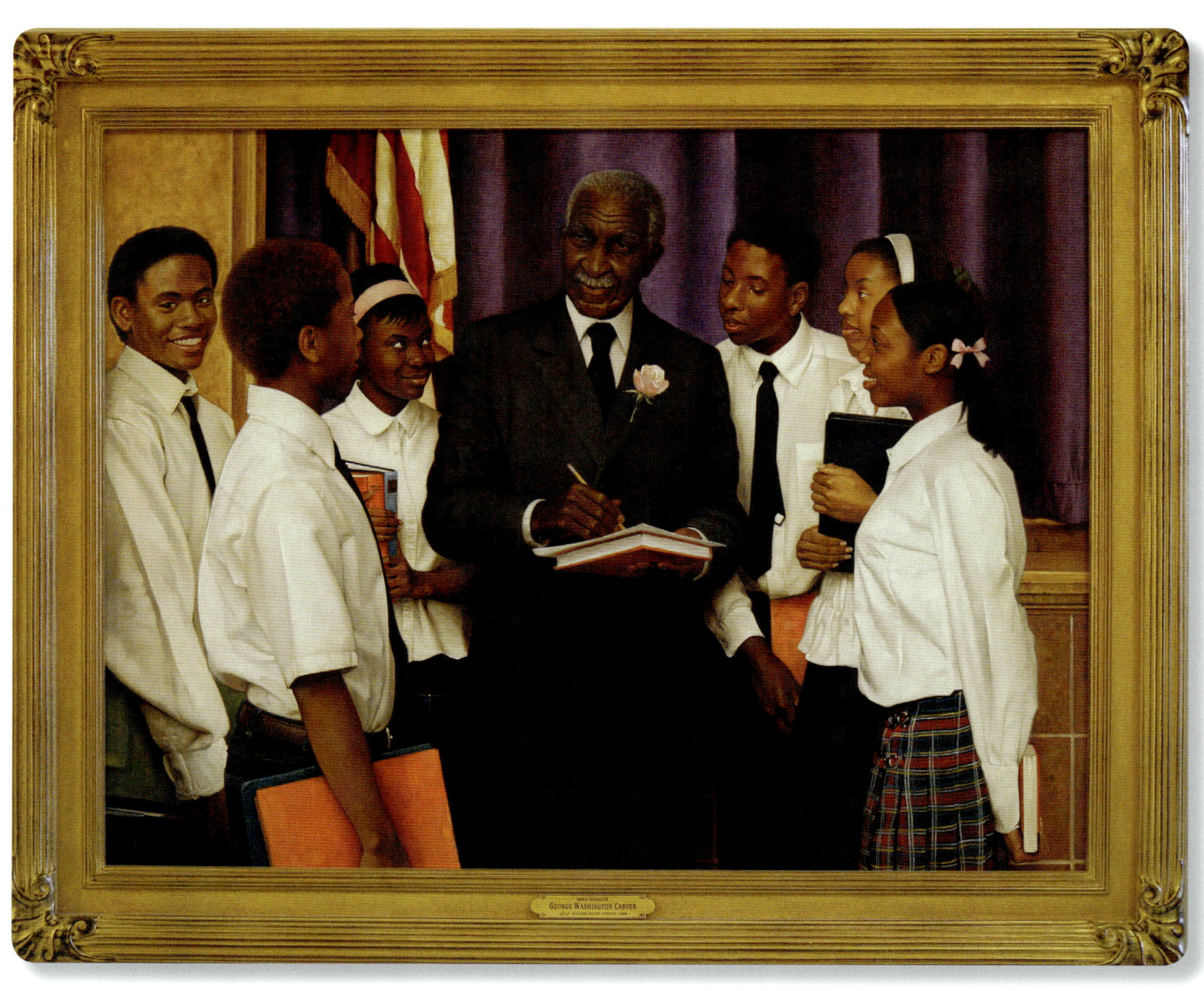
GEORGE WASHINGTON CARVER

MISS ALICE ROBERTSON

BY MIKE WIMMER

24 x 30, oil/canvas

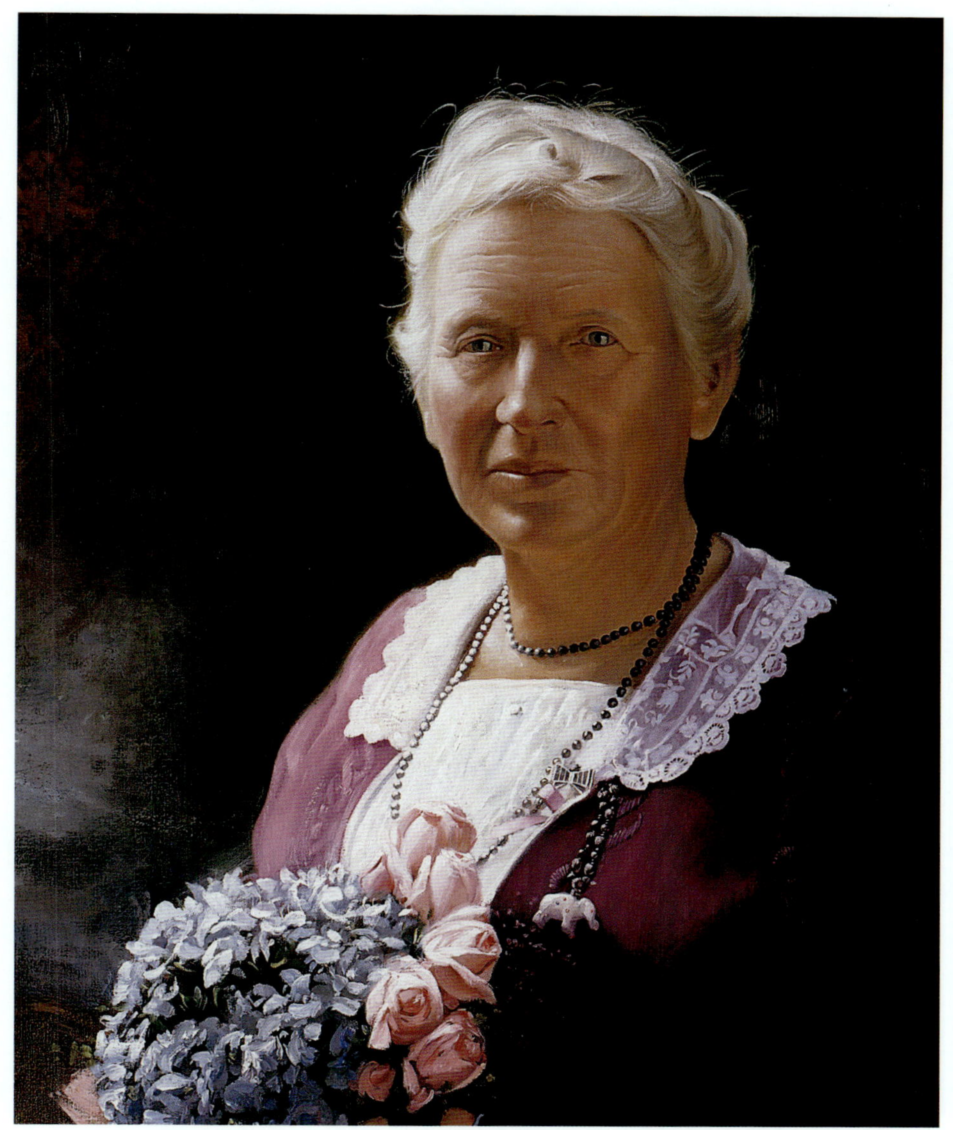

Oklahoma's first congresswoman, Alice Robertson was fondly known as "Miss Alice." From Muskogee, she was elected to Congress in 1920 and was the first woman to preside over the U. S. House of Representatives. She was only the second female member of the House. Earlier she had served as the nation's first woman postmaster of a Class A post office and founded Henry Kendall College, which became the University of Tulsa. Senator Charles Ford sponsored her portrait. Giclées of this portrait are on on display at the Alice Robertson Elementary School in Muskogee, Alice Robertson Elementary School in Tulsa, and The University of Tulsa.

GEORGE WASHINGTON CARVER IN TULSA (FACING)

BY MIKE WIMMER

40 x 30, oil/canvas

George Washington Carver was born into slavery but overcame many obstacles to become one of the most prestigious scientists of his time. He revolutionized research methods and agricultural processes. In May, 1929, he attended the dedication ceremony of the Tulsa junior high school bearing his name. More than 3,000 citizens were present. Carver, a meek and gentle man, was awed by the appearance of his name on the school, saying it affected him more than any honor he had yet received. The painting was sponsored by Senator Maxine Horner.

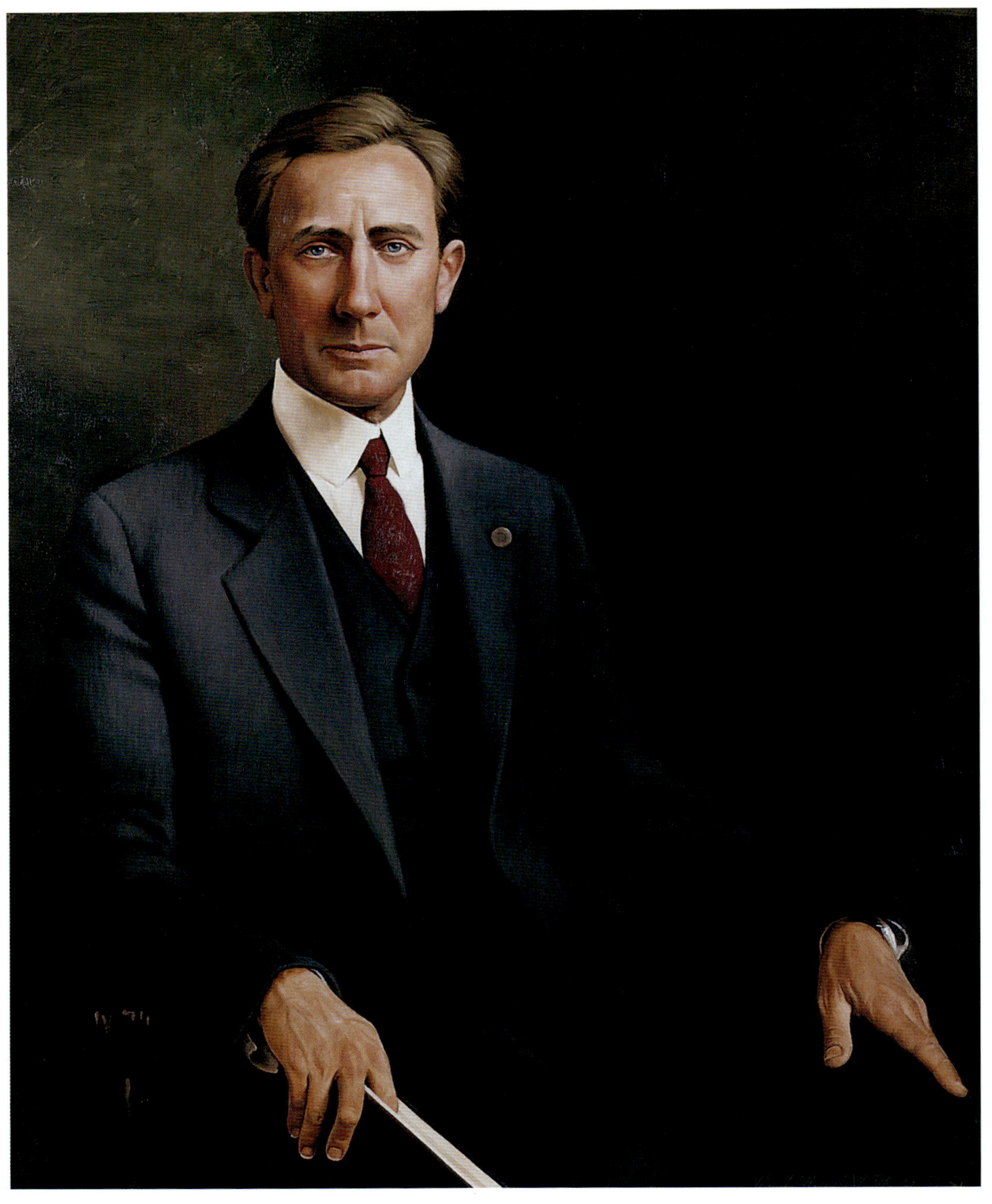

SENATOR HENRY S. JOHNSTON

BY MIKE WIMMER

30 x 36, oil/canvas

Henry S. Johnston was the first president pro tempore of the Oklahoma State Senate. A lawyer from Perry, he was a delegate to the constitutional convention and the first legislature. He later served as governor of Oklahoma from 1927 until he was impeached and removed from office in 1929. He was again elected to the senate and served with many of the same members who had participated in his removal. He was a popular Oklahoma leader who lived out his life in Perry until his death in 1965. His portrait was sponsored by Senator Robert Milacek of Waukomis.

SOLOMON LAYTON (FACING)

BY CHRISTOPHER NICK

32 x 41, oil/canvas

Solomon Layton designed more than 100 public, educational, and commercial buildings in Oklahoma. His most prominent work was the state's capitol. In a ceremony on Statehood Day, November 16, 1915, he was joined by local members of the Freemasons in laying the cornerstone of the capitol. Layton's portrait was sponsored by the Oklahoma chapter of the American Institute of Architects.

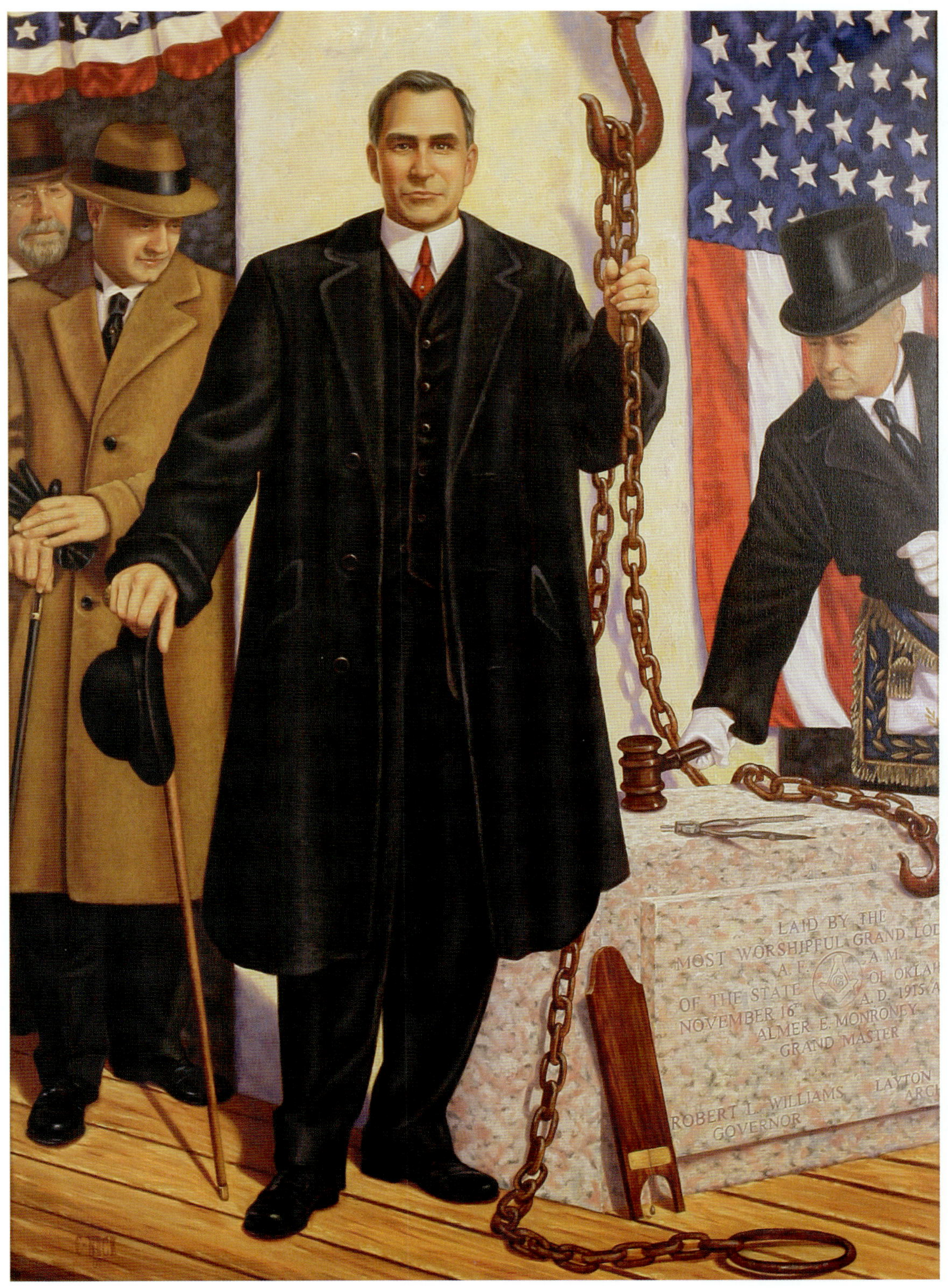
LAID BY THE
MOST WORSHIPFUL GRAND
A. F. A. M.
OF THE STATE OF
NOVEMBER 16TH A. D. 1915
ALMER E. MONRONEY
GRAND MASTER
ROBERT L. WILLIAMS
GOVERNOR
LAYTON

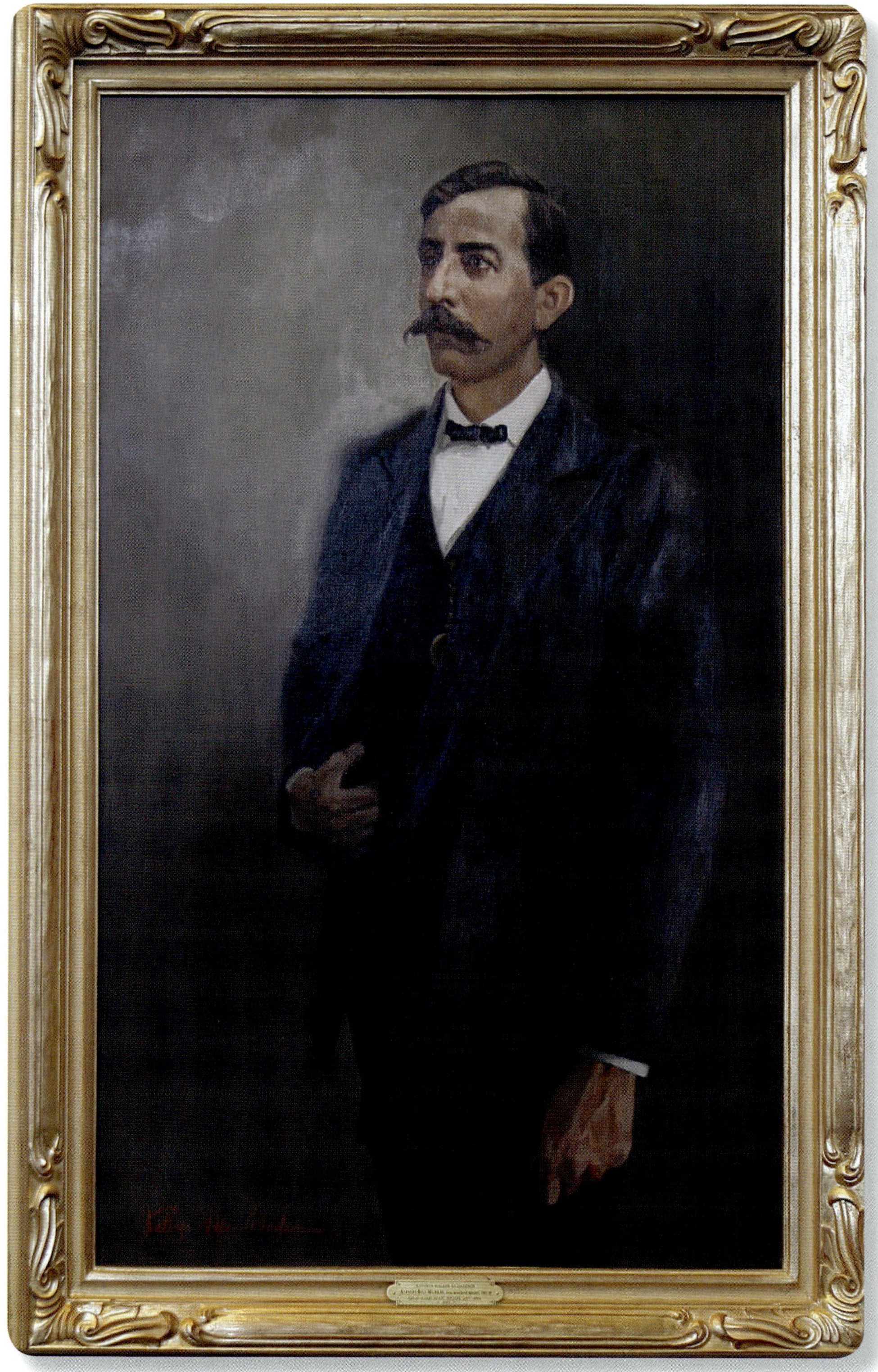

ALFALFA BILL MURRAY

BY KATHRYN WALKER RICHARDSON

30 x 48, oil/canvas

Oklahoma's most colorful political leader, William H. "Alfalfa Bill" Murray, was president of the state constitutional convention, first Speaker of the House of Representatives, a member of the United States Congress, and governor of Oklahoma from 1931 to 1935. He called out the National Guard more times than any other governor of the state and is legendary for standing up to federal judges and offering to rent the governor's mansion for office space during the Great Depression. His portrait was sponsored by House Speaker Larry Adair.

ARTHUR N. DANIELS

BY KATHRYN WALKER RICHARDSON

30 x 48, oil/canvas

A territorial representative from El Reno, Arthur N. Daniels was elected the first Speaker of the Oklahoma House of Representatives when it convened in Guthrie on August 29, 1890. His election was a surprise because Daniels was a Populist and Republicans controlled the territorial legislature. Daniels's portrait was sponsored by Senator Charles Ford.

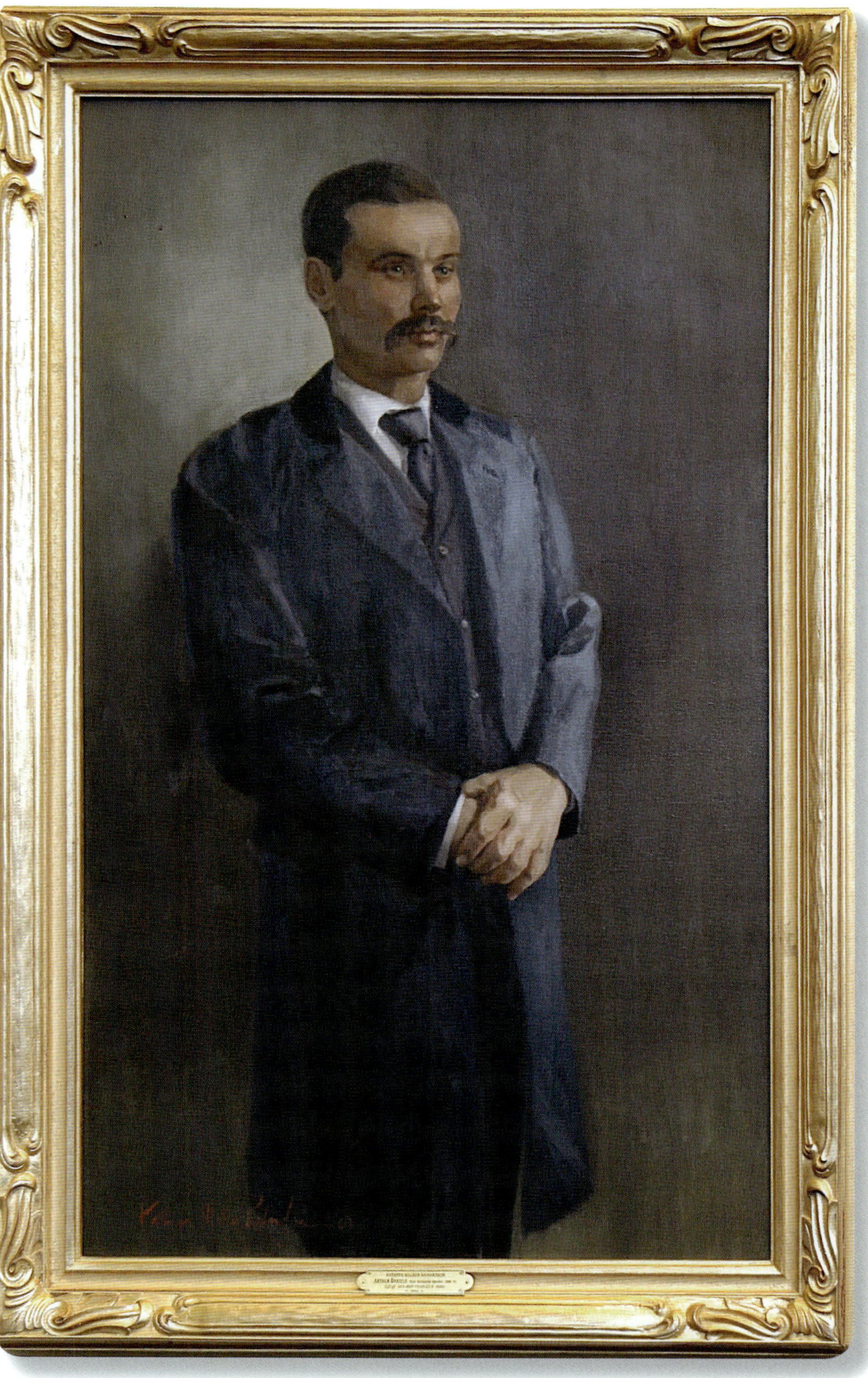

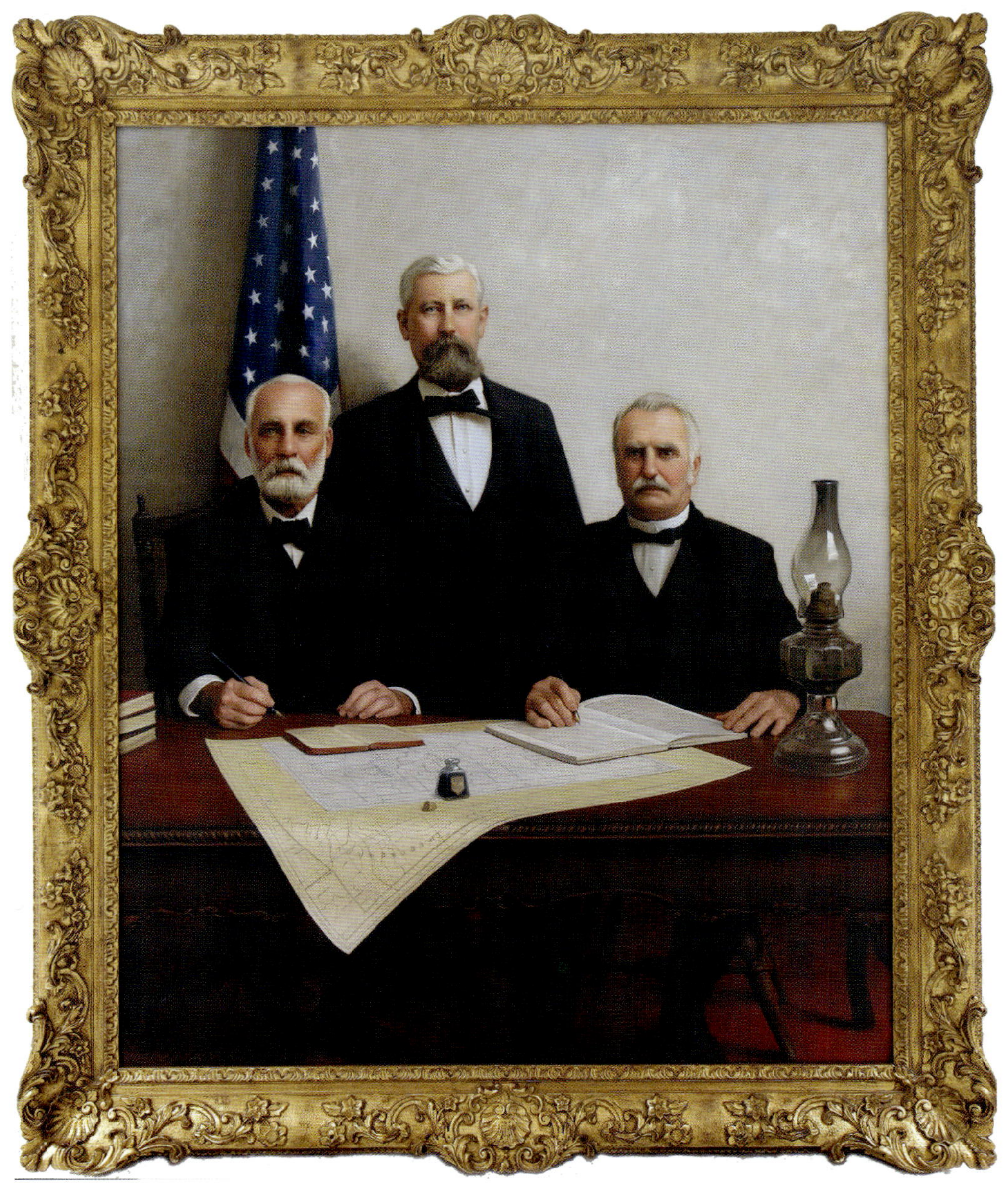

DAWES COMMISSION

BY MIKE WIMMER

50 x 60, oil/canvas

Named for its first chairman, Henry L. Dawes, the Dawes Commission was authorized by Congress to carry out the law that took communally-held national lands of the Five Civilized Tribes and divided them into single allotments for individual tribal members. The commission was appointed by President Grover Cleveland and spent several years developing a final roll of qualified members of the tribes. The portrait was sponsored by the Paul and Helen Sisk Charitable Trust.

COURT OF CRIMINAL APPEALS (FACING)

BY MIKE WIMMER

43 x 58, oil/canvas

Oklahoma is unique in that its state constitution gives final appellate authority to two courts. The state's Supreme Court has the final say in civil cases, but the Court of Criminal Appeals is the court of last resort in criminal cases. This painting shows the first three judges of the Court of Criminal Appeals, Henry M. Furman of Ada, H. G. Baker of Muskogee, and Thomas H. Doyle of Perry, all appointed by Governor Charles Haskell in 1907. The painting was a gift of Senator Charles Ford and Friends of the Court.

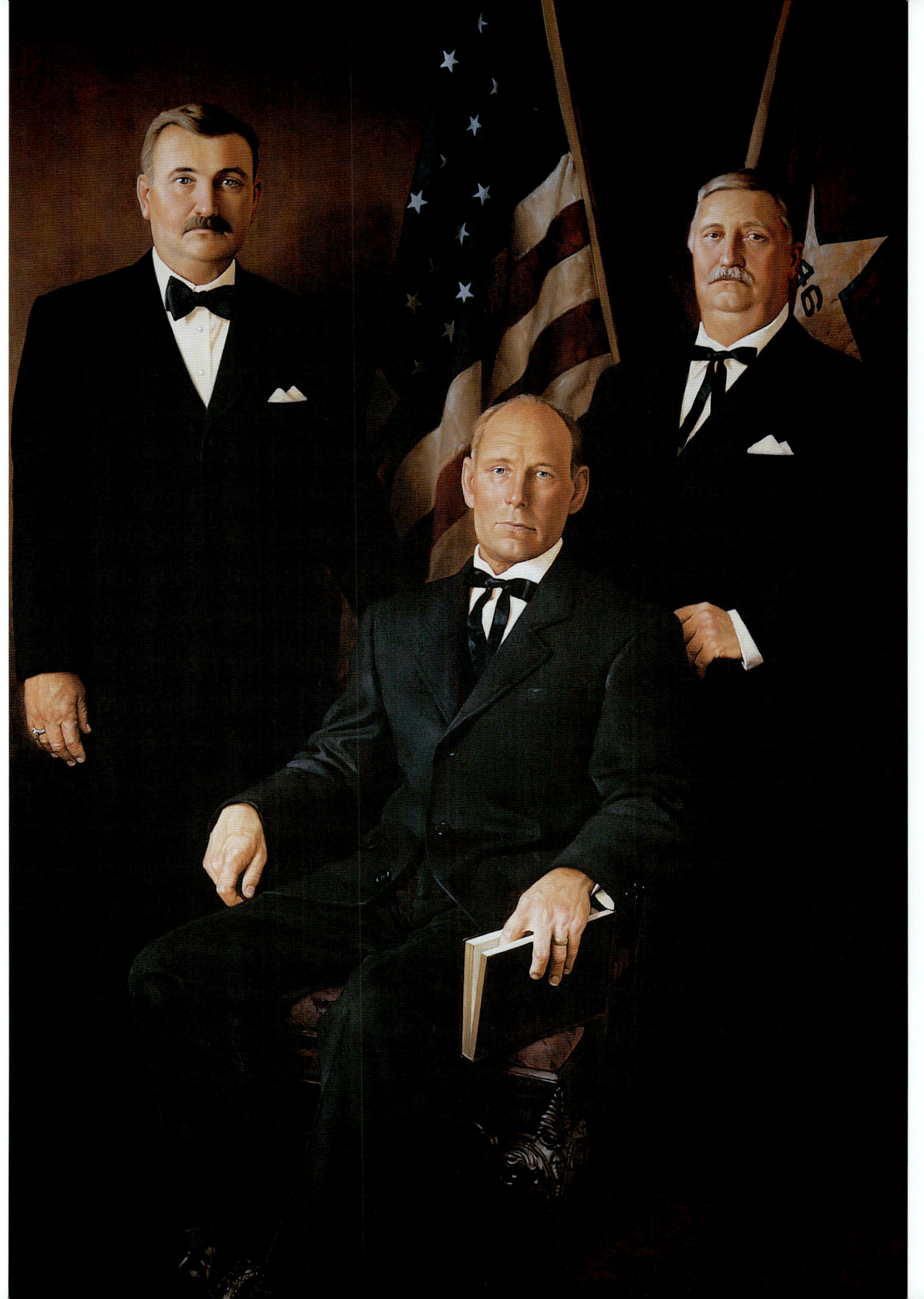
46

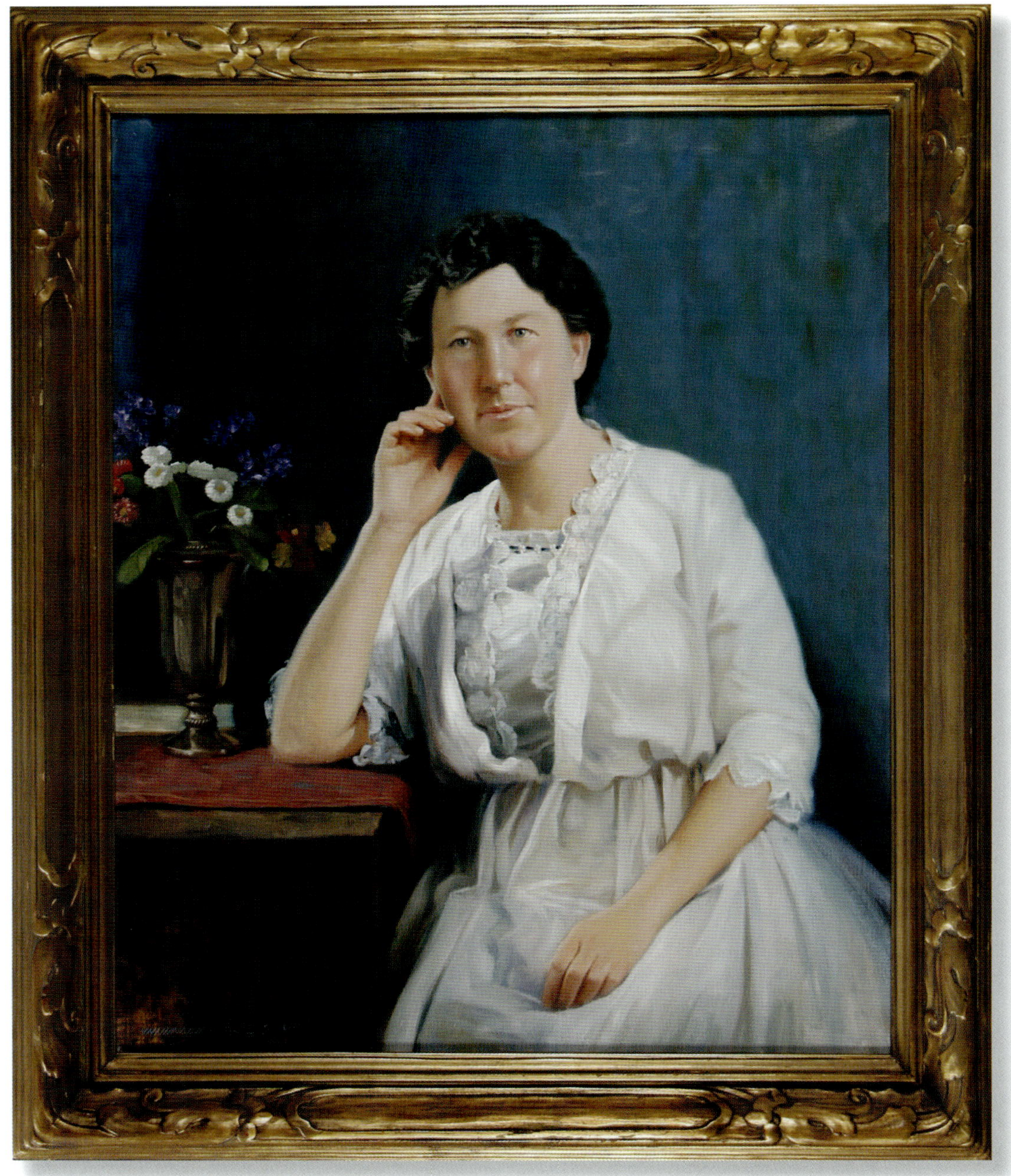

REPRESENTATIVE BESSIE S. MCCOLGIN

BY MIKE WIMMER

25 x 30, oil/canvas

Amelia Elizabeth "Bessie" McColgin was the first woman to serve in the Oklahoma House of Representatives. Settling with her husband in Roger Mills County in 1903, she taught school in her home and was postmaster at Ridgeton in 1904. In 1920, McColgin was elected to the house of representatives and served in the eighth legislature. Her portrait was sponsored by her family and Congressman Frank Lucas.

MRS. LAMAR LOONEY (FACING)

BY MIKE WIMMER

24 x 30, oil/canvas

Mirabeau Lamar Looney was born in Alabama and moved to southwestern Oklahoma Territory in 1892. Widowed, she became a public servant, serving as county treasurer and county clerk in Harmon County. In 1920, she was elected Oklahoma's first female state senator. She remained the only woman to serve in the state senate until 1928. She became a lawyer at age 52 and died in 1935. Her portrait was sponsored by the 2005 State Senate Women's Caucus.

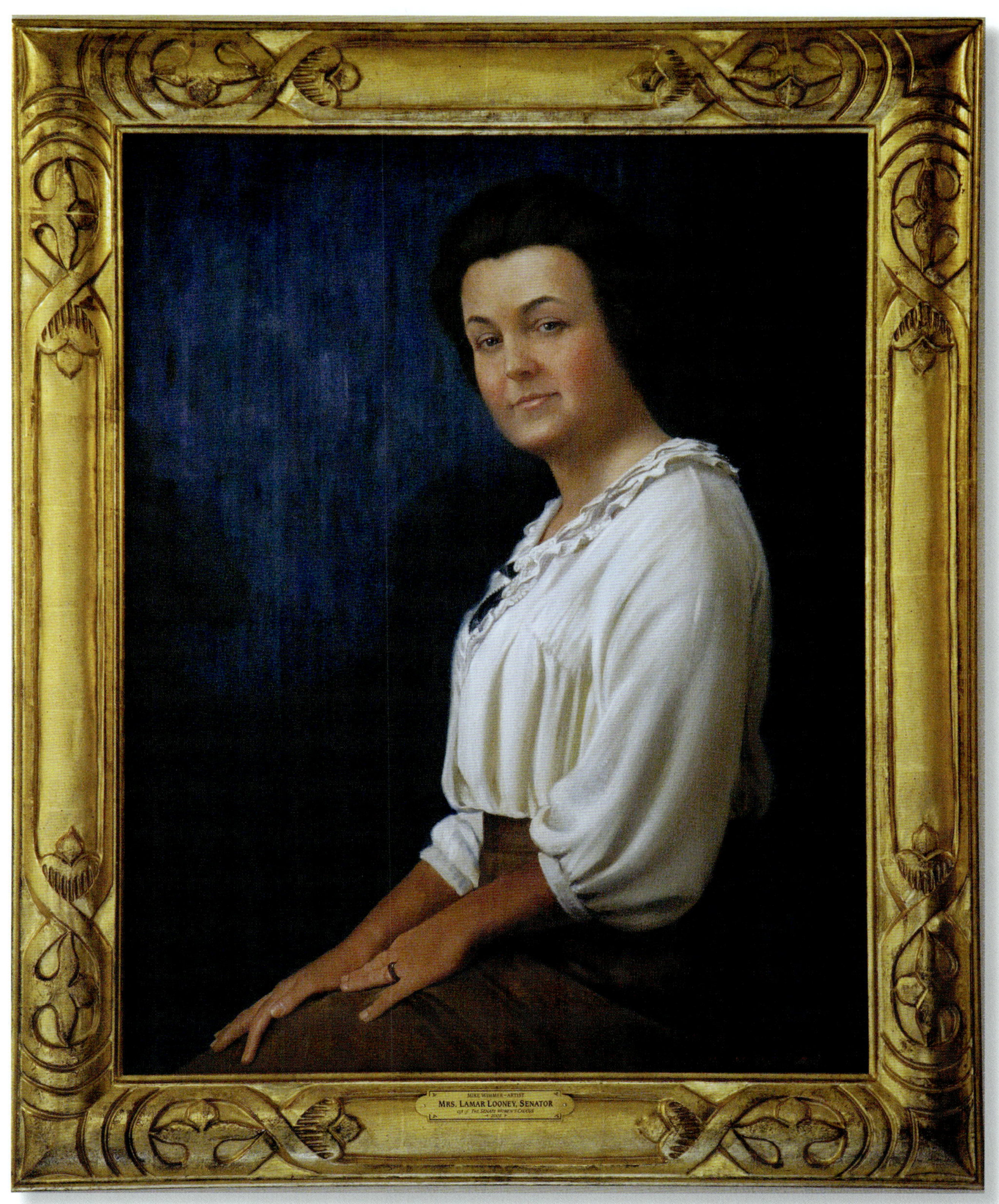
Mike Wimmer—Artist
Mrs. Lamar Looney, Senator

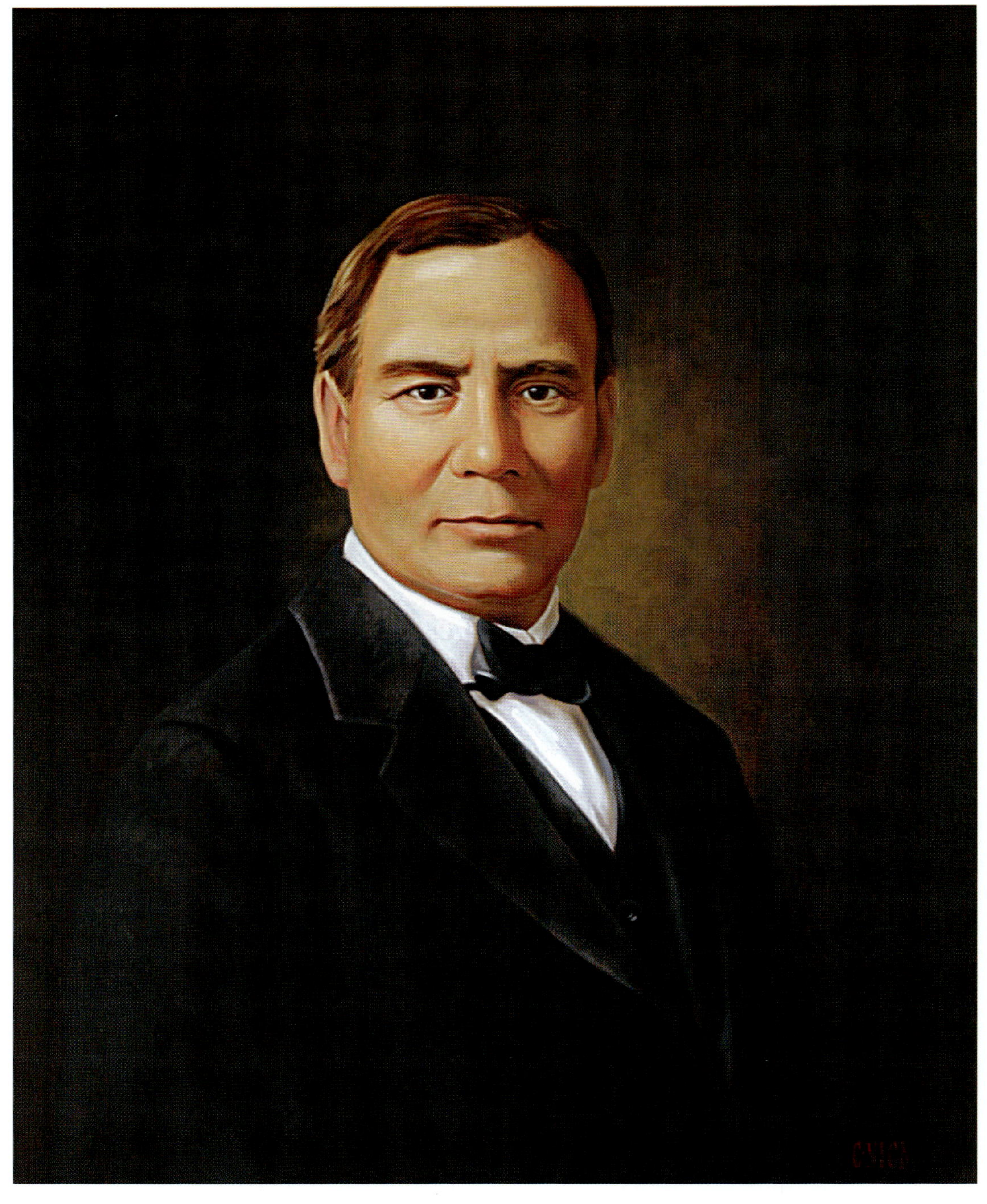

HOUSTON BENGE TEEHEE

BY CHRISTOPHER NICK

25 x 30, oil/canvas

Houston Benge Teehee, Cherokee, was born in Sequoyah County. After his education at the Cherokee Male Seminary and Fort Worth University, he entered banking, practiced law, and served two terms (1910-1914) in the Oklahoma House of Representatives. After his appointment to the position of registrar of the United States Treasury (a position now called secretary of the Treasury) during the administration of Woodrow Wilson (1915–1919), his signature appeared on all federal notes and bonds. It is said that he signed his name to documents representing more money than had any person in history up to his time. He died in 1953. Chris Benge, Tulsa, speaker of the Oklahoma House of Representatives, is a relative of Houston Teehee. The portrait was sponsored by Cherokee Nation Tourism.

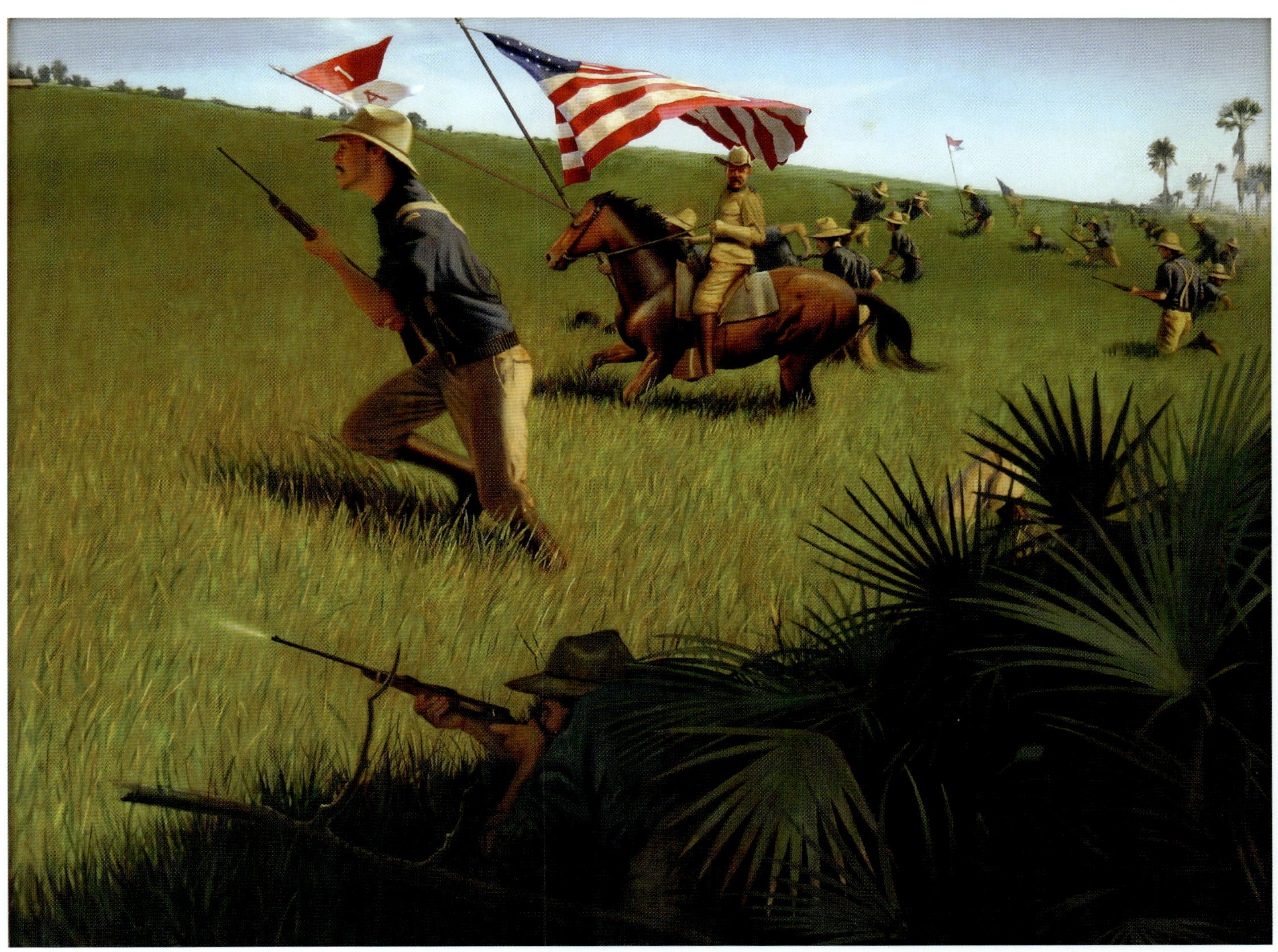

FRANK FRANTZ—
ROUGH RIDER AND TERRITORIAL GOVERNOR

BY TIMOTHY TYLER

30 x 40, oil/canvas

Frank Frantz, the final governor of Oklahoma Territory, rode with Theodore Roosevelt's Rough Riders in the Spanish-American War. Frantz jointed the cavalry at age 26 and traveled to Cuba where the Rough Riders engaged the Spanish in the Battle of Las Guasimas. The following day, the Rough Riders fought the fiercest battle of the conflict, the Battle of San Juan Hill. After the war, Frantz settled in Enid, Oklahoma, and opened a hardware and lumber business. When Roosevelt became president of the United States, Frantz used his friendship with his former commander to gain appointment as governor of Oklahoma Territory. The painting was sponsored by Senator Patrick Anderson and the citizens of Enid.

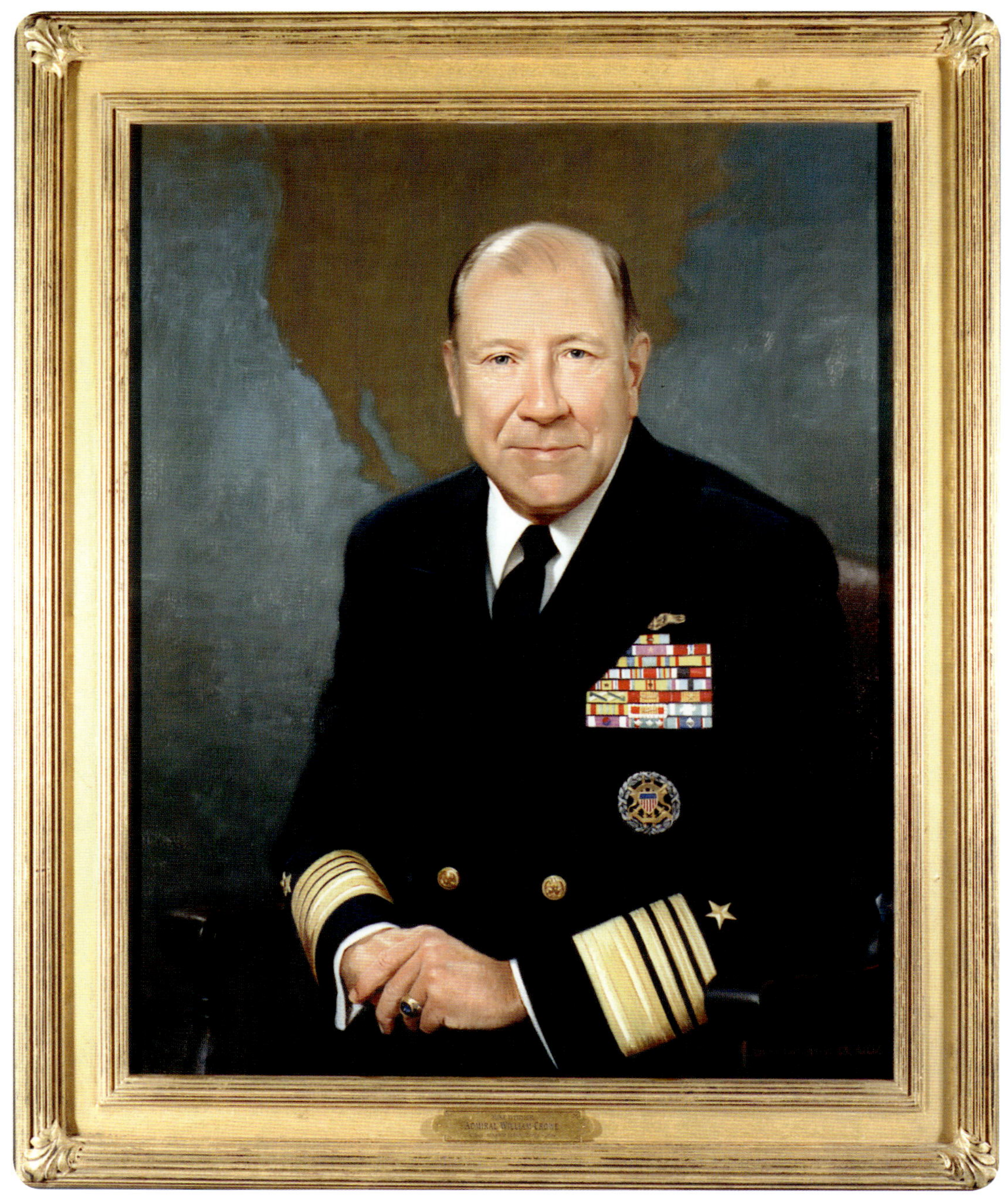

ADMIRAL WILLIAM J. CROWE, JR.

BY MIKE WIMMER

24 x 30, oil/canvas

William J. Crowe, Jr. grew up in Oklahoma City and received his education at the University of Oklahoma, the U. S. Naval Academy, Stanford University, and Princeton University. His navy career was spectacularly exemplary. Attaining the four-star rank, Admiral Crowe was commander in chief of NATO forces in southern Europe and commander in chief of Pacific forces, the largest geographic command in the American military. In 1985, President Ronald Reagan appointed Crowe chairman of the joint chiefs of staff, the nation's highest military position. His portrait was sponsored by Senator Glenn Coffee.

ALEXANDER POSEY

BY MIKE WIMMER

21 x 18, oil/canvas

Creek poet, humorist, and journalist Alexander Posey became internationally known for writing political satire in what became known as the Fus Fixico Letters. He began writing poetry while a student at Bacone College. He was one of the first Native Americans to own a newspaper, gaining widespread recognition as a journalist who used wit and humor to capture the interest of his readers. He drowned in 1908 at the age of 34. The portrait was sponsored by Senator Jerry Smith, his wife, Sally Howell-Smith, and the Creek Nation.

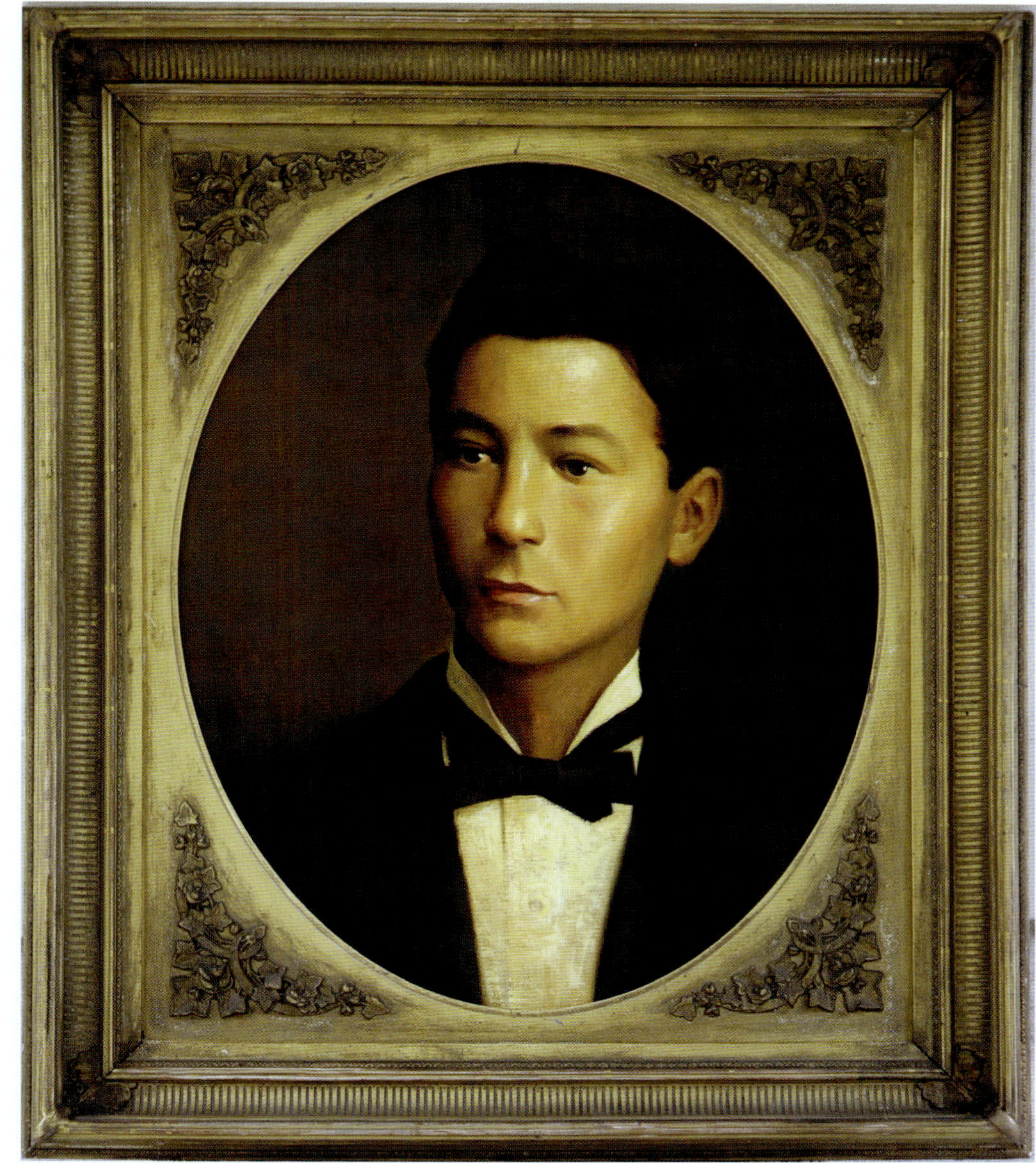

WILL ROGERS

BY BORIS GORDON

70 x 40, oil/canvas

Will Rogers, "Oklahoma's favorite son," posed for this portrait in 1931, at the height of his careers as an actor and newspaper columnist. For many years, the portrait was on permanent loan for performances of the Will Rogers Follies in Branson, Missouri. Through the efforts of State Senator Charles Ford, the portrait was returned to its permanent home in the state senate.

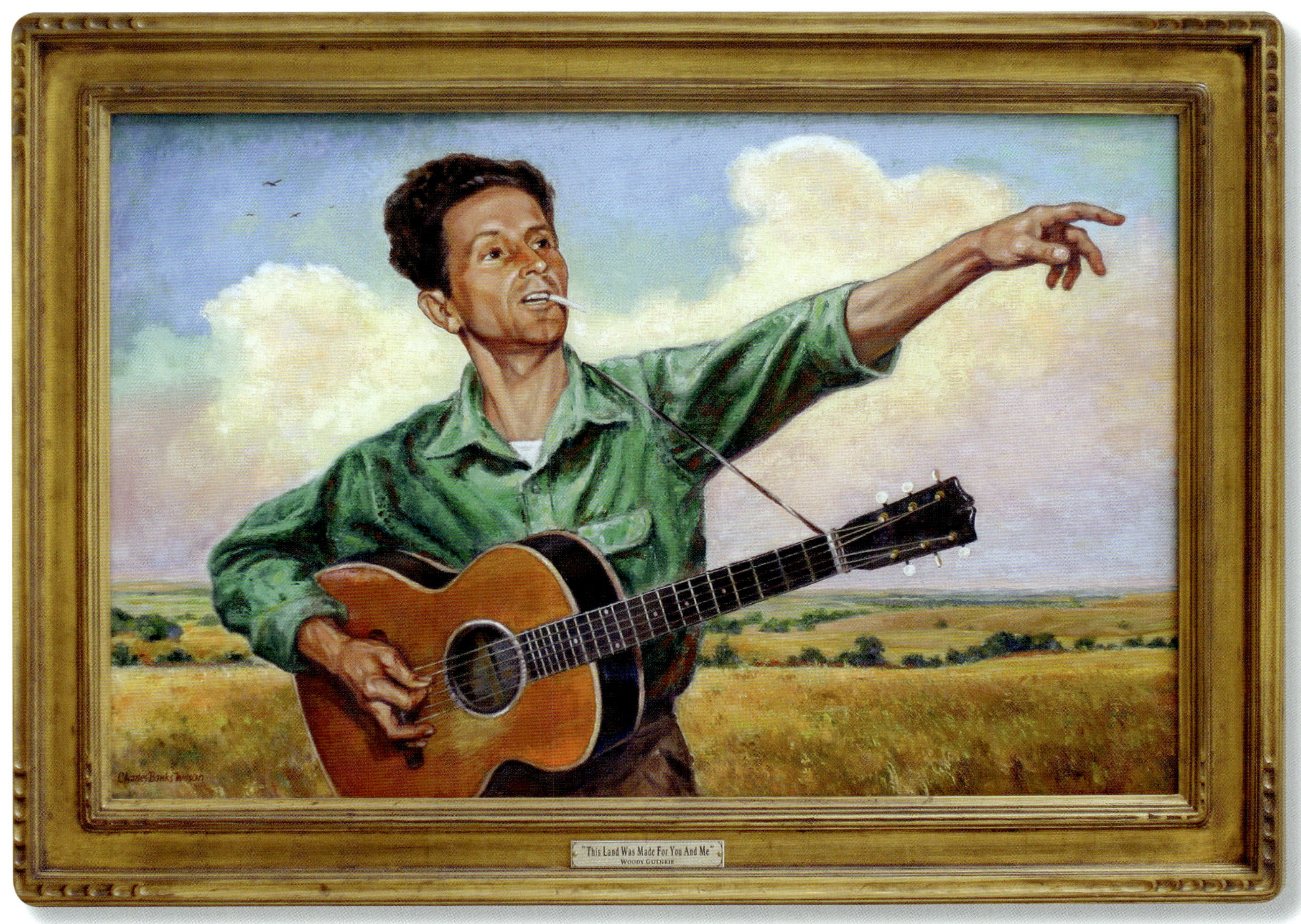

WOODY GUTHRIE

BY CHARLES BANKS WILSON

25 x 30, oil/canvas

Born in Okemah, Oklahoma, Woody Guthrie traveled among migrants during the Dust Bowl of the 1930s accumulating stories and life experiences for nearly 1,000 songs. The self-taught folk singer became America's first true folk hero. Among his classic songs were "This Land is Your Land" and "Oklahoma Hills." Credited with influencing subsequent generations of songwriters and performers, including Bob Dylan, Guthrie died in 1967. His portrait was sponsored by the *Oklahoma Gazette.*

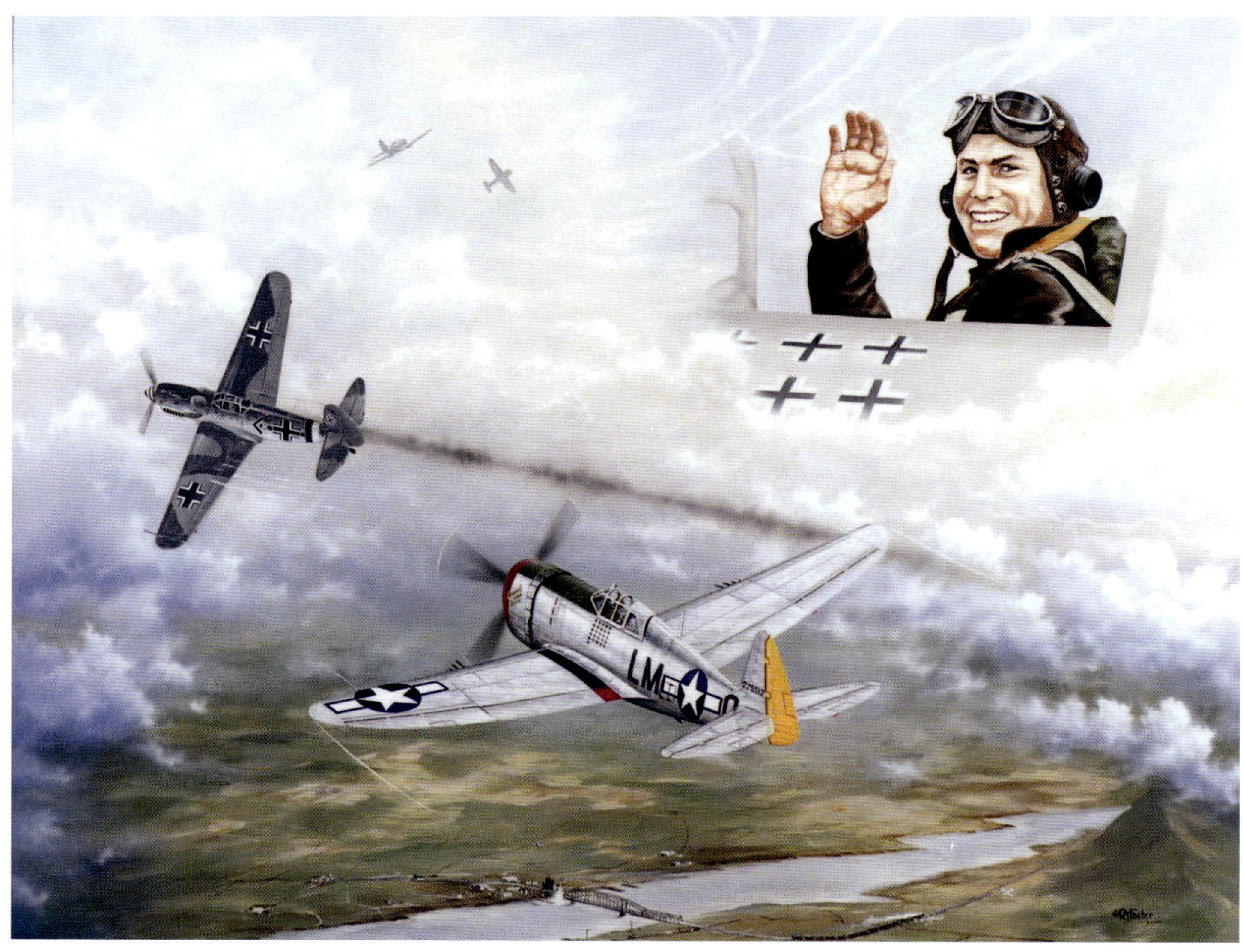

COLONEL ROBERT S. JOHNSON

BY R.T. FOSTER

36 x 48, acrylic/canvas

Robert S. Johnson, from Lawton, was Oklahoma's highest scoring fighter pilot of World War II. Colonel Johnson shot down 28 German aircraft. His final two kills allowed him to surpass Captain Eddie Rickenbacker's total of 26 enemy planes downed in World War I. Johnson's portrait and depiction of him shooting down a German aircraft was sponsored by Tom and Hillary Clark of Tulsa.

GENERAL TINKER AND TINKER FIELD

BY R. T. FOSTER

30 x 36, oil/canvas

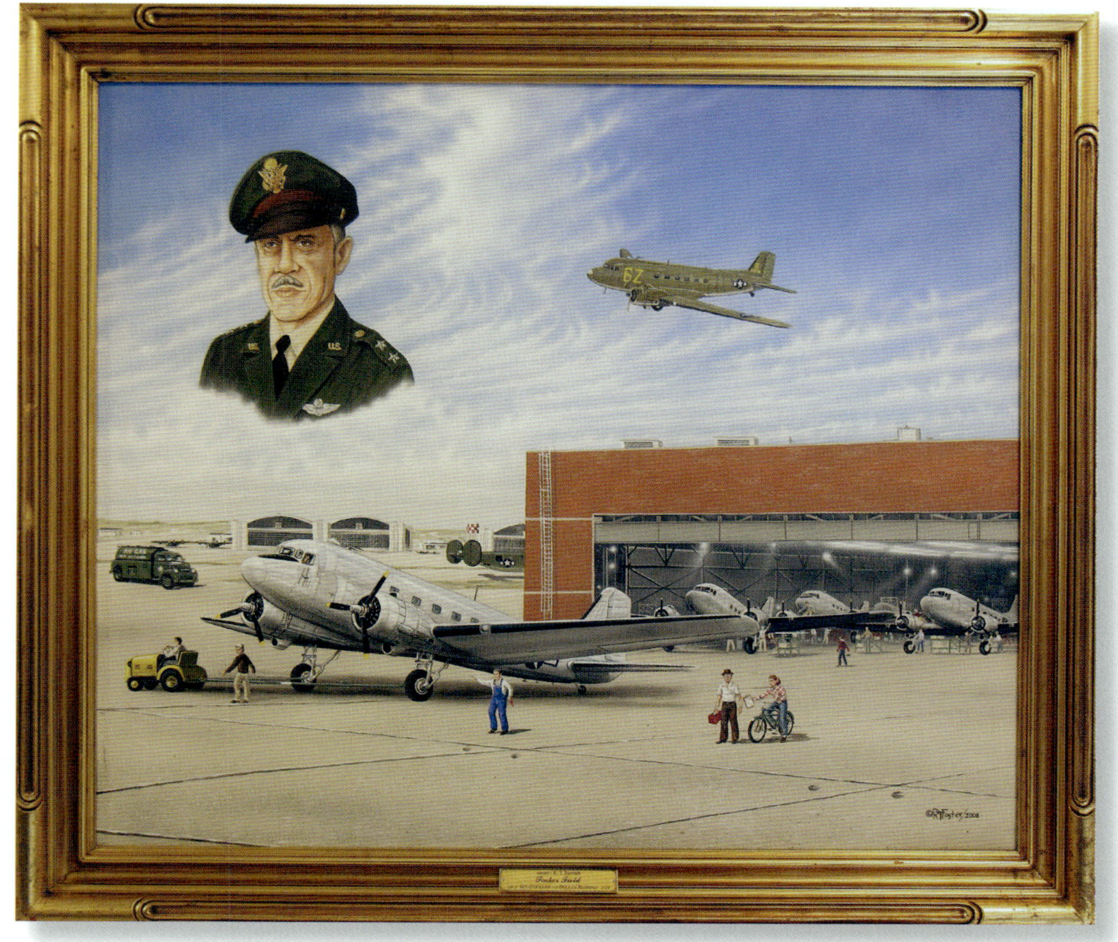

Tinker Air Force Base in Midwest City began as Tinker Field, a maintenance and supply depot, in 1940. During World War II, workers at Tinker repaired bombers for combat and built half the C-47 Skytrains used in the war. The base was named in honor of Major General Clarence L. Tinker, a native of Pawhuska, Oklahoma, who was killed during an attack on Wake Island in the early months of World War II. The painting was sponsored by State Senator Cliff Aldridge and his wife, DeeAnn.

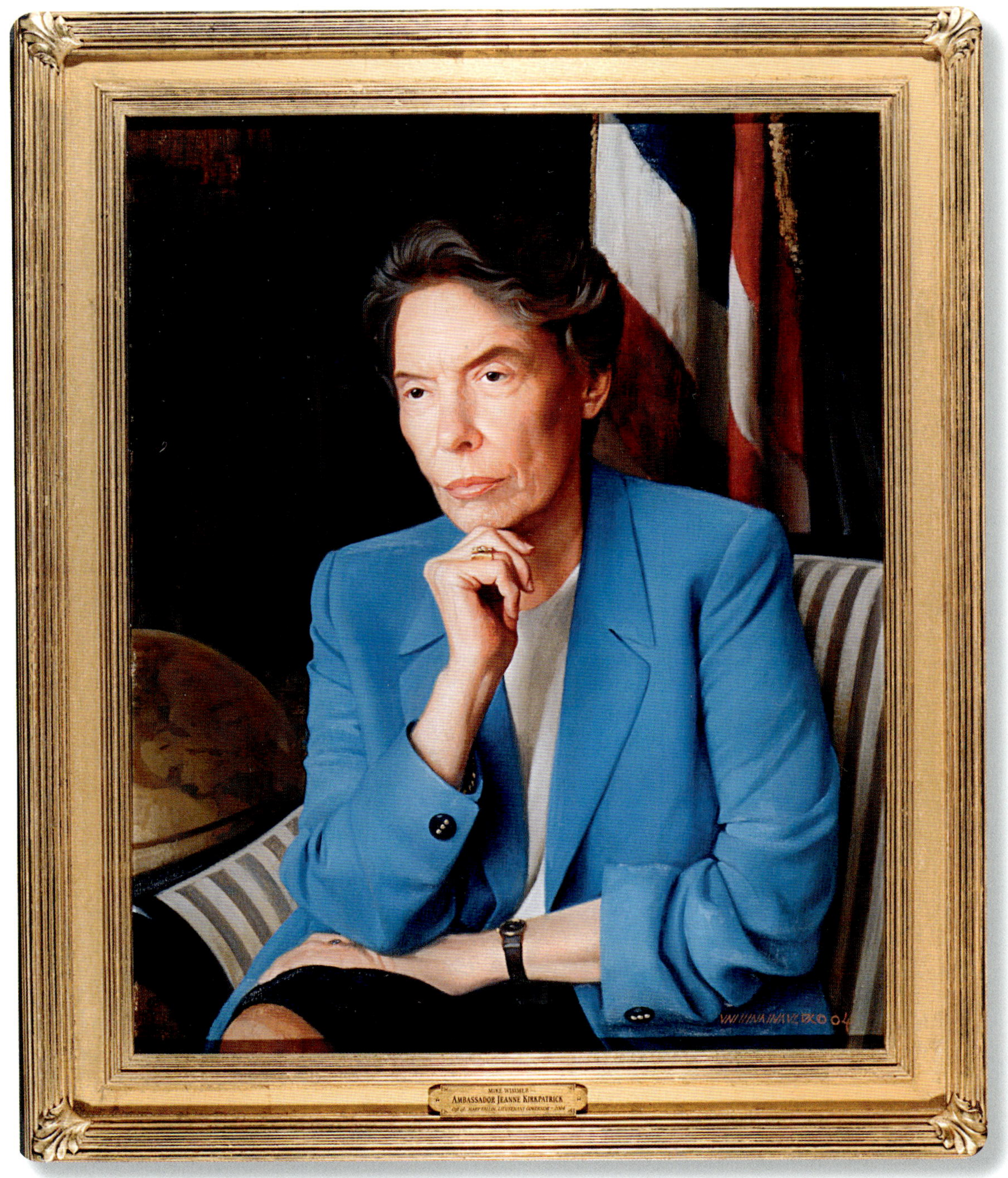

AMBASSADOR JEANE J. KIRKPATRICK

BY MIKE WIMMER

24 x 30, oil/canvas

Lieutenant Governor Mary Fallin sponsored the portrait of Jeane J. Kirkpatrick, the first female U. S. ambassador to the United Nations. Kirkpatrick was born in Duncan and educated at Barnard College and Columbia University. She was appointed to the United Nations post by President Ronald Reagan. She served in other administrations and became one of the nation's most respected experts on geopolitical issues. She died in 2006.

SENATOR STRATTON TAYLOR

BY MIKE WIMMER

30 x 36, oil/canvas

Members of the senate in 1999 sponsored the portrait of Stratton Taylor of Claremore, 37th president pro tempore of the Oklahoma State Senate. Taylor was elected to the Oklahoma House of Representatives at age 22 and advanced to the senate four years later. He was the only member of his high school graduating class at Alluwe, Oklahoma, to graduate from college.

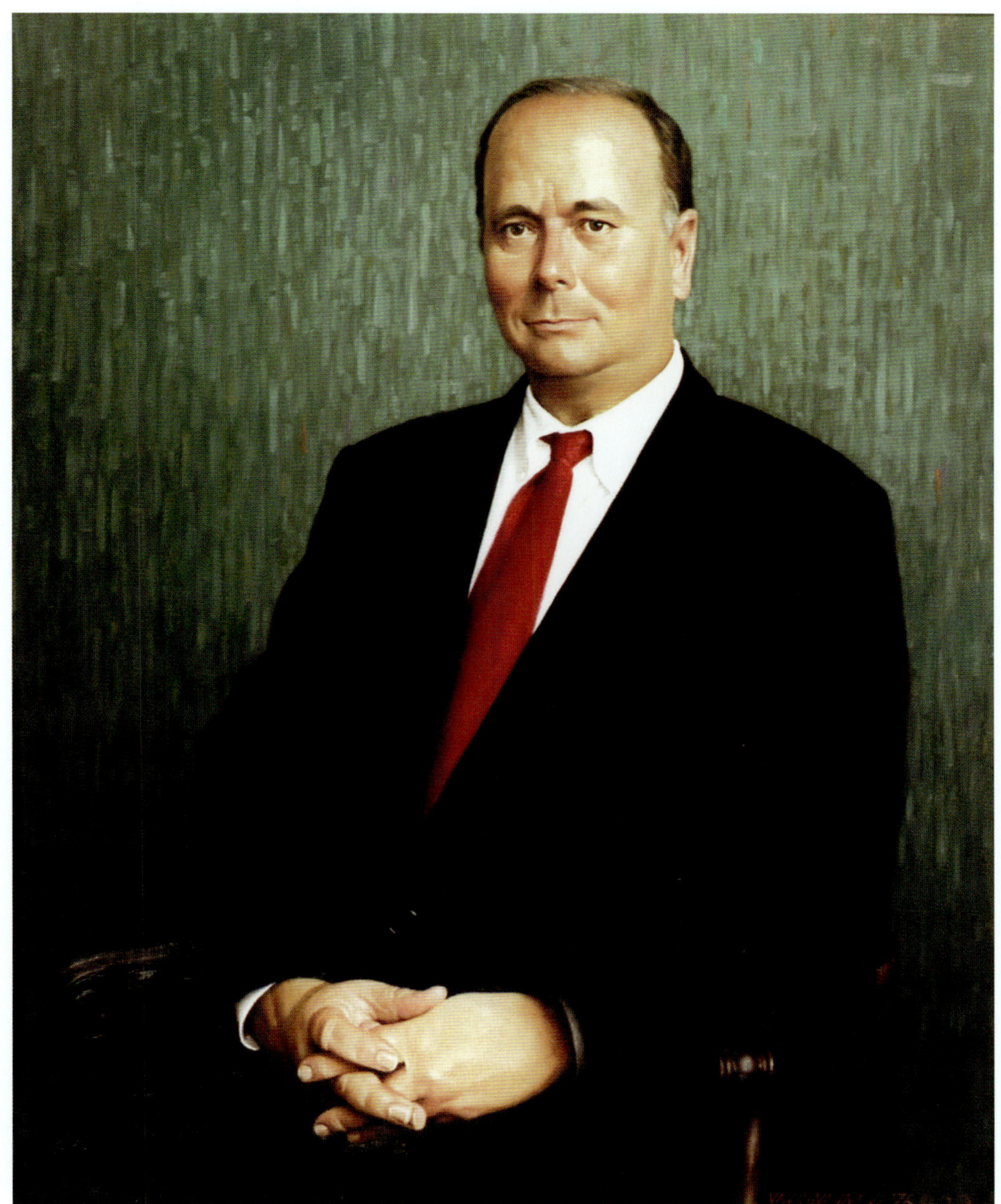

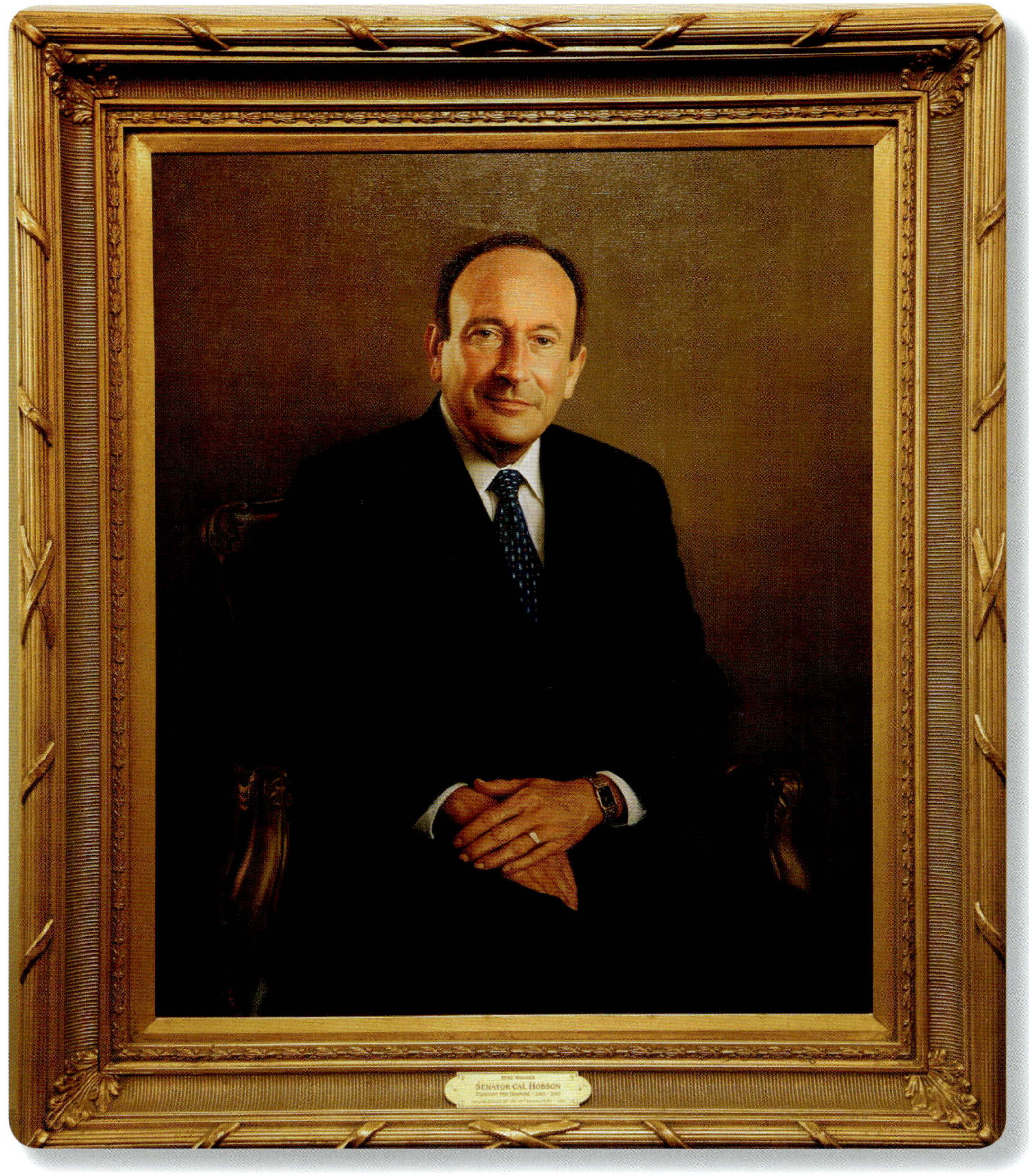

SENATOR CAL HOBSON

BY MIKE WIMMER

30 x 36, oil/canvas

Members of the state senate sponsored this portrait of Calvin Hobson, 35th president pro tempore of the senate, in 2003. Hobson, of Lexington, graduated from the University of Oklahoma and is a retired colonel in the Oklahoma National Guard. He served in both the state senate and the Oklahoma House of Representatives.

STATE SENATOR GLENN COFFEE

BY MIKE WIMMER

30 x 36, oil/canvas

When Republicans equaled Democrats in the number of seats occupied in the state senate, Senator Glenn Coffee was elected Republican leader and became co-president pro tempore from 2006 to 2008. In the 2008 general election, Republicans assumed control of the senate for the first time in history and Coffee became president pro tempore. He is an attorney in Oklahoma City. His portrait was sponsored by members of the state senate.

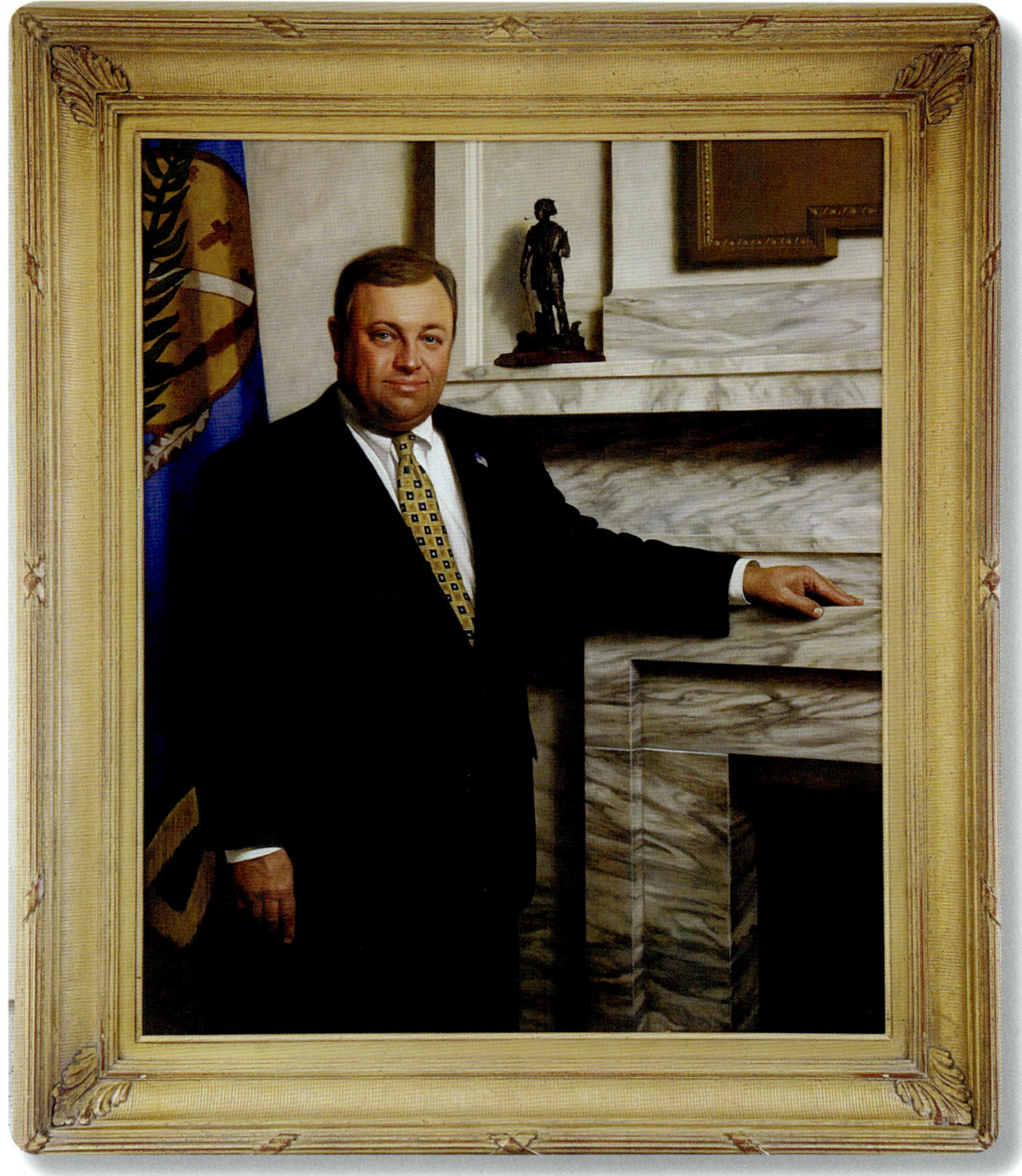

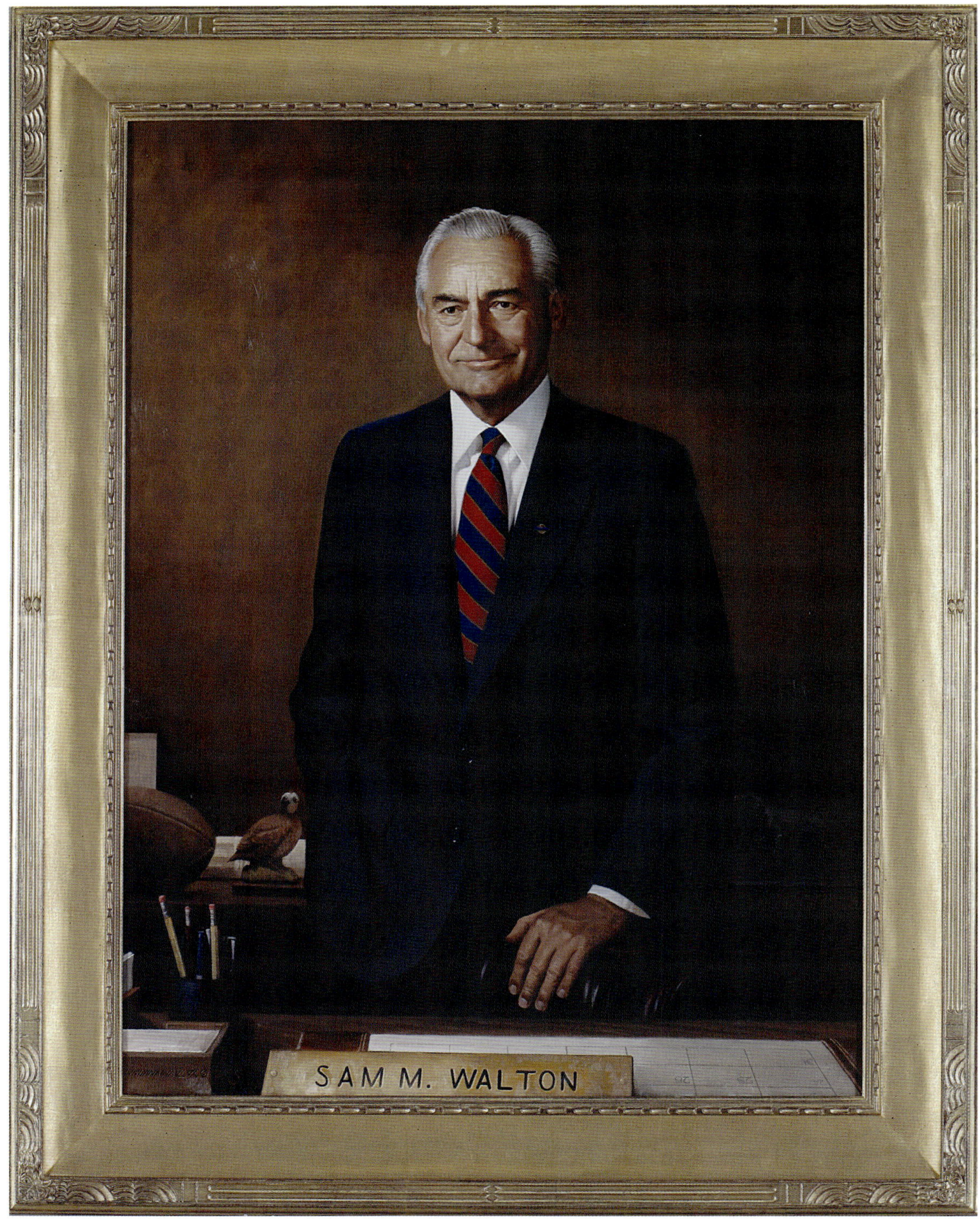

SAM WALTON

BY MIKE WIMMER

32 x 42, oil/canvas

The Wal-Mart Foundation sponsored the portrait of Samuel Moore “Sam” Walton, born in Kingfisher, Oklahoma. He opened his first Wal-Mart store in Rogers, Arkansas, in 1962 and lived to see his company become the world’s largest retailer and the nation’s largest private employer. When he died in 1992, he was the world’s second richest man. *Time Magazine* named Walton one of the 100 most influential people of the twentieth century.

STATE SENATOR MIKE MORGAN

BY MIKE WIMMER

30 x 36, oil/canvas

State Senator Mike Morgan of Stillwater was president pro tempore of the Oklahoma State Senate and part of history's first power-sharing arrangement in 2006 when Republicans and Democrats held an equal number of seats in the senate. Morgan and Republican Glenn Coffee were co-presidents pro tempore in 2006 and 2007. Because of constitutional term limits, Senator Morgan left the legislature after the 2008 election. An attorney, Morgan was educated at Oklahoma State University and the University of Tulsa. His portrait was sponsored by members of the Oklahoma State Senate.

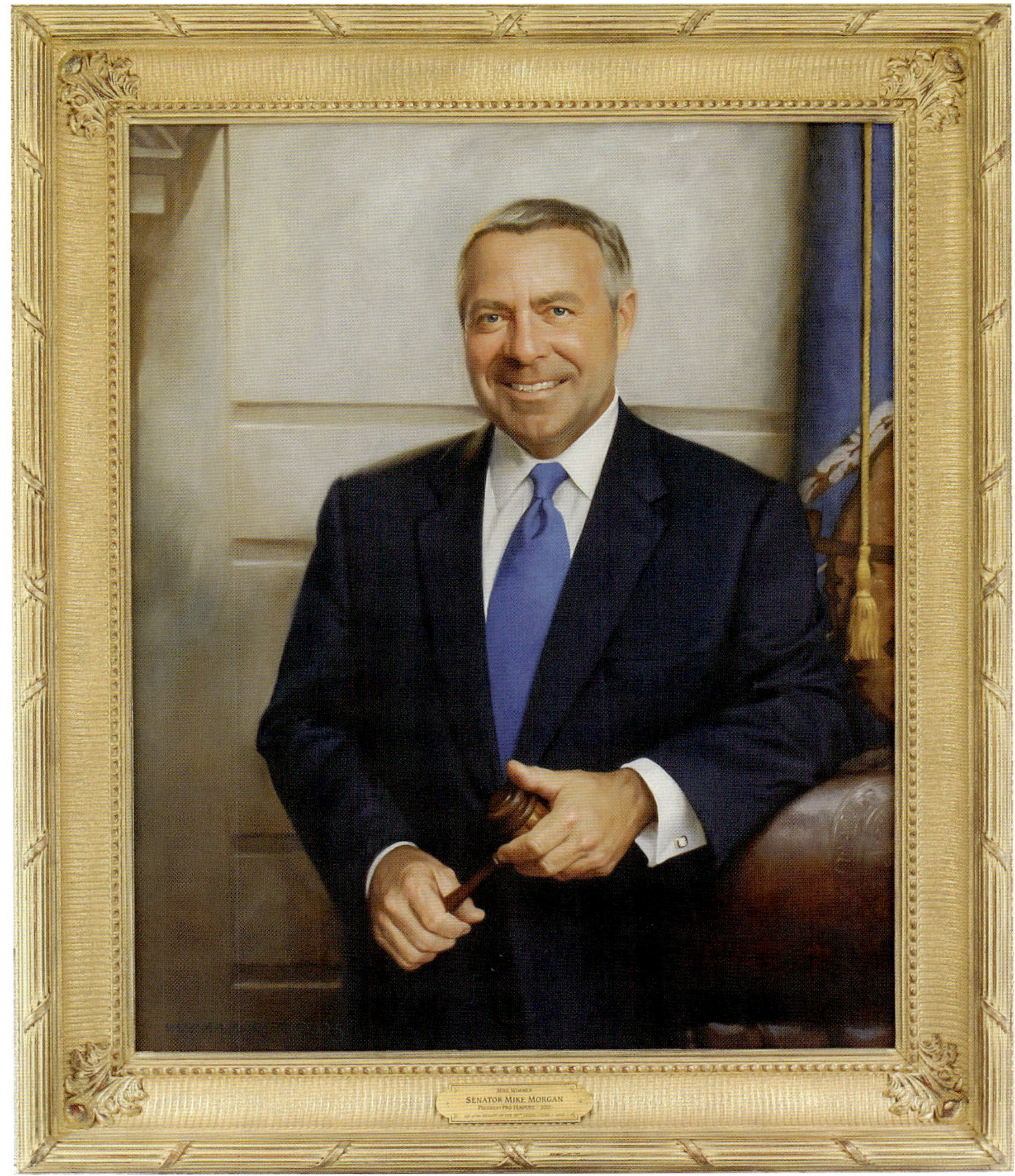

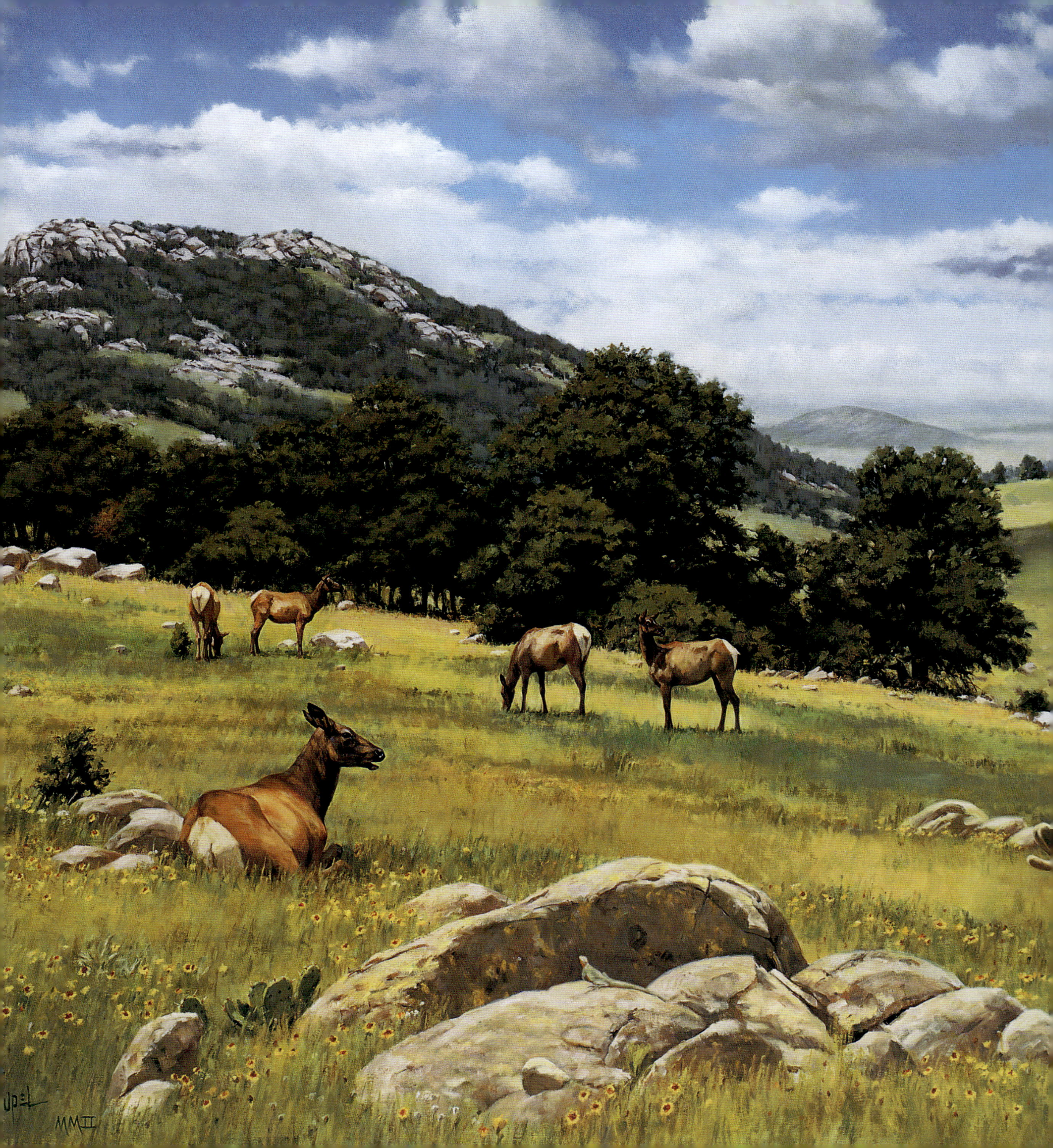

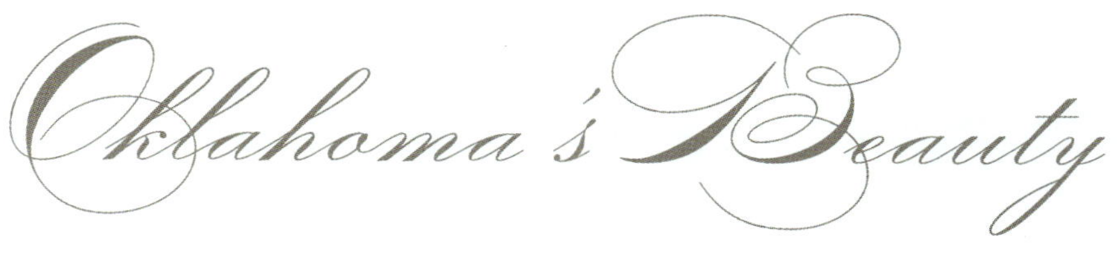

LANDSCAPES

RANDY RAMER, Curator, Gilcrease Museum

Oklahomans are defined by their landscape. From earliest times, our opportunities and challenges have been shaped in some important ways by our surroundings—not just by the economies and livelihoods derived from natural resources, but by the terrain, the earth, and the natural world itself. For over a century, the Oklahoma character has been shaped by windswept grasslands and rolling prairies, rugged canyons and dense forests, winding rivers that rise and fall at the whim of the seasons—by the place on earth in which we live. The themes found within the paintings of the Senate Art Collection are as diverse as the Oklahoma landscape itself. More than renderings of regional topography, they are visual keys to the state's distinctive spirit. They are celebrations of a common heritage.

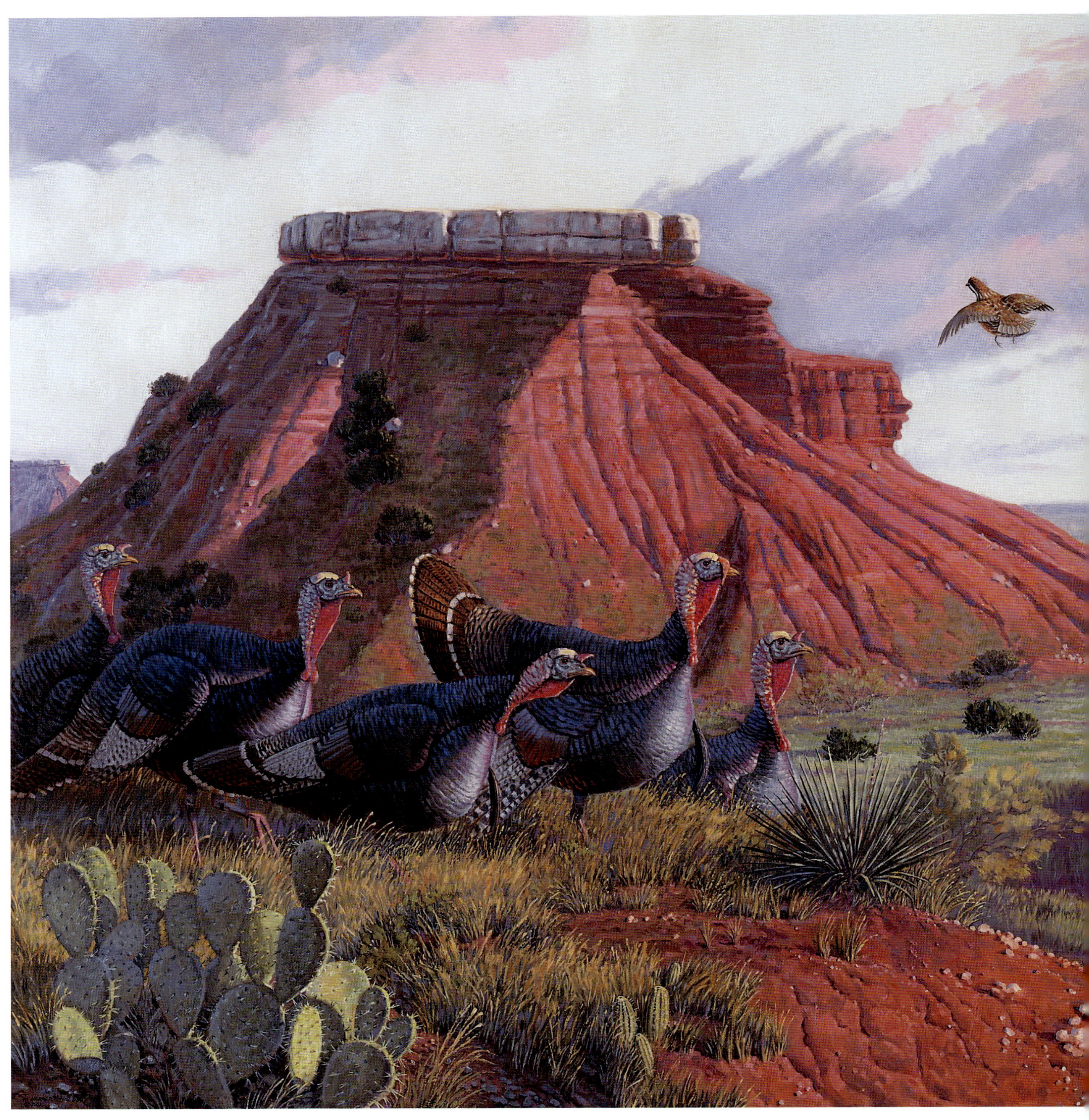

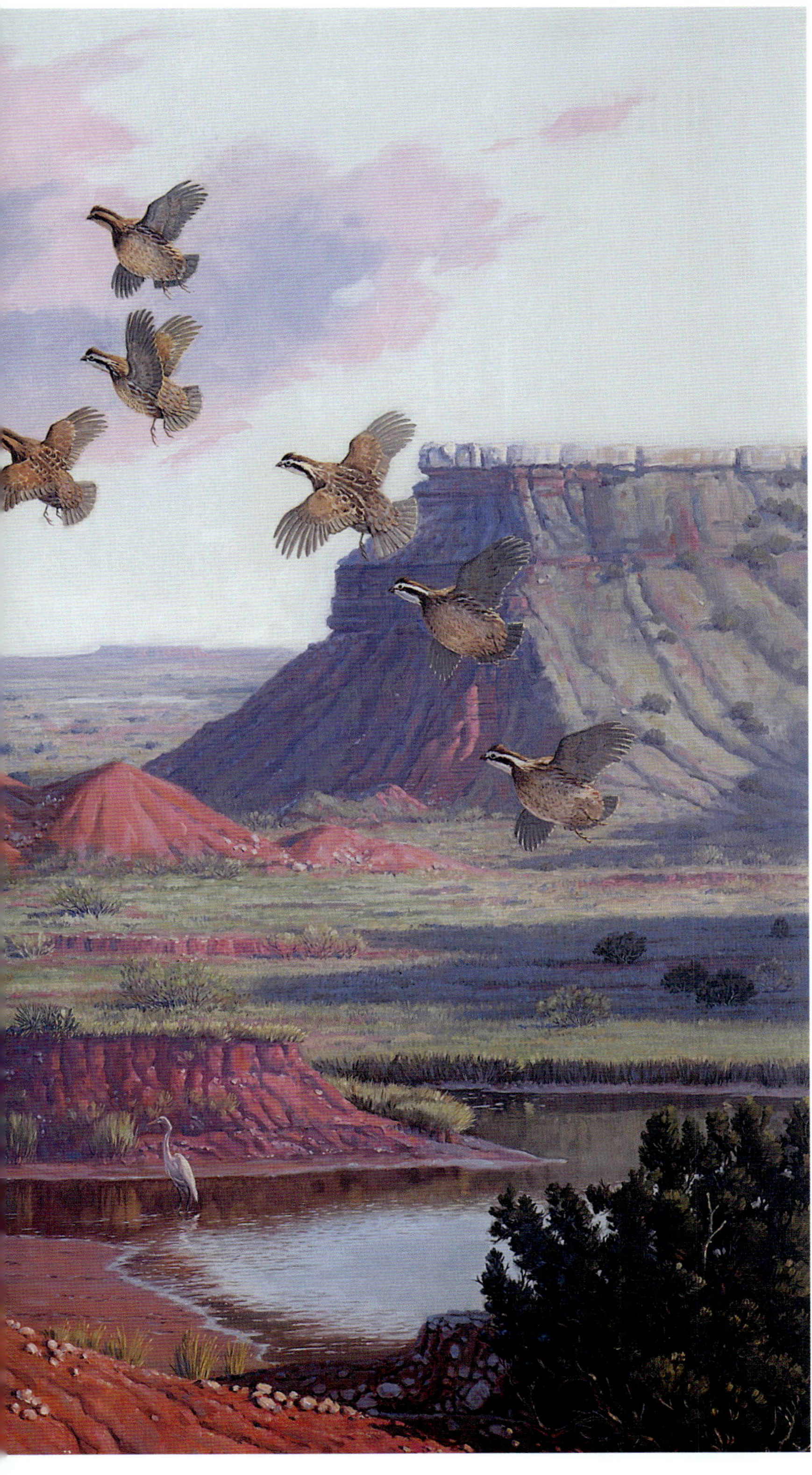

GAME BIRDS AT GLASS MOUNTAIN

BY HAROLD T. HOLDEN

60 x 96, oil/canvas

Patty and Joe Cappy of Tulsa sponsored this painting that depicts the Glass Mountains, also called the Gloss Mountains, northwest of Fairview in Major County. The sun bounces off the face of the selenite crystal rocks, the background chosen by the artist to show game birds indigenous to northwest Oklahoma.

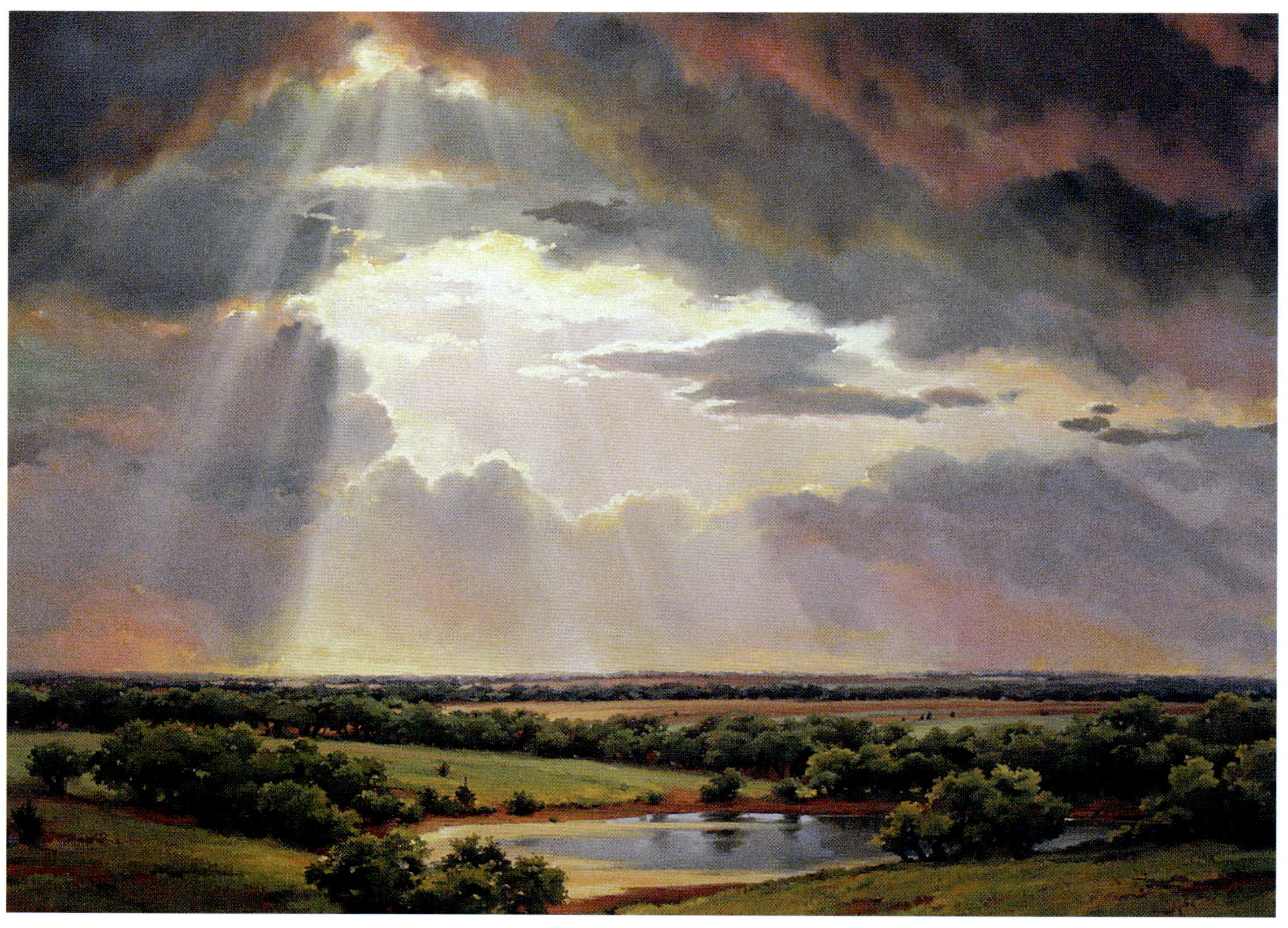

SHOWERS OF SUNSHINE

BY LINDA TUMA ROBERTSON

60 x 84, oil/canvas

The landscape of Grady County is shown from the H. E. Bailey Turnpike about one-quarter mile south of the tollbooth gate. Oklahoma sunshine showers the countryside. The family of Rob McCune of Oklahoma City sponsored the painting.

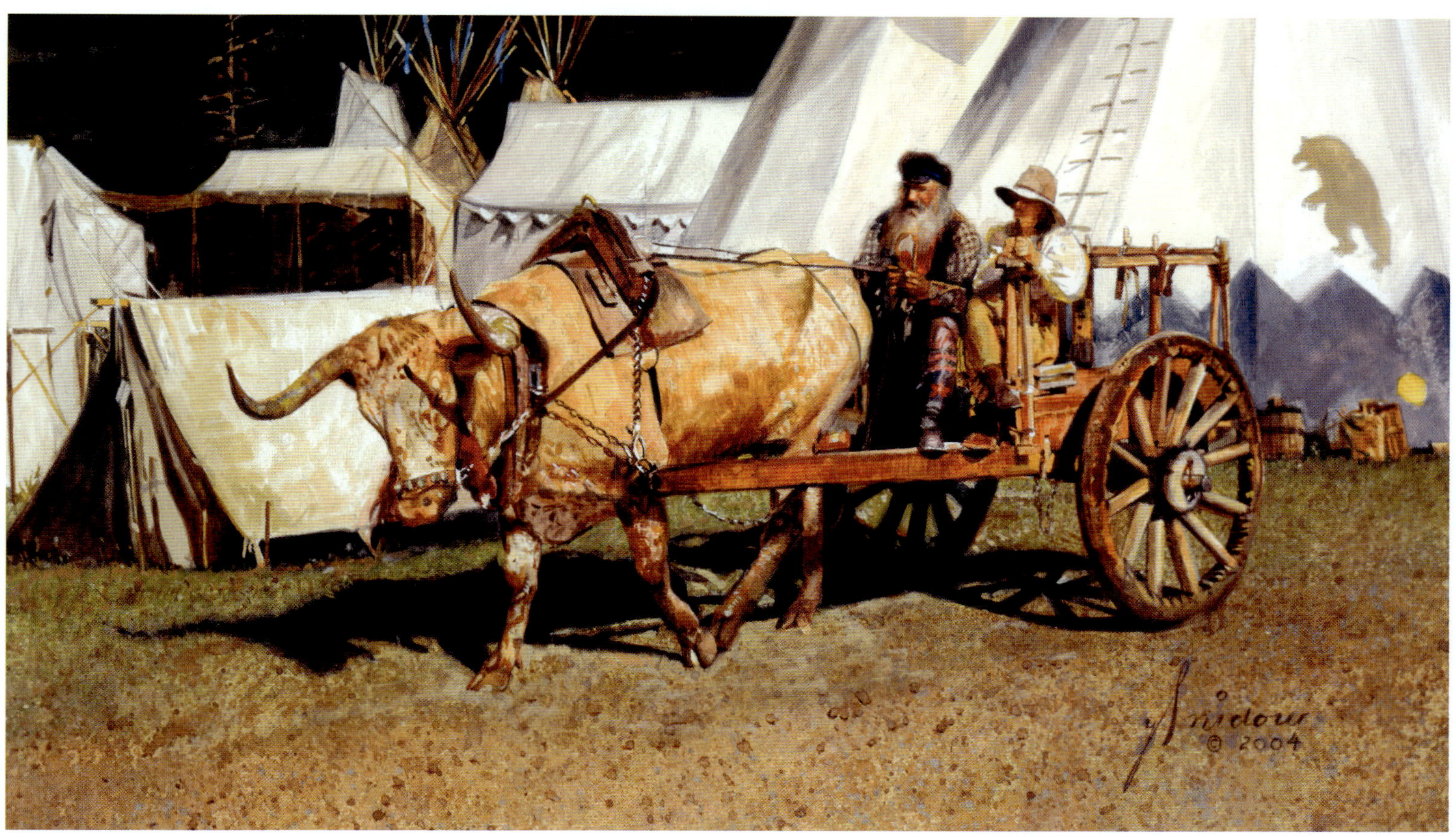

BUFFALO SKINNER'S CART

BY GORDON SNIDOW

30 x 17, gouache/canvas

Buffalo were once so plentiful on the Great Plains that trains might stop and wait hours for herds to pass. In 1867 General Philip Sheridan, commander of U. S. troops in the West, pledged to bring peace to the plains by killing off the animals. Hundreds of hunters were hired to indiscriminately kill them for their hides. Skins were stretched, baled, and shipped to markets. By 1875, the great herd was practically extinct. The painting was sponsored by the Harold Stuart Foundation.

DUGOUT SODDY ON THE PRAIRIE

BY WAYNE COOPER

72 x 120, oil/canvas

The Kerr Foundation sponsored this depiction of early pioneer family life in the sod houses that dotted western Oklahoma's landscape after a series of land openings. A pioneer woman tends to her chickens while her husband sharpens an ax on a grindstone. The wash pot and rifle leaning against the wall symbolize the harsh and sometimes dangerous life on the windswept prairie. Made from cheap, readily-available building material, sod houses were cool in the summer and easy to heat in the winter. The only remaining sod house in Oklahoma is at Aline and is preserved by the Oklahoma Historical Society.

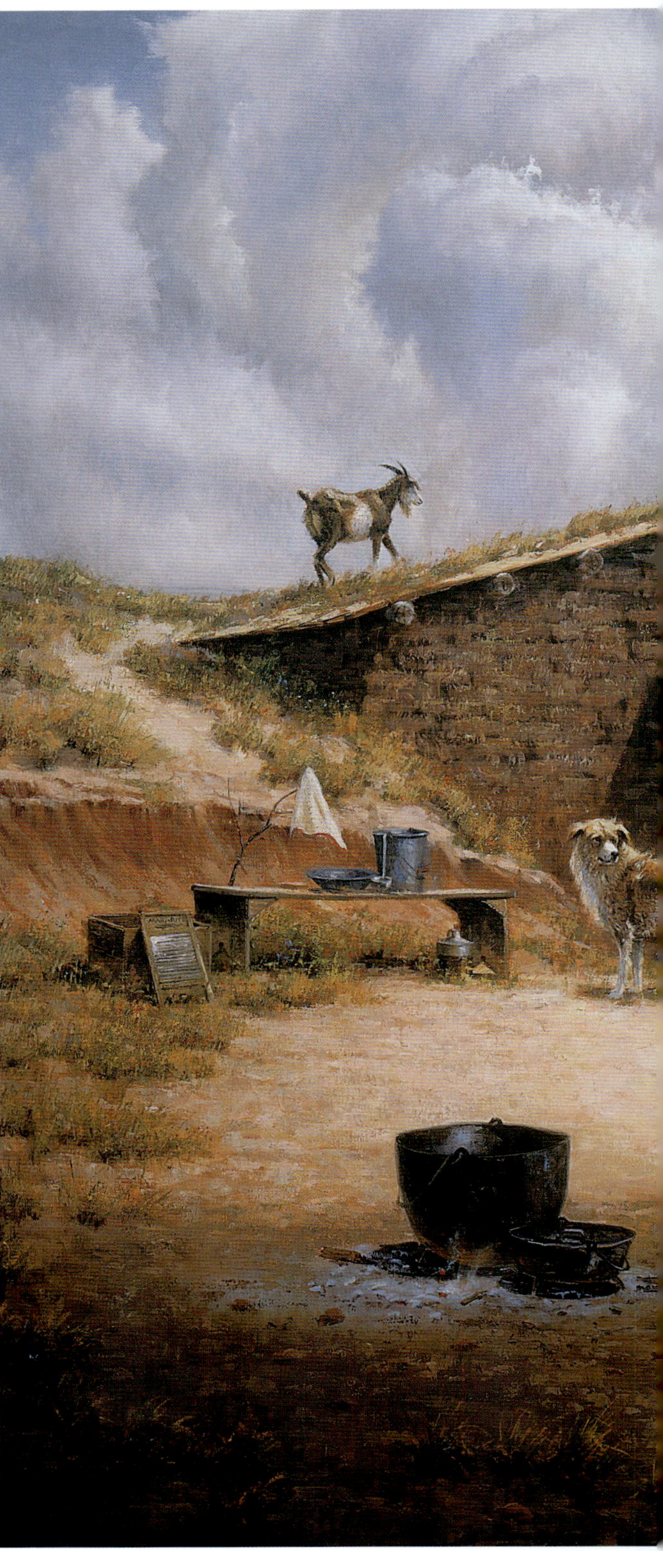

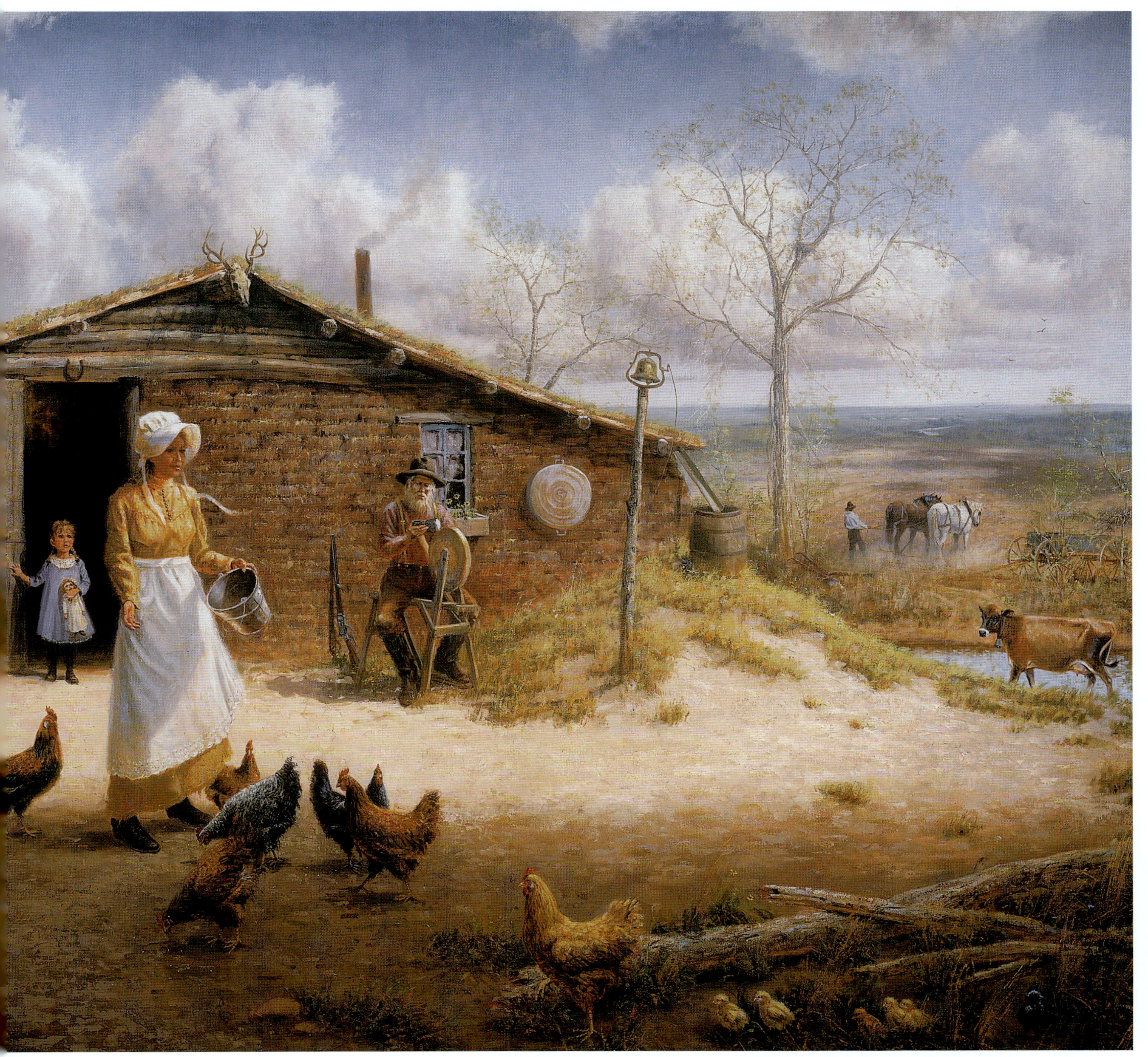

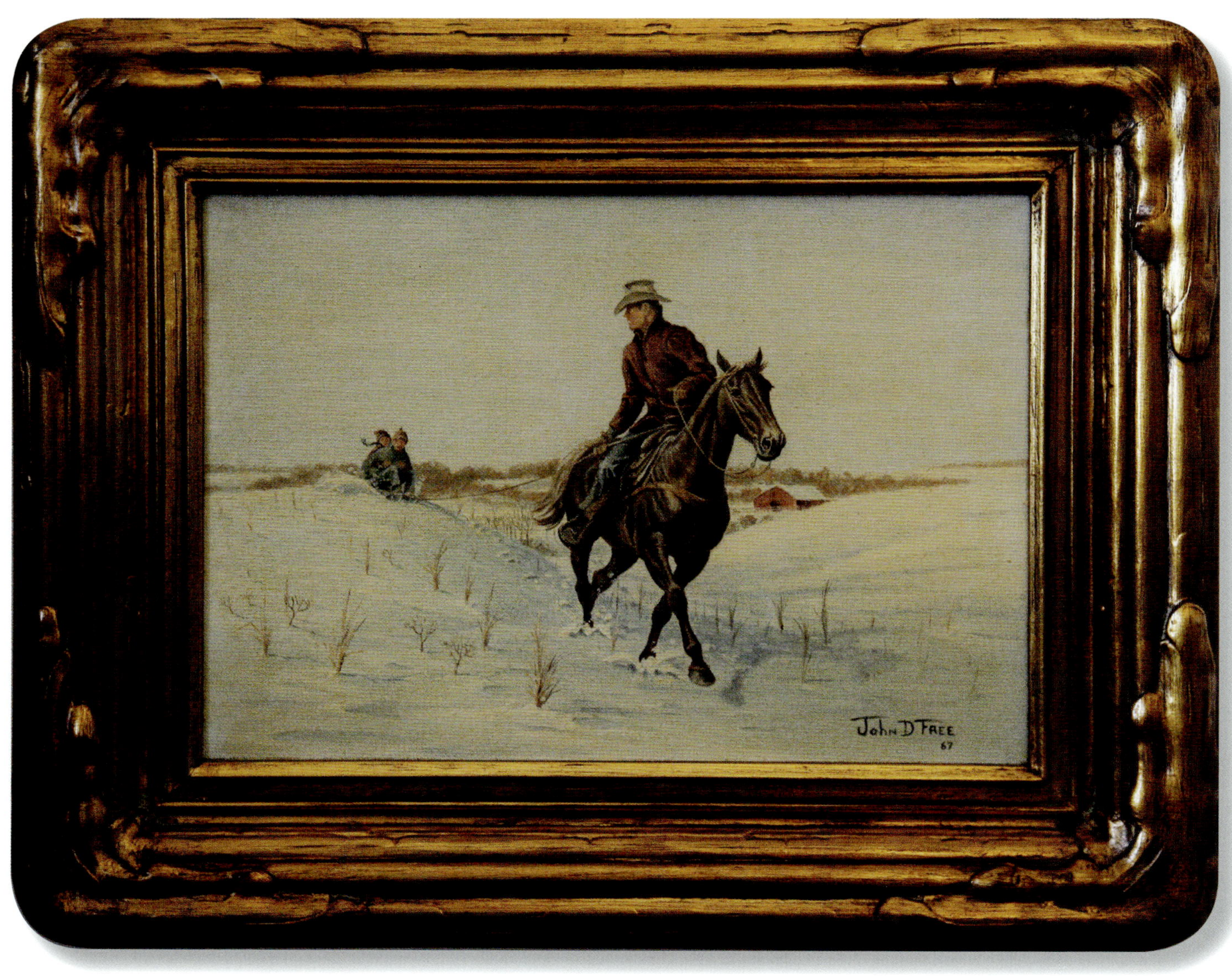

TOO EARLY TO PLOW

BY JOHN FREE

10 x 14, oil/boar

The artist John Free first used this painting as his personal Christmas card. It depicts a lively use for an Osage County family's horse in the snowy days of winter before spring planting. Sponsored by Senator Charles Ford.

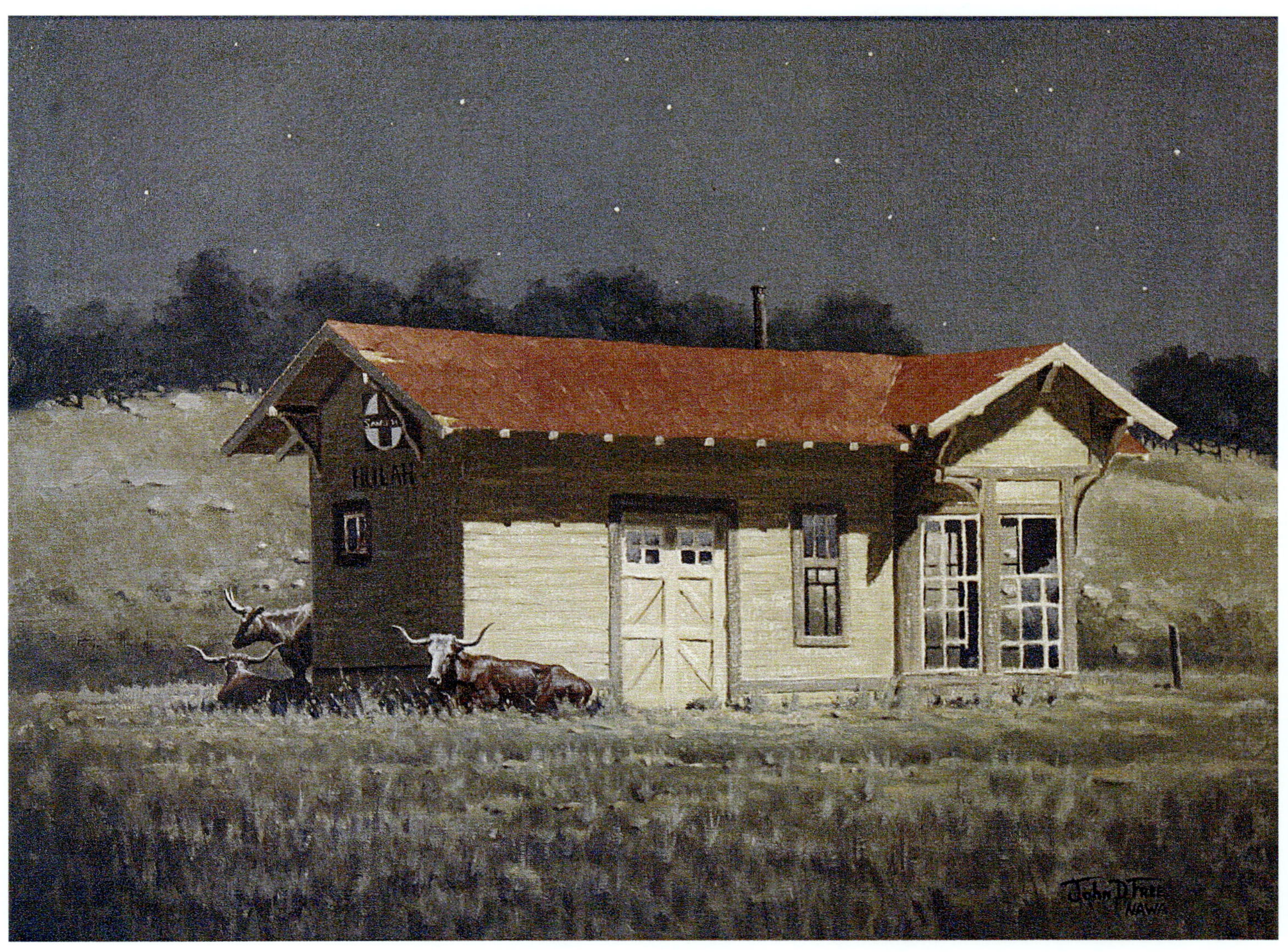

HULAH STATION AND CROSSBELL STEERS

BY JOHN FREE

16 x 22, oil/canvas

Hulah Station was a railroad stop whose name is the Osage word for "eagle." The abandoned station house began a second life when owners of the Crossbell Ranch moved remnants of the old town at Hulah Station to their property to serve as storage for hay. Sponsored by Senator Charles Ford.

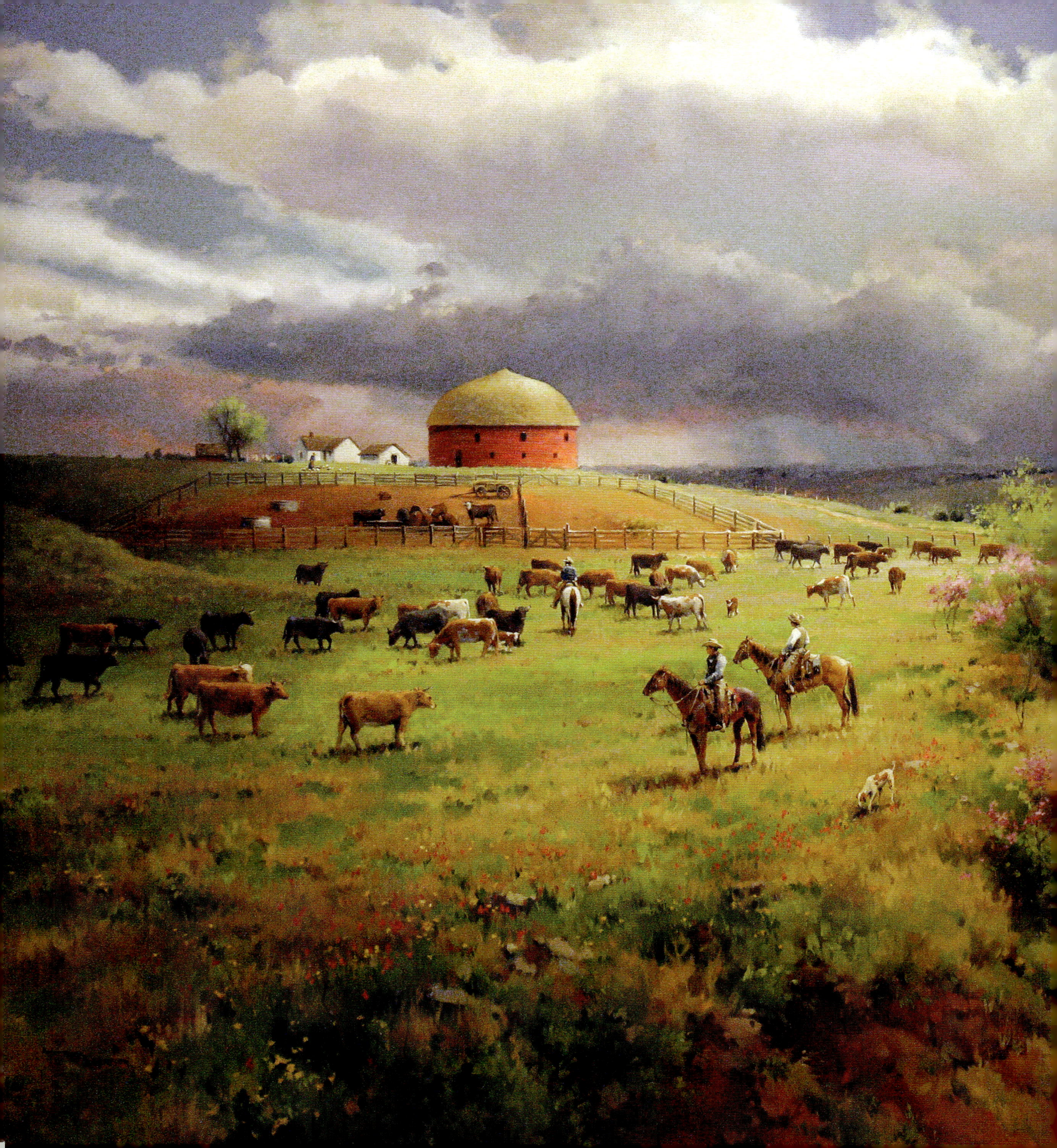

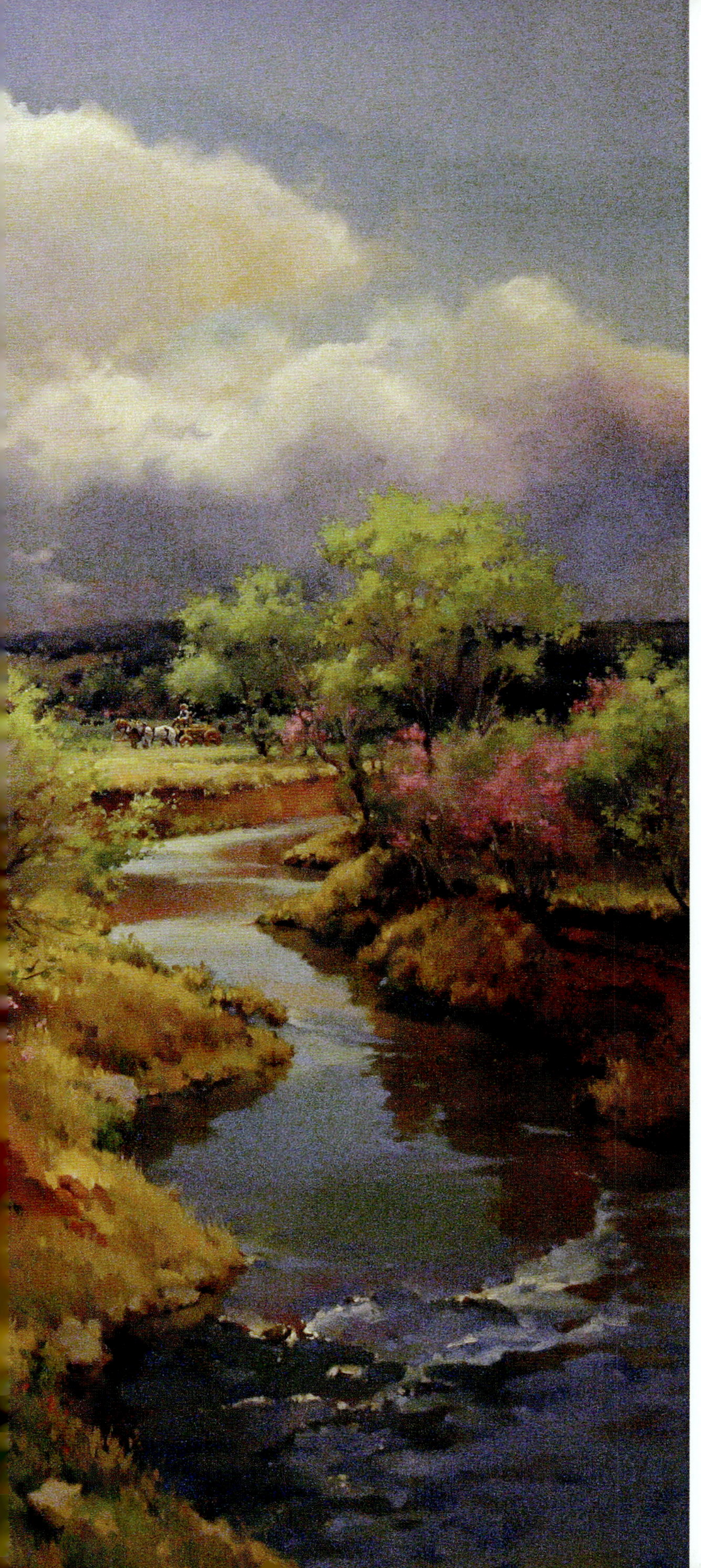

ARCADIA ROUNDUP

BY LINDA TUMA ROBERTSON

60 x 84, oil/canvas

One of Oklahoma's most notable manmade features is the round barn at Arcadia. William Harrison Odor and his neighbors began construction on the barn in 1898. Odor believed a round barn would withstand the force of Oklahoma tornadoes. Rafters were formed from green lumber soaked in water from nearby Deep Fork River. The round barn is two stories high, with a diameter of 60 feet and a height of 45 feet. After Route 66 was built adjacent to the barn it became a tourist attraction along the "Mother Road." The painting of a roundup at Arcadia with the barn in the background was sponsored by State Representative Ray Vaughn of Edmond and his wife Suzanne.

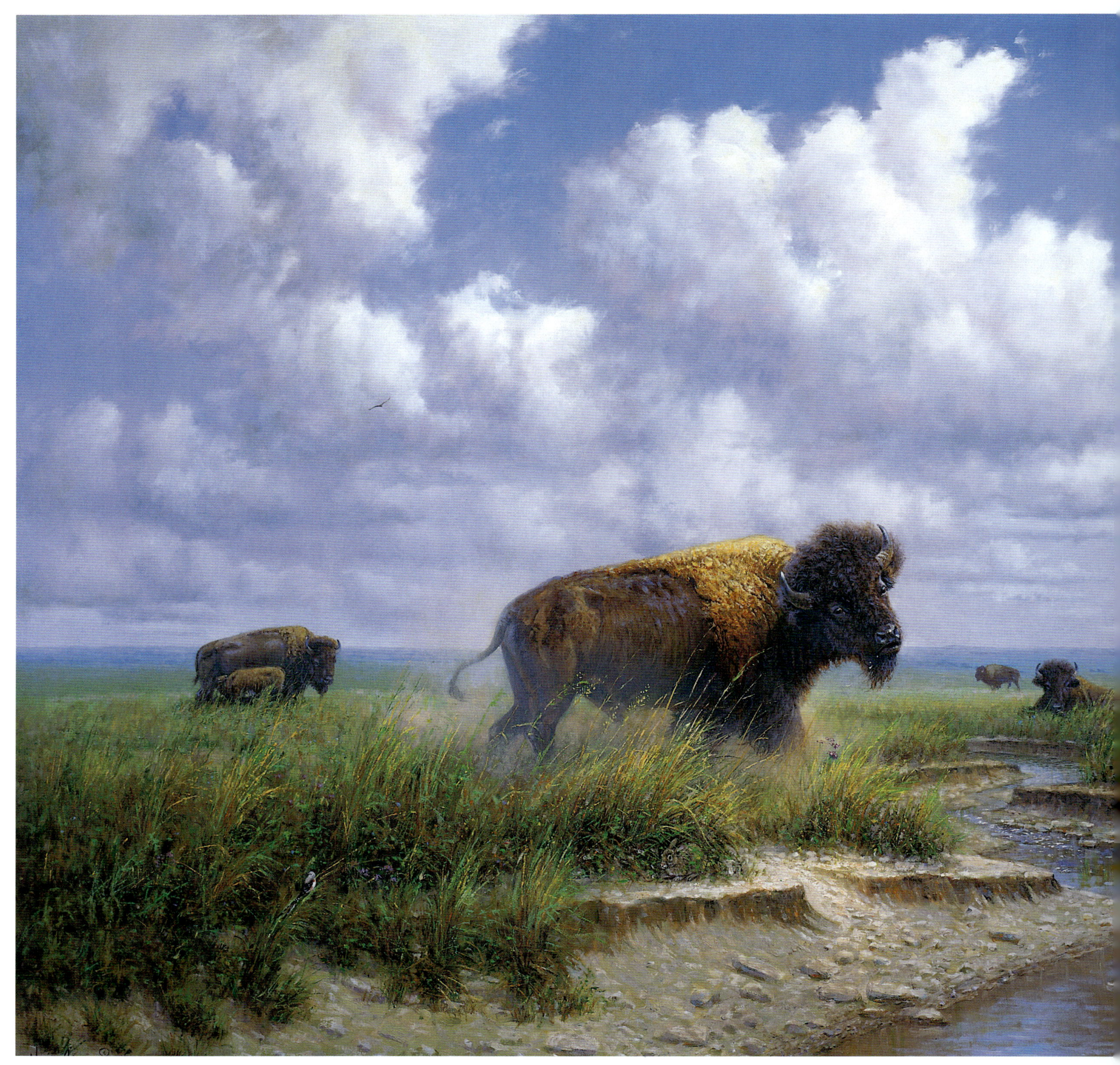

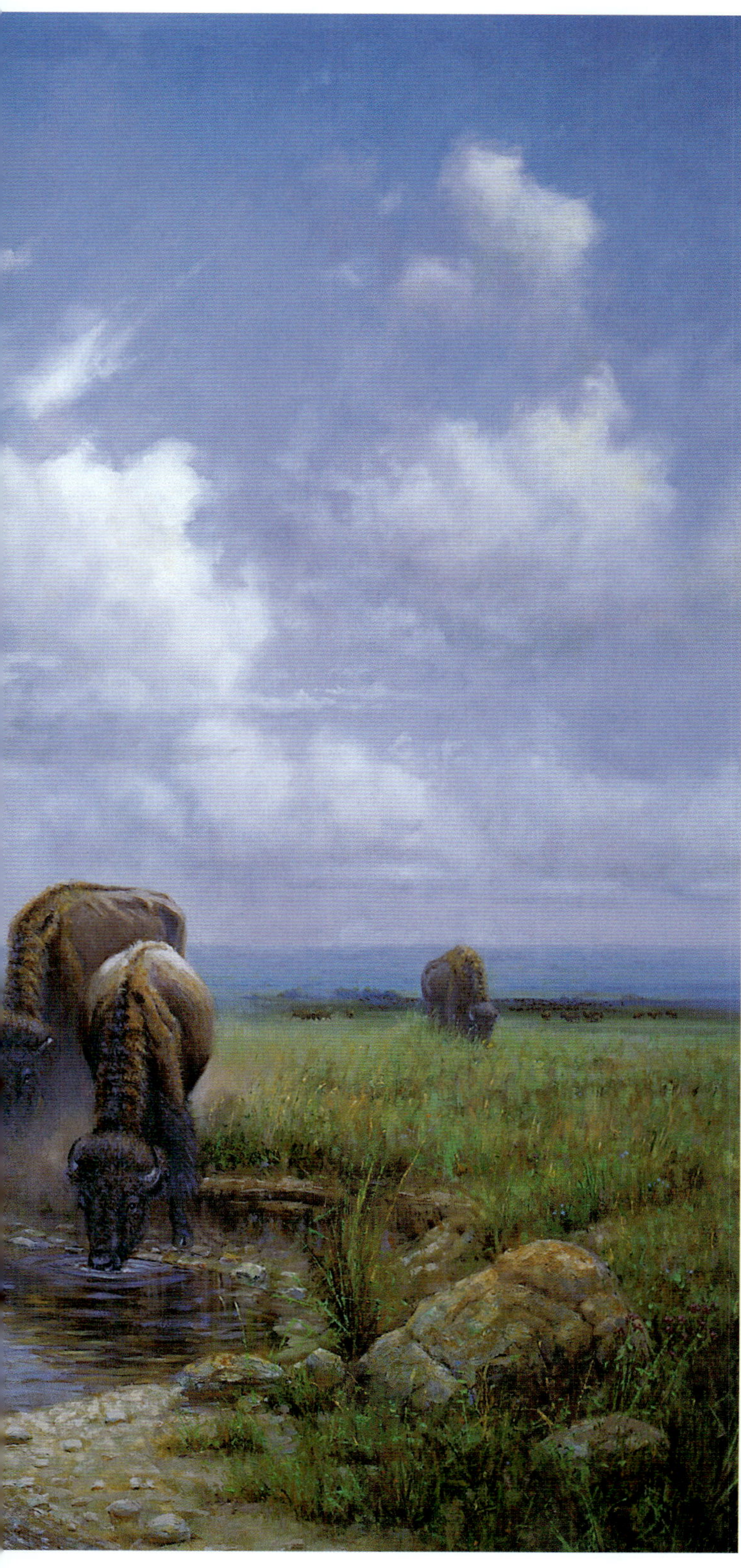

TALLGRASS PRAIRIE

BY WAYNE COOPER

60 x 96, oil/canvas

The rich diversity of plants and animals that made up the tallgrass prairie is depicted in this painting sponsored by the Williams Companies of Tulsa. The tallgrass prairie once spanned 14 states and covered more than 140 million acres. In 1989, the Nature Conservancy bought the 29,000-acre Barnard Ranch in northern Oklahoma as the cornerstone of the Tallgrass Prairie Reserve.

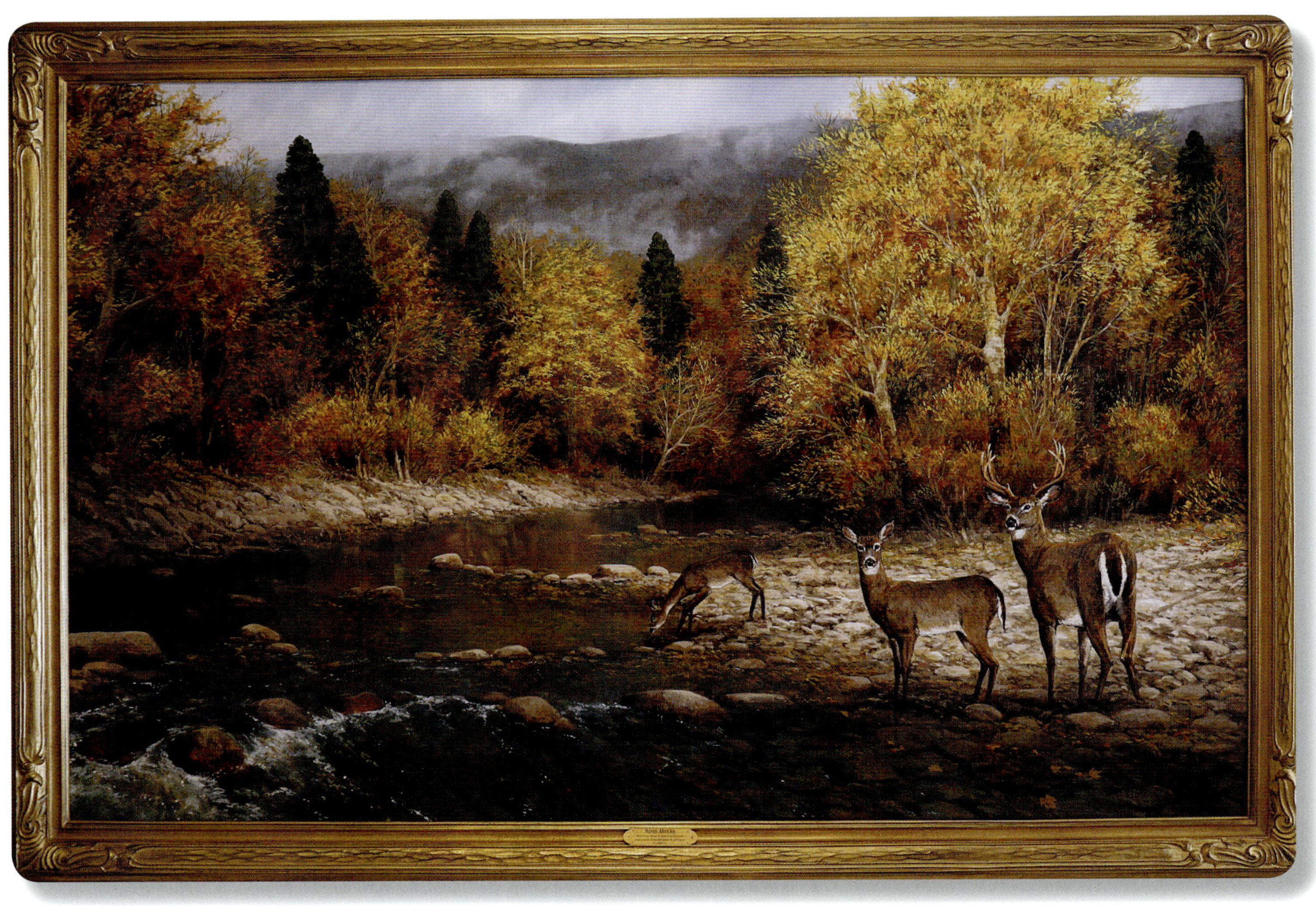

WHITETAIL DEER IN CHOCTAW COUNTRY

BY ROSS MYERS

60 x 96, oil/canvas

Whitetail deer were a principal source of meat for the Choctaw Indians when they were removed from their homeland in the southeastern United States and given lands in southeast Oklahoma in the 1830s. The artist found this scene on the banks of a stream called Big Creek that flows into the Black Fork of the Poteau River in LeFlore County. The painting was a gift to the people of Oklahoma from the family of the late Senator John R. McCune of Oklahoma City.

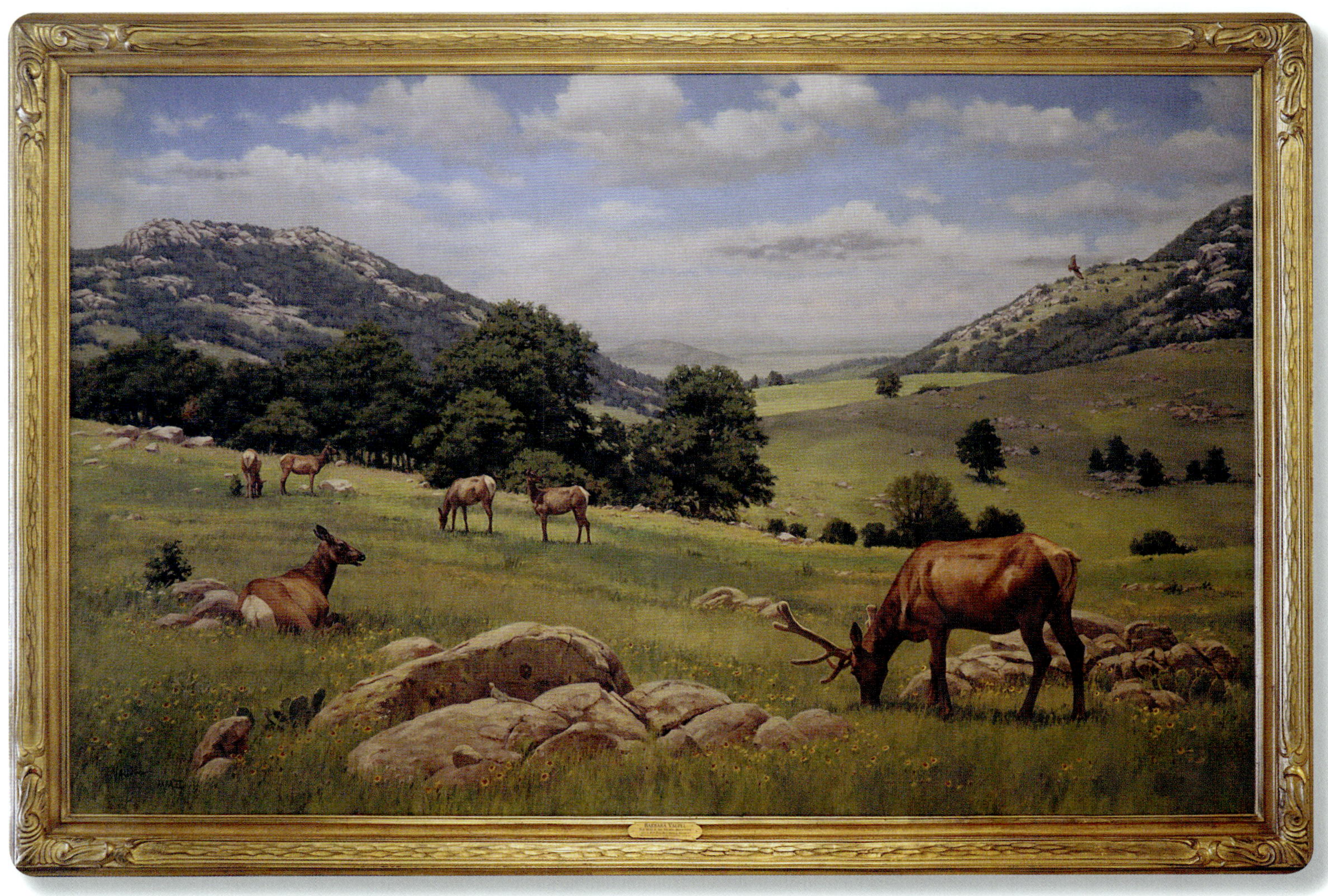

ELK HERD IN THE WICHITA MOUNTAINS

BY BARBARA VAUPEL

60 x 96, oil/canvas

This painting shows elk grazing on a peaceful stretch of grassland bordered by rising granite mountains in southwest Oklahoma. Elk were indigenous to the Wichita Mountains but were exterminated by the late 1800s. A year after Oklahoma statehood, the city of Wichita, Kansas, donated a single bull elk to the Wichita Mountains Wildlife Refuge. Three years later, the federal government added elk that are ancestors of the current population. The artist creates a spring scene with a blanket of wildflowers and the young bull elks' antlers still encased in velvet. The painting was sponsored by State Representative Don McCorkell of Tulsa.

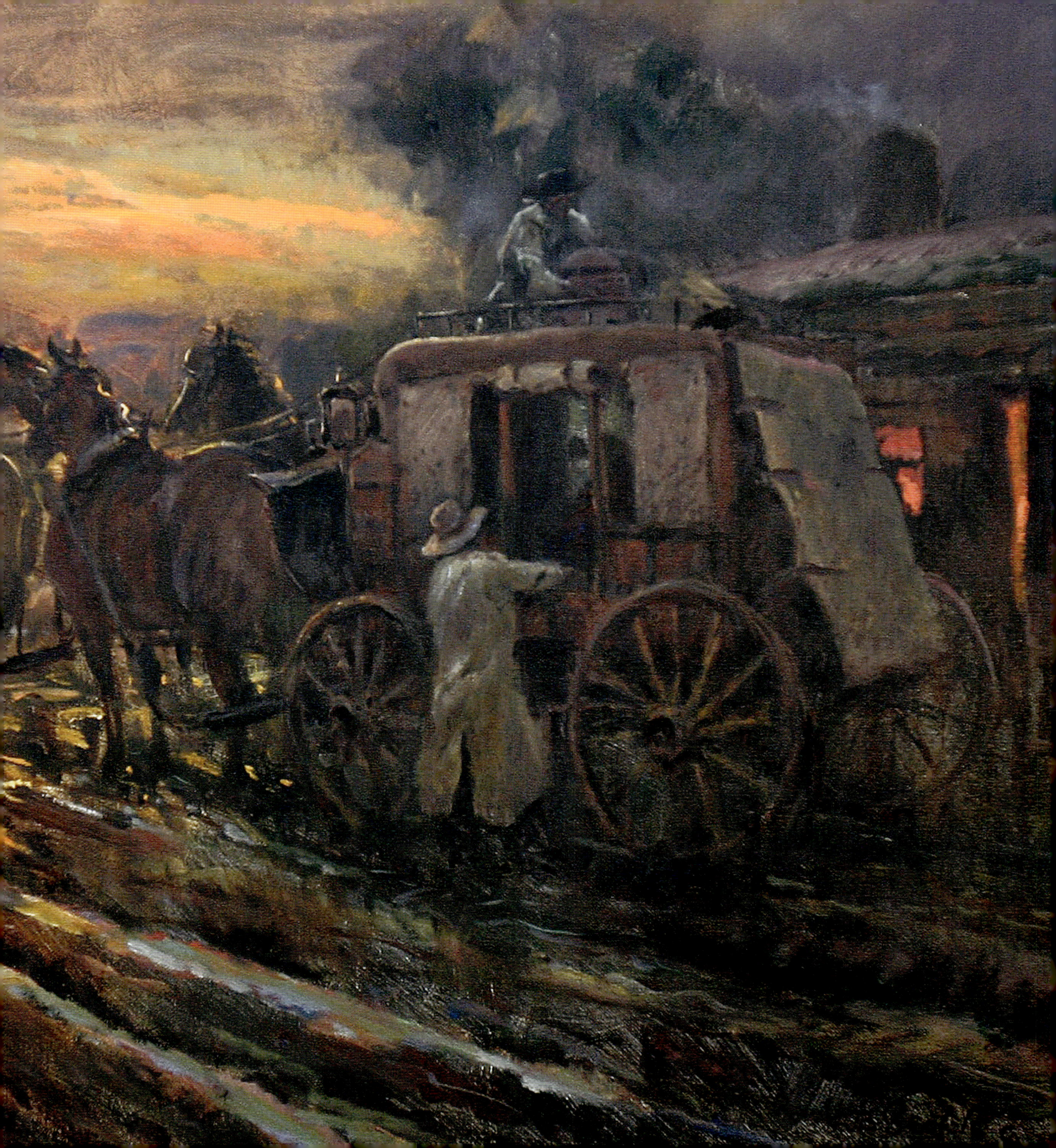

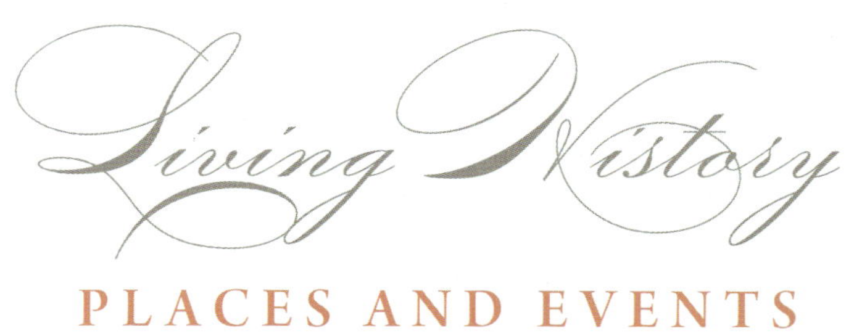

PLACES AND EVENTS

KIMBERLY ROBLIN, Associate Curator

Characterized, idolized, vilified, and romanticized, the American West has often been defined through dichotomies: cowboys and Indians, outlaws and lawmen, mythology and history. Through it all it has retained its rugged reputation as a time untamed, unforgiving, and unwilling to suffer fools. Inherently compelling, it forges a dramatic image of windswept plains and horizon-spanning sunsets, cattle drives and wagon trains, warbonnets and Winchesters, where East met West and changed the ways of both forever. Defined within this legacy and landscape is Oklahoma, the land of tallgrass prairies and Ozark foothills, with a history as diverse as its landscape.

Far older than its century of statehood would suggest, Oklahoma claims a unique heritage of confluence and resilience. While its history is most closely associated with that of the frontier West, it is important to remember the breadth and scope of this state's past. The art of the Senate Collection pays tribute to this history, honoring events that occurred in or are associated with Oklahoma. Some works feature Native Americans and pioneer settlers, familiar elements of Oklahoma history. Others, such as *Battle of Round Mountain* and *Surrender of General Stand Watie,* illustrate the less familiar topic of Indian Territory's involvement in the Civil War. Not only depicting events long in the past, however, the collection also includes *Attack of Battleship Oklahoma at Pearl Harbor, The U.S.S. Oklahoma Memorial at Pearl Harbor,* and *Comanche Code Talkers at Omaha Beach.* Each portrays a scene relating to the Second World War. From pre-Territory days through pioneer settlement, from the Civil War to the Second World War, the art of the Senate Collection conveys the long and proud history of our state.

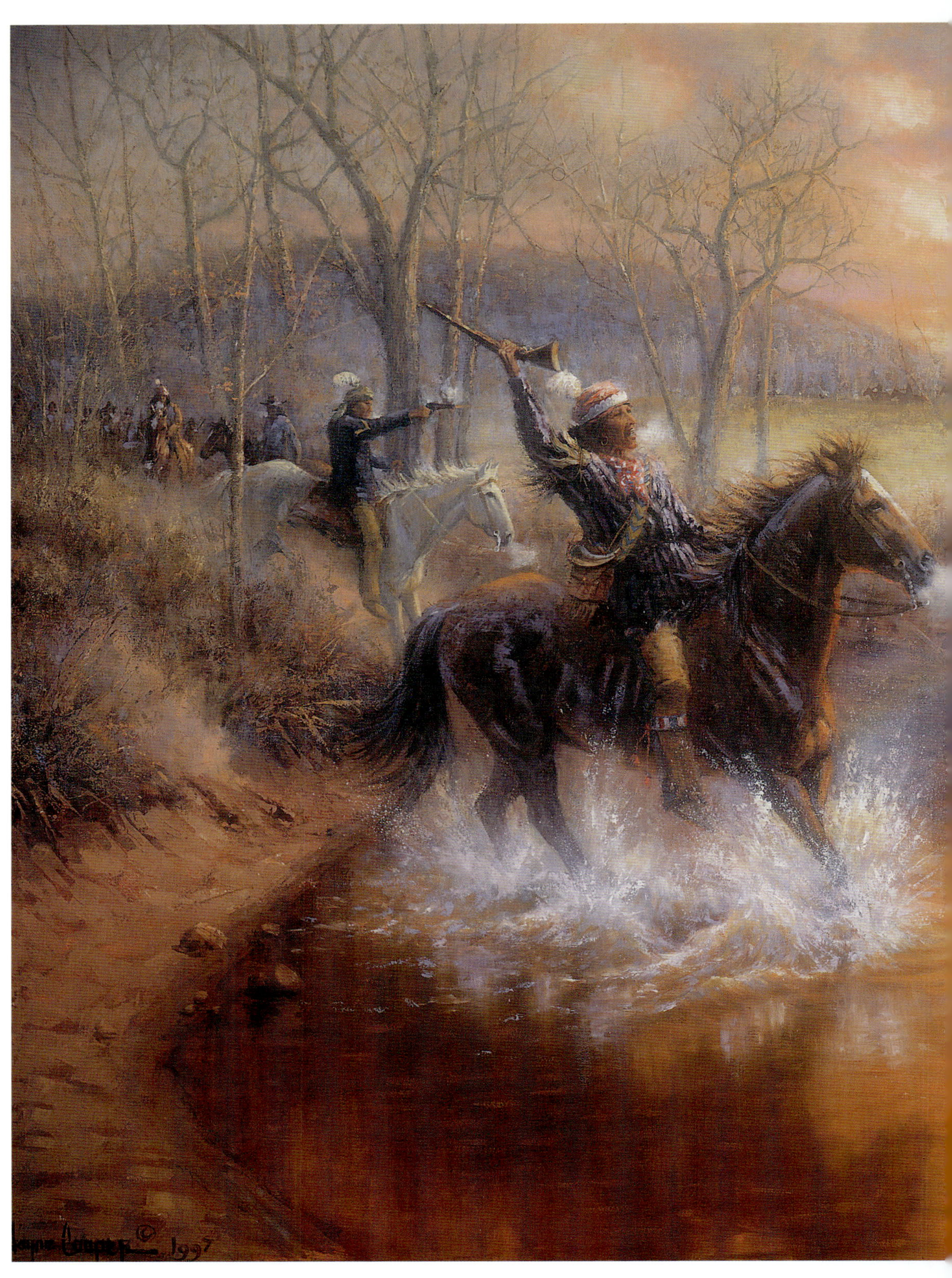

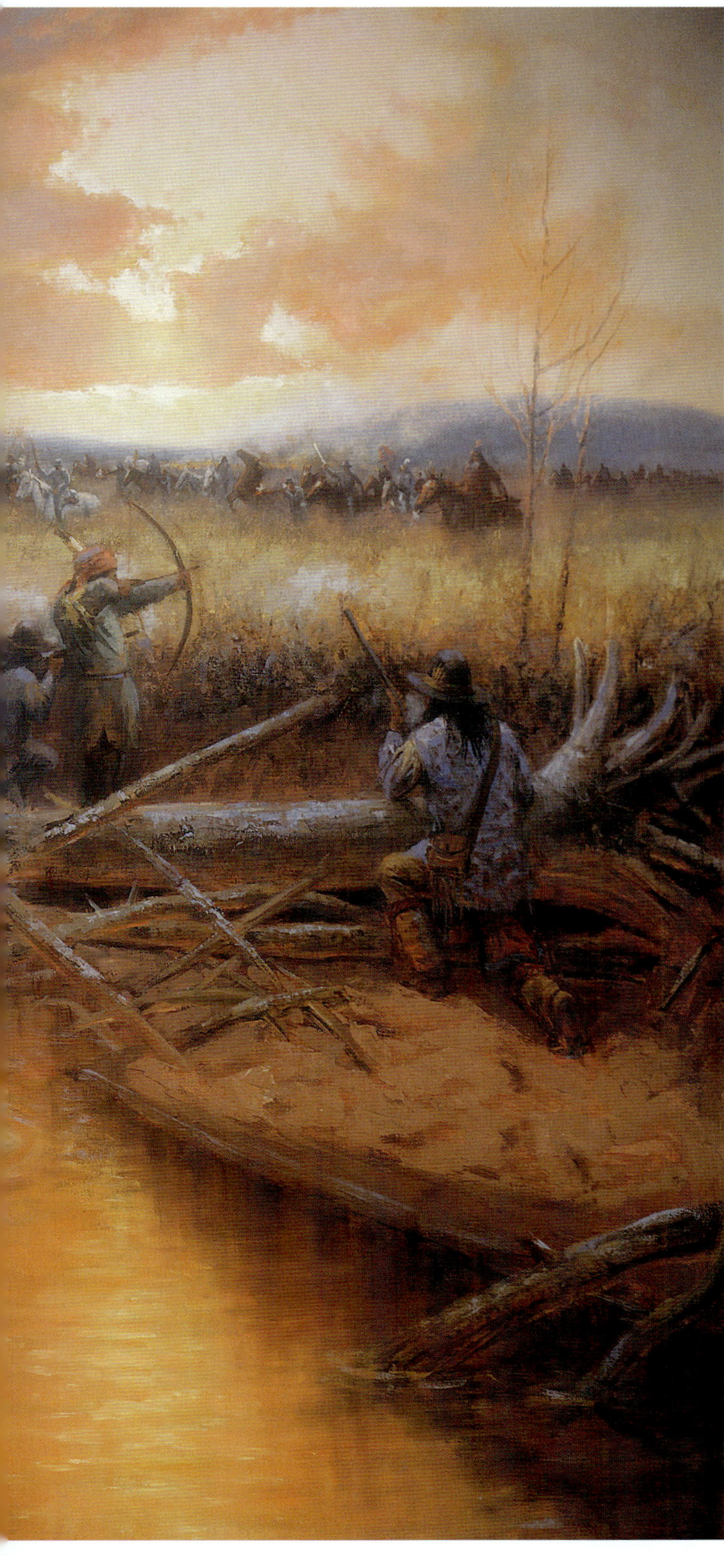

BATTLE OF ROUND MOUNTAIN

BY WAYNE COOPER

36 x 48, oil/canvas

The first major Civil War battle fought in what would become Oklahoma was the Battle of Round Mountain. Confederate Colonel Douglas H. Cooper and troops from the First Choctaw and Chickasaw Regiment were pursuing 9,000 Creeks under the leadership of Opothle-Yahola. The Creeks were headed to Kansas to seek Union protection. Because historians disagree about the exact location of the battle, the artist visited two similar areas and arrived at a composition that resembled both places. The painting was sponsored by State Senator Ted Fisher of Sapulpa.

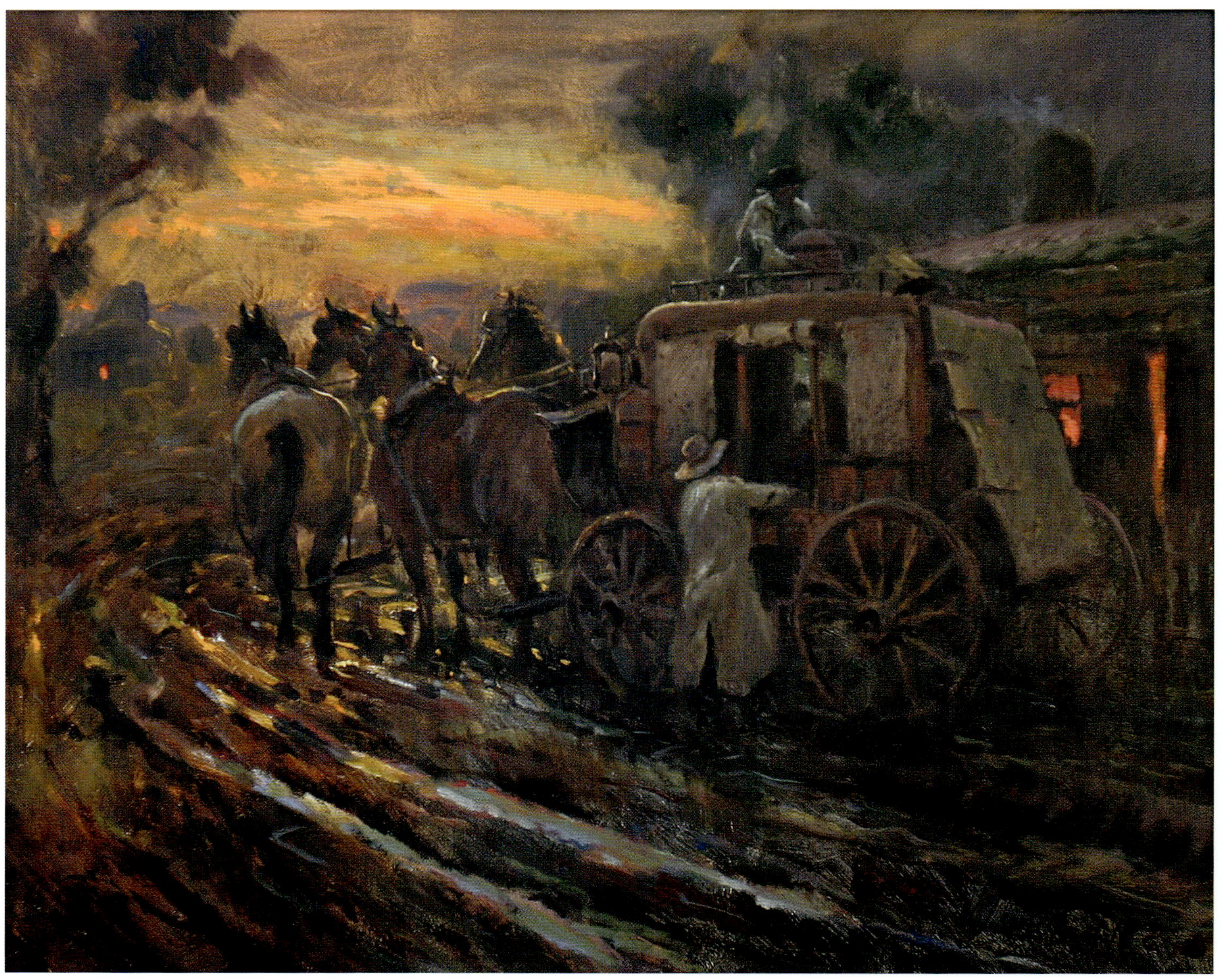

BUTTERFIELD STAGE AT BOGGY DEPOT

BY JOE BEELER

16 x 20, oil/canvas

The Butterfield Overland Mail Company carried mail from St. Louis, Missouri, to San Francisco, California, twice weekly between 1858 and 1861. To avoid mountain snows, it took the southern route through Oklahoma. The high quality coaches carried passengers as well as mail. One Oklahoma stop was Boggy Depot, home of Choctaw Chief Allen Wright, who suggested the name "Oklahoma" for the proposed Indian Territory. In 1907, the word was made the official state name. William Lobeck and Kathryn Taylor sponsored the painting.

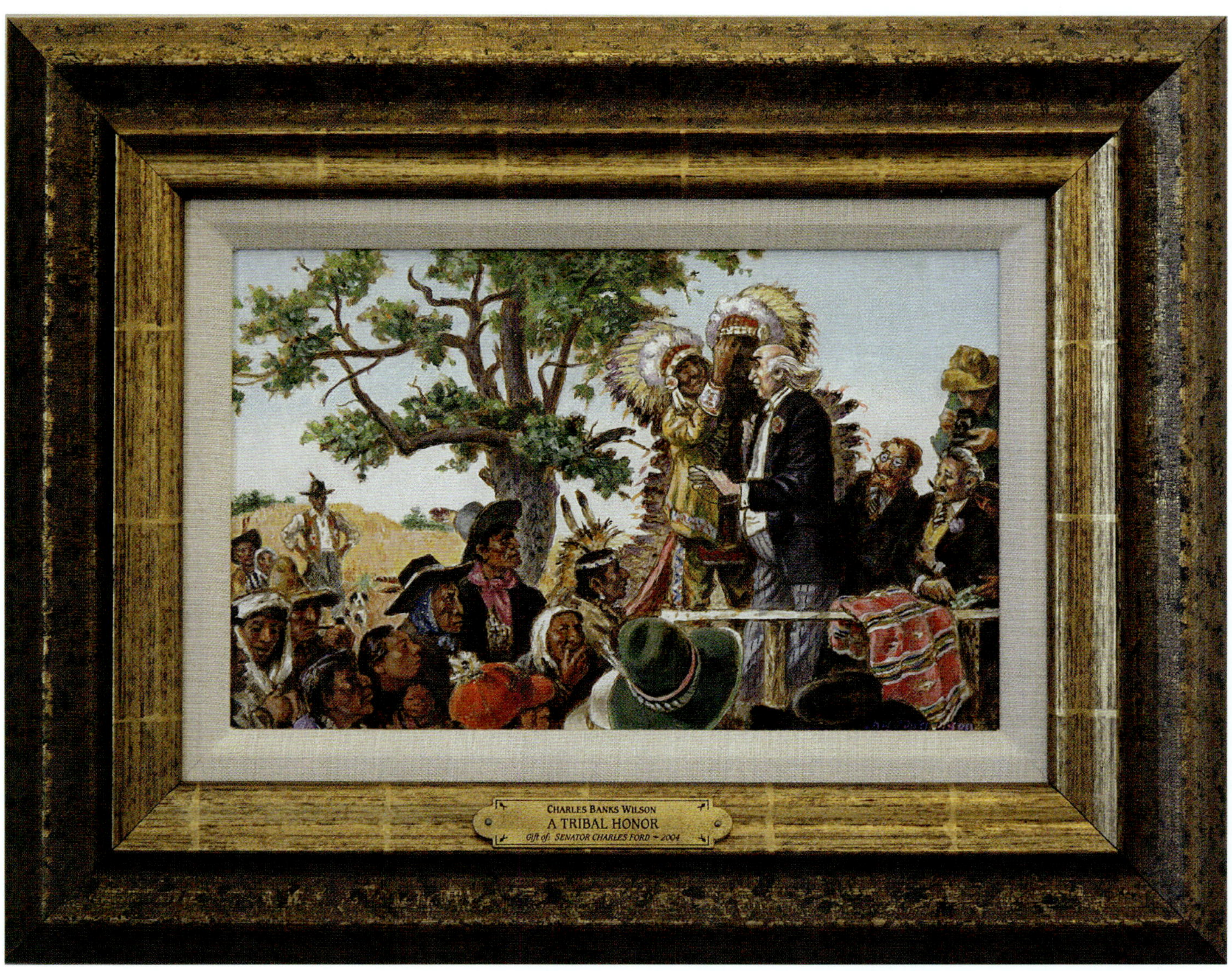

A HIGH HONOR

BY CHARLES BANKS WILSON

12 x 18, oil/canvas

An early Oklahoma politician at a "speaking" with Native Americans. A headdress is being presented to the politician as a high honor. Sponsored by Senator Charles Ford.

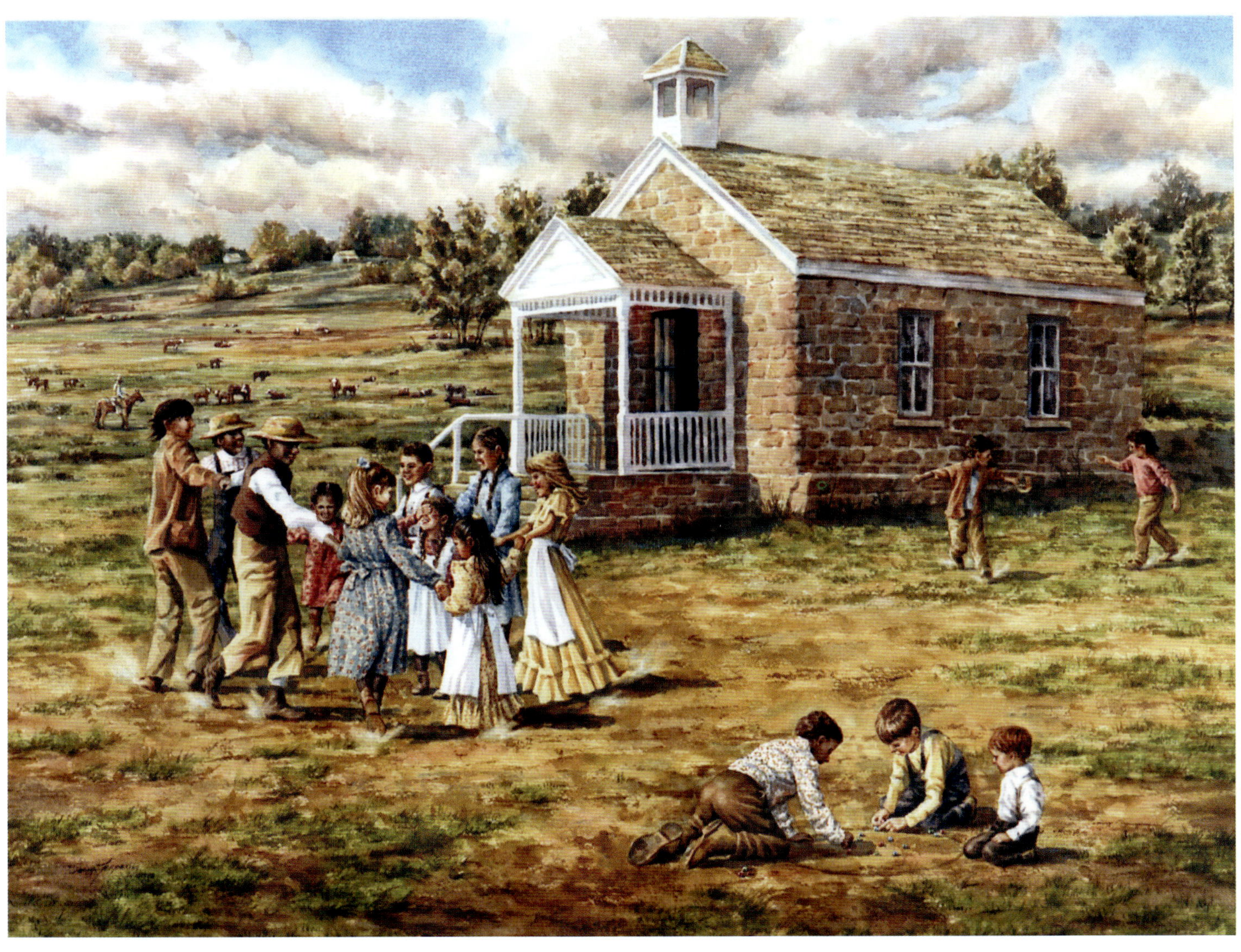

COMMUNITY OF BOLING SPRINGS

BY SONJA TERPENING

30 x 40, watercolor

The school was the center of the Boling Springs community in Craig County where Indians, blacks, and whites peacefully coexisted. Will Rogers visited the area many times when he worked as a ranch hand. Senate President Pro Tempore Stratton Taylor of Claremore sponsored the painting that depicts children from various ethnic groups playing together on the school ground during recess.

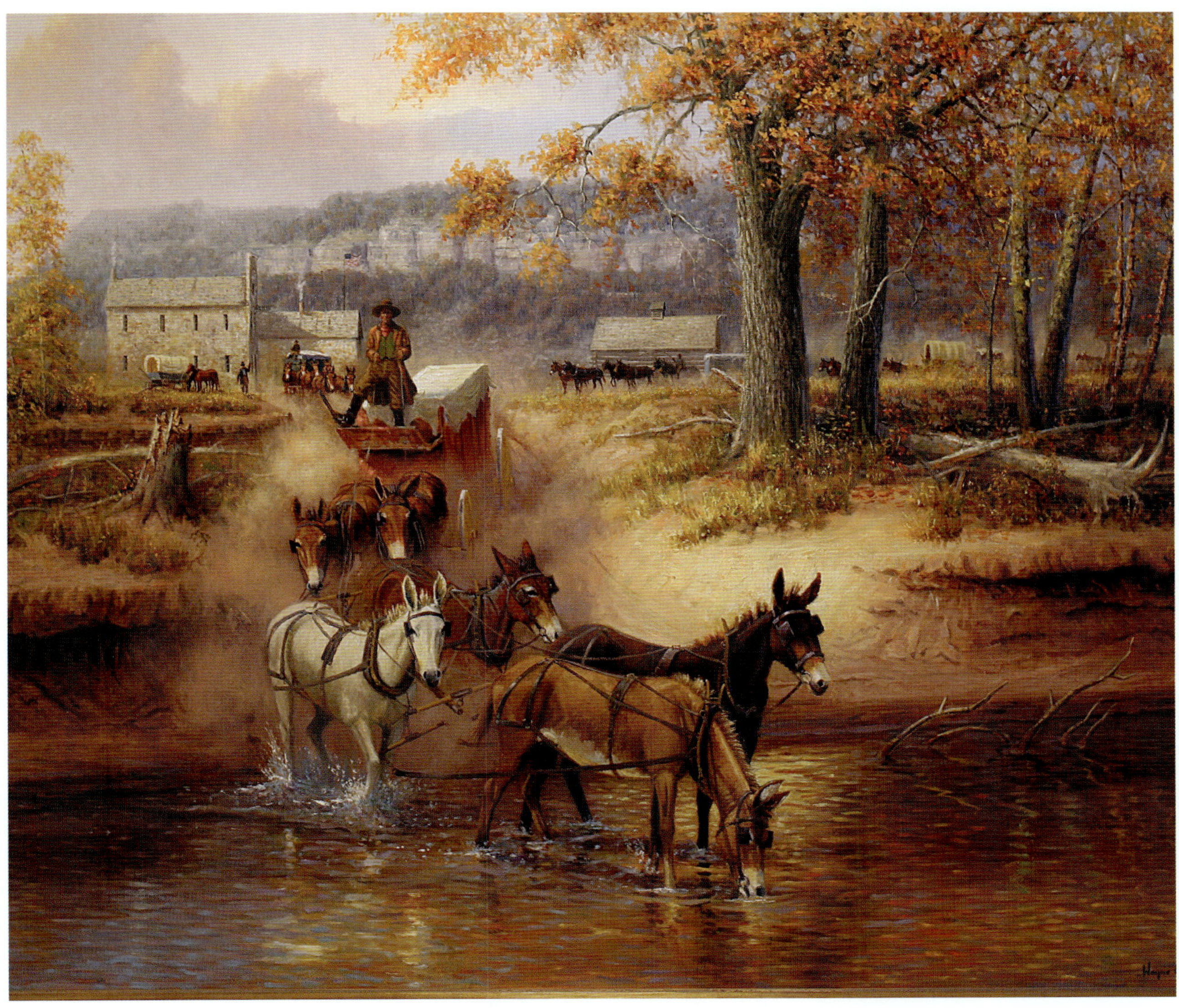

CALIFORNIA ROAD

BY WAYNE COOPER

72 x 96, oil/canvas

Sponsored by Senator Joe McGraw of Tulsa and his wife, Carol, the painting depicts travelers on the California Road in Indian Territory.

With the discovery of gold in California in 1848, thousands of settlers headed west from Fort Smith, Arkansas, and followed the trail along the south bank of the South Canadian River. Emigrants made the Edwards Trading Post in present Hughes County one of the busiest commercial enterprises in the territory. Wagon ruts can still be seen along the trail that lost its importance with the coming of the railroads.

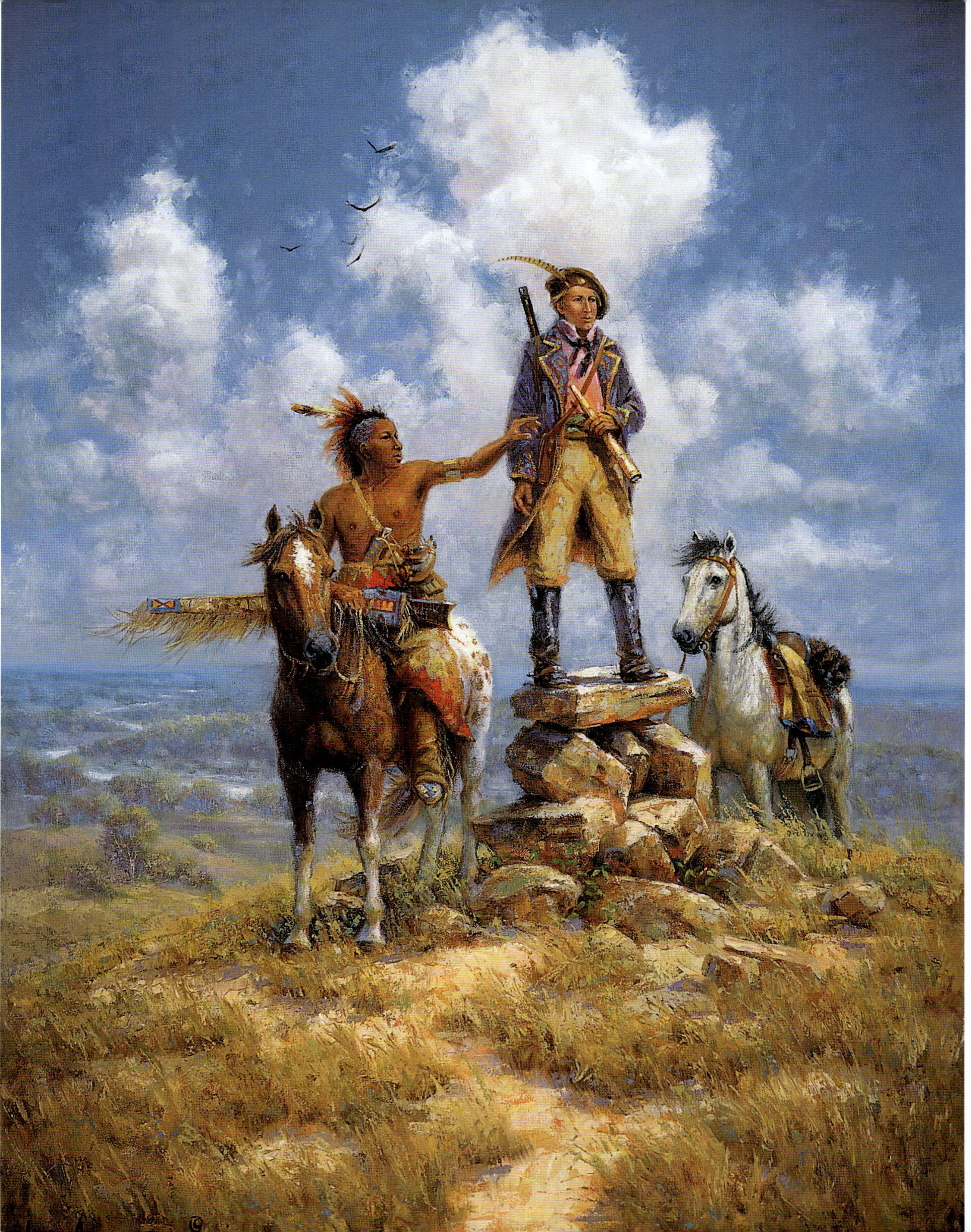

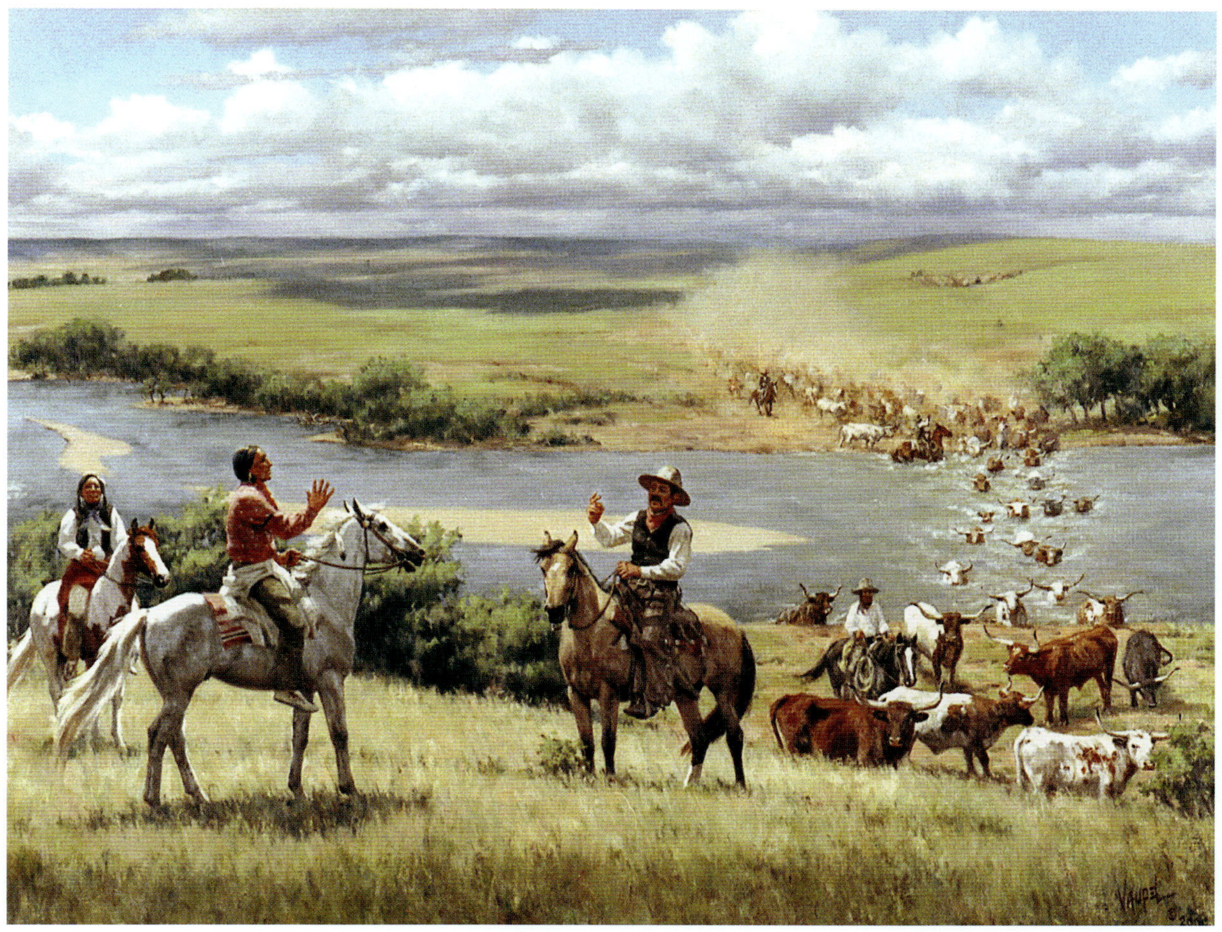

FRIENDS FOR A DAY—OCTOBER 12, 1832 (FACING)

BY WAYNE COOPER

30 x 40, oil/canvas

State Senator Ben Brown of Oklahoma City sponsored this painting depicting the friendship between Count Albert-Alexandre de Portales, a 21-year-old member of Washington Irving's party, and a young Osage boy who brought a stray pony into Irving's camp. Portales made the boy his personal squire after rescuing him from Cherokees who believed the pony was stolen and ordered the boy flogged. Irving recorded his 1832 travels through future Oklahoma in 1832 in *A Tour on the Prairies.*

GREAT WESTERN CATTLE TRAIL—1890S

BY BARBARA VAUPEL

30 x 40, oil/canvas

After the Civil War four major cattle trails were blazed across future Oklahoma for moving Texas longhorns to railheads in Kansas. This scene, crossing the Canadian River near Camargo in Dewey County, is on the Great Western Trail established by John Lytle in 1874. More than 300,000 cattle were moved north on the trail until the coming of railroads made the famous cattle trails obsolete. The painting was sponsored by the late State Senator Robert M. Kerr of Altus.

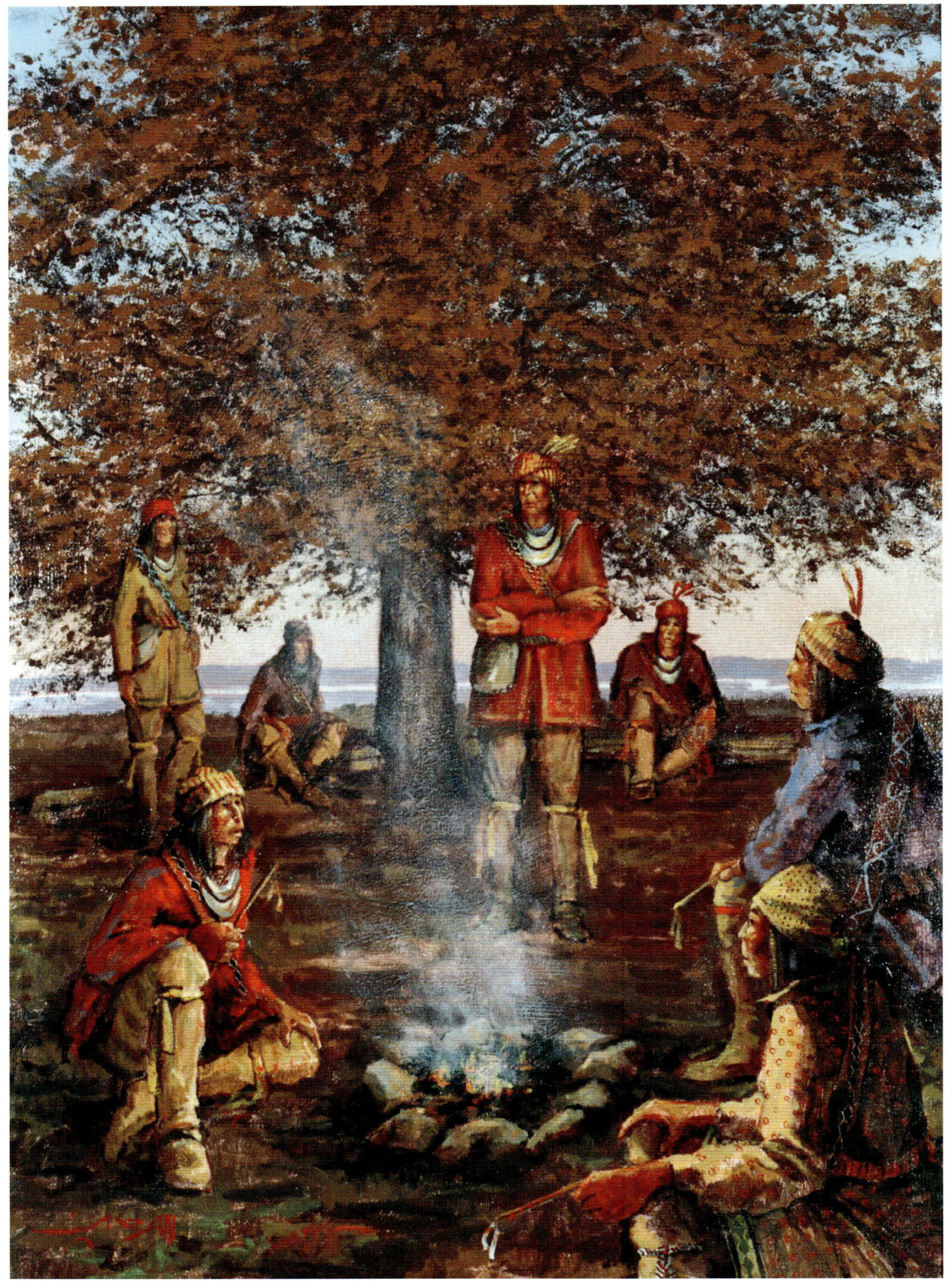

CREEK COUNCIL OAK TREE

BY MIKE LARSEN

30 x 40, oil/canvas

The founding of Tulsa is depicted in this painting sponsored by Governor Frank Keating and First Lady Cathy Keating. On a hill along the Arkansas River, Creeks held their first council, celebrating their arrival and depositing ashes brought from their ancestral home in Alabama. Some called the new town Tallasi, after a Creek town that had existed since the sixteenth century. Historians believe the name Tulsa is derived from the Creek word *Tallasi.*

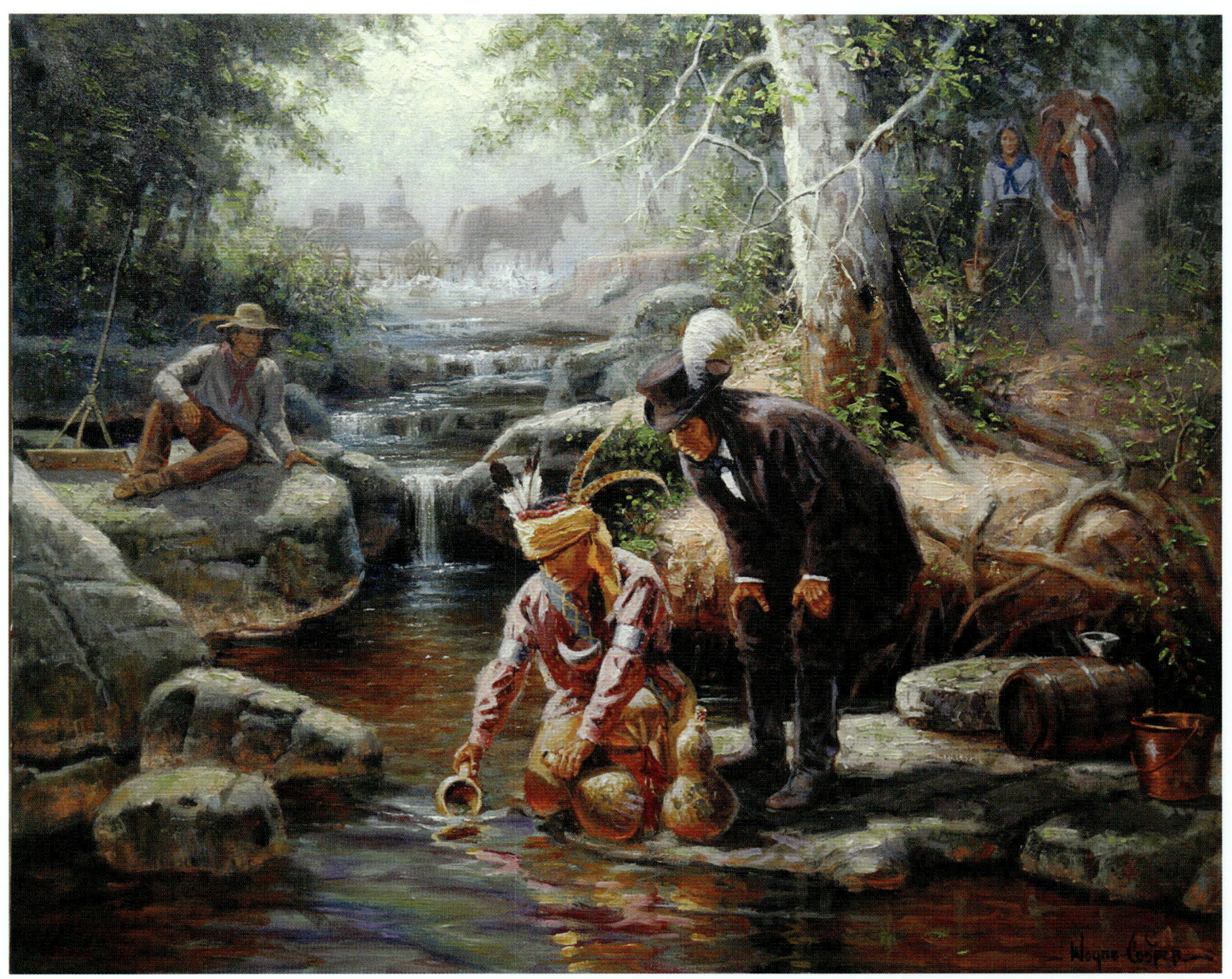

THE MAGIC OF PETROLEUM

BY WAYNE COOPER

72 x 96, oil/canvas

Long before oil derricks dotted the Oklahoma landscape, Native Americans and settlers used oil springs for medicinal purposes. Well-known springs were located near Tahlequah in the Cherokee Nation and at Boyd Springs, northeast of present Ardmore, in the Chickasaw Nation. Indians gathered at Boyd Springs and lighted their camps with gas by placing a tube or gun barrel in the ground. A natural oil spring near Caddo in Bryan County drew so many visitors that a hotel was opened nearby. Later, oil wells were drilled and Oklahoma became a major producer of petroleum. The painting was sponsored by ONEOK, Inc.

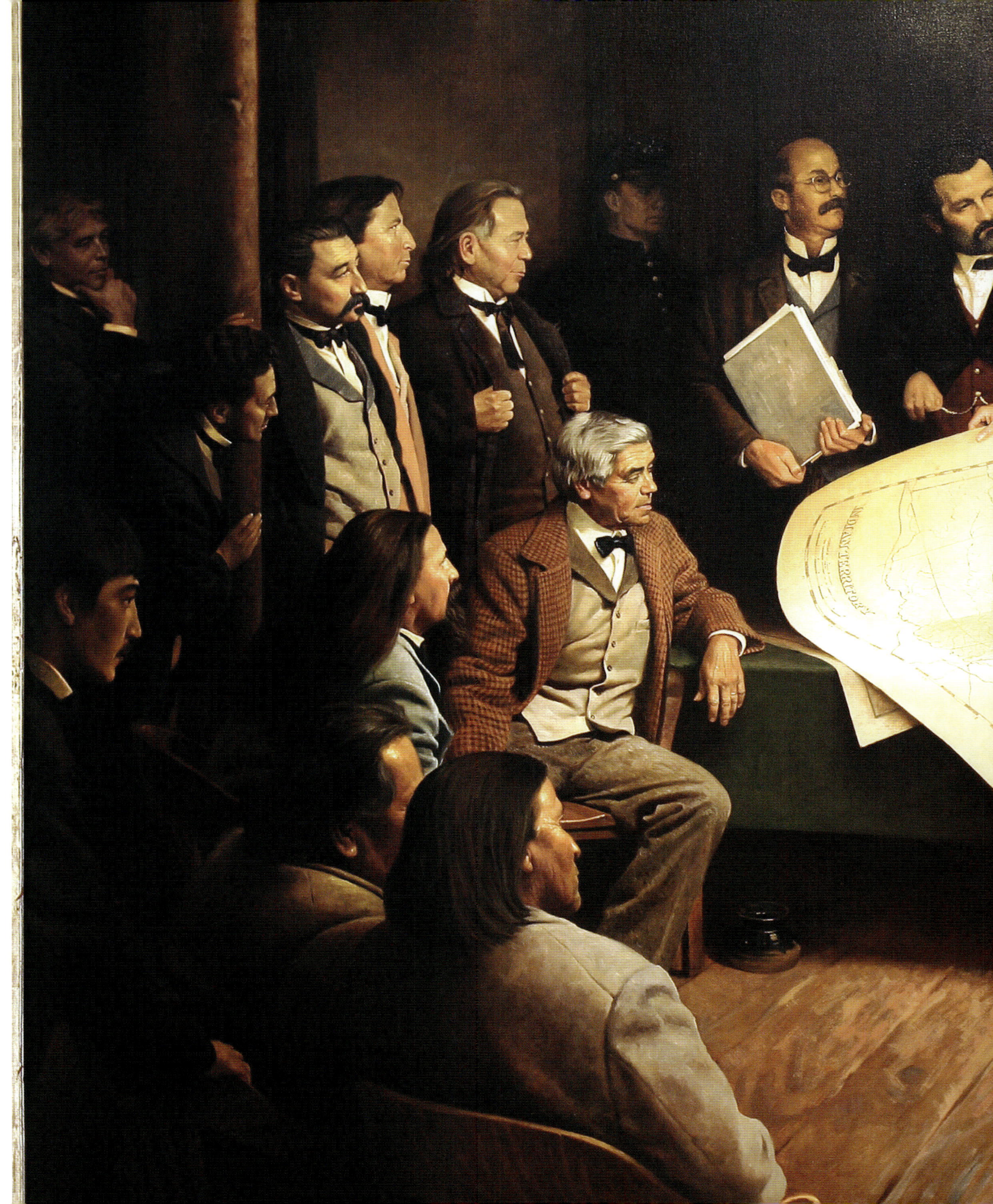

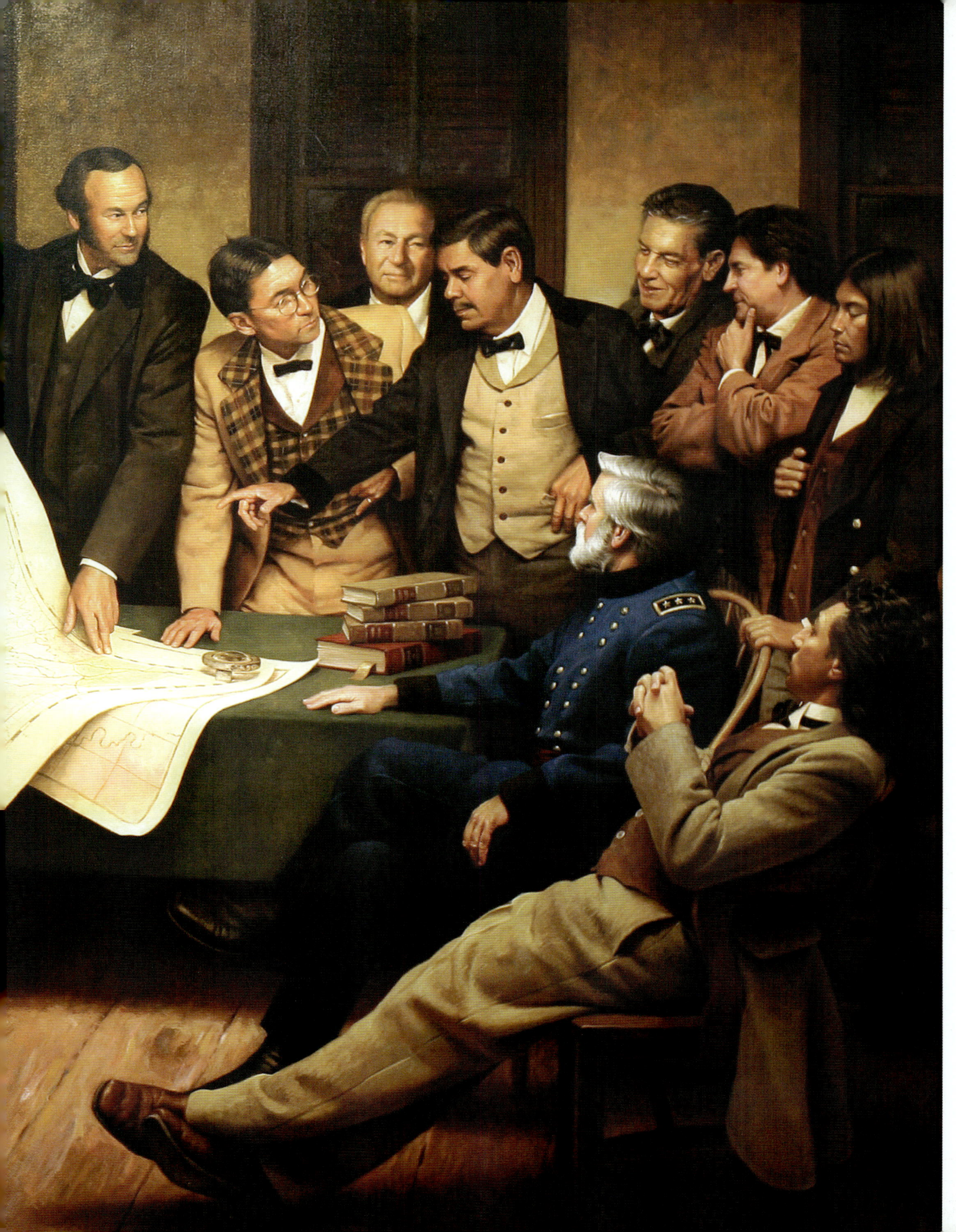

(PREVIOUS PAGES)
FORT SMITH COUNCIL—1865
BY MIKE WIMMER

90 x 56, oil/canvas

After the Civil War the federal government convened a council at Fort Smith to renegotiate treaties with Indian tribes who fought with the Confederacy during the Civil War. It was suggested at the council on September 8, 1865, that tribes should join together in a common government in Indian Territory. Choctaw Chief Allen Wright suggested the word "Oklahoma," taken from two Choctaw words meaning "land of the red men." The tribes objected to most peace terms presented, but formally agreed to meet in Washington, D. C., the following year. Lilah B. Marshall and Paula Marshall sponsored the painting.

MEDICINE BLUFF AT FT. SILL 1870S (AT RIGHT)
BY BARBARA VAUPEL

40 x 30, oil/canvas

In 1868 the U. S. Army decided to built a new post near Medicine Bluff to handle unrest among Indians in the Red River area. The Kiowas called Fort Sill, founded by General Philip Henry Sheridan, *Tso-Kada-Hagya,* which meant "where the soldiers lived at Medicine Bluff." Fort Sill was named after General Joshua W. Sill, killed at the Battle of Stone River, Tennessee, in 1862. The painting, sponsored by Senators Sam Helton and Jim Maddox, depicts a peaceful encampment of Kiowas at the base of Medicine Bluff.

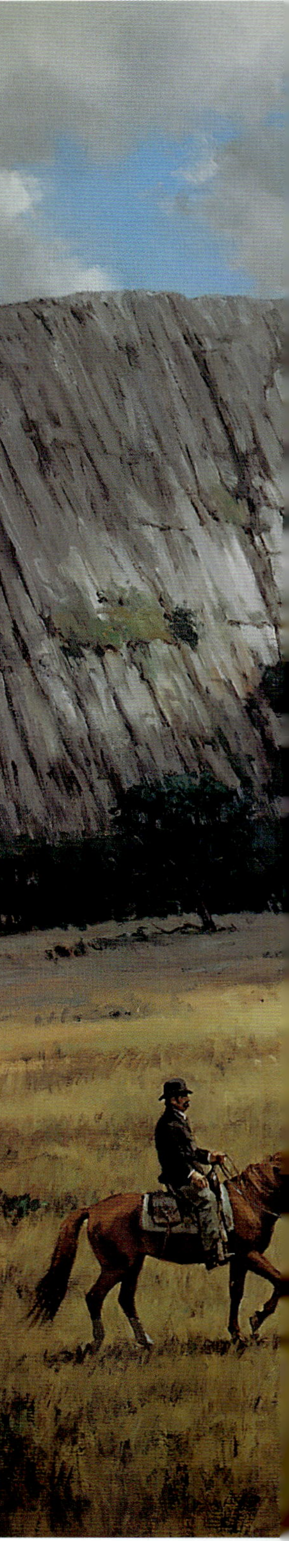

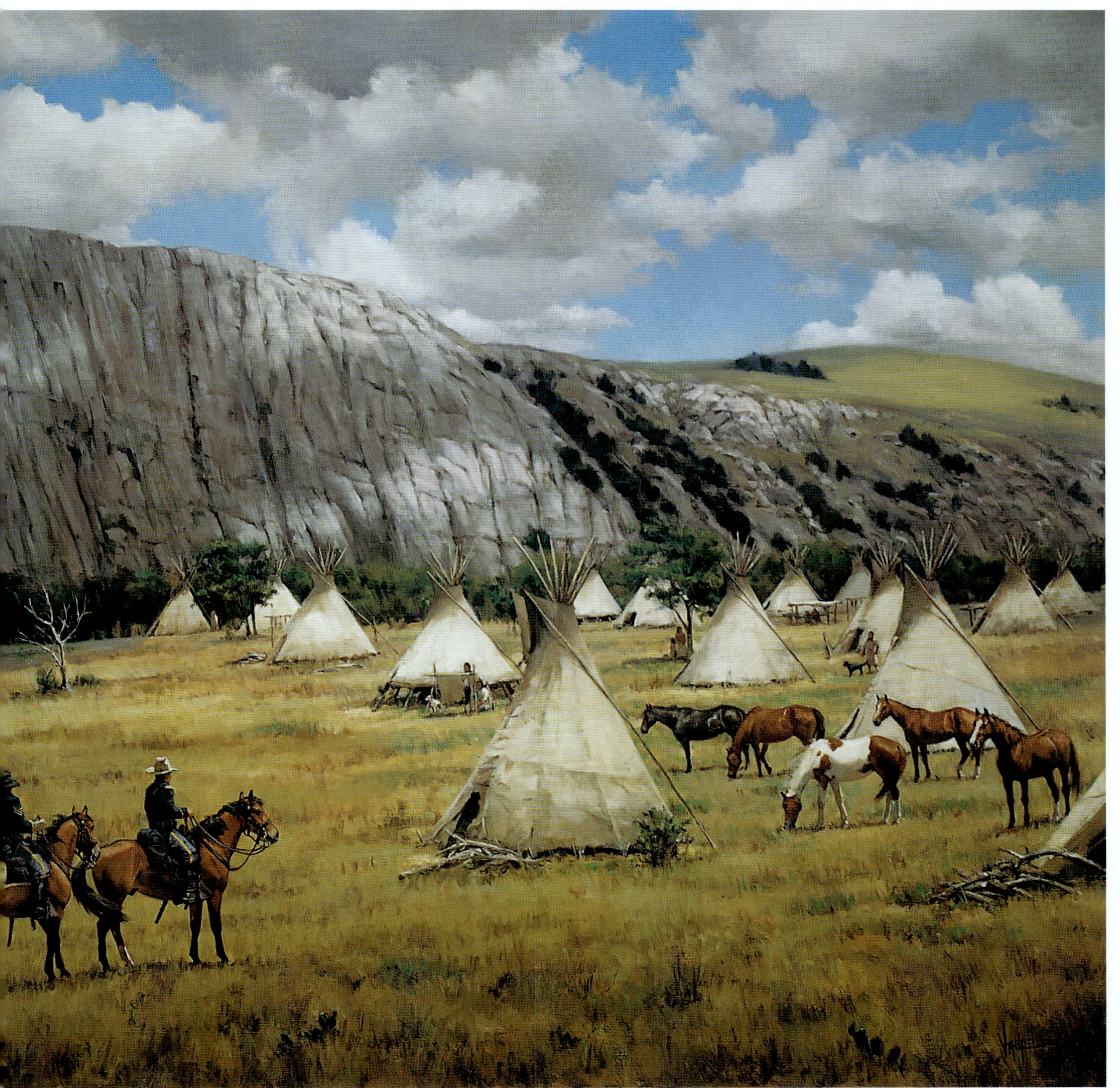

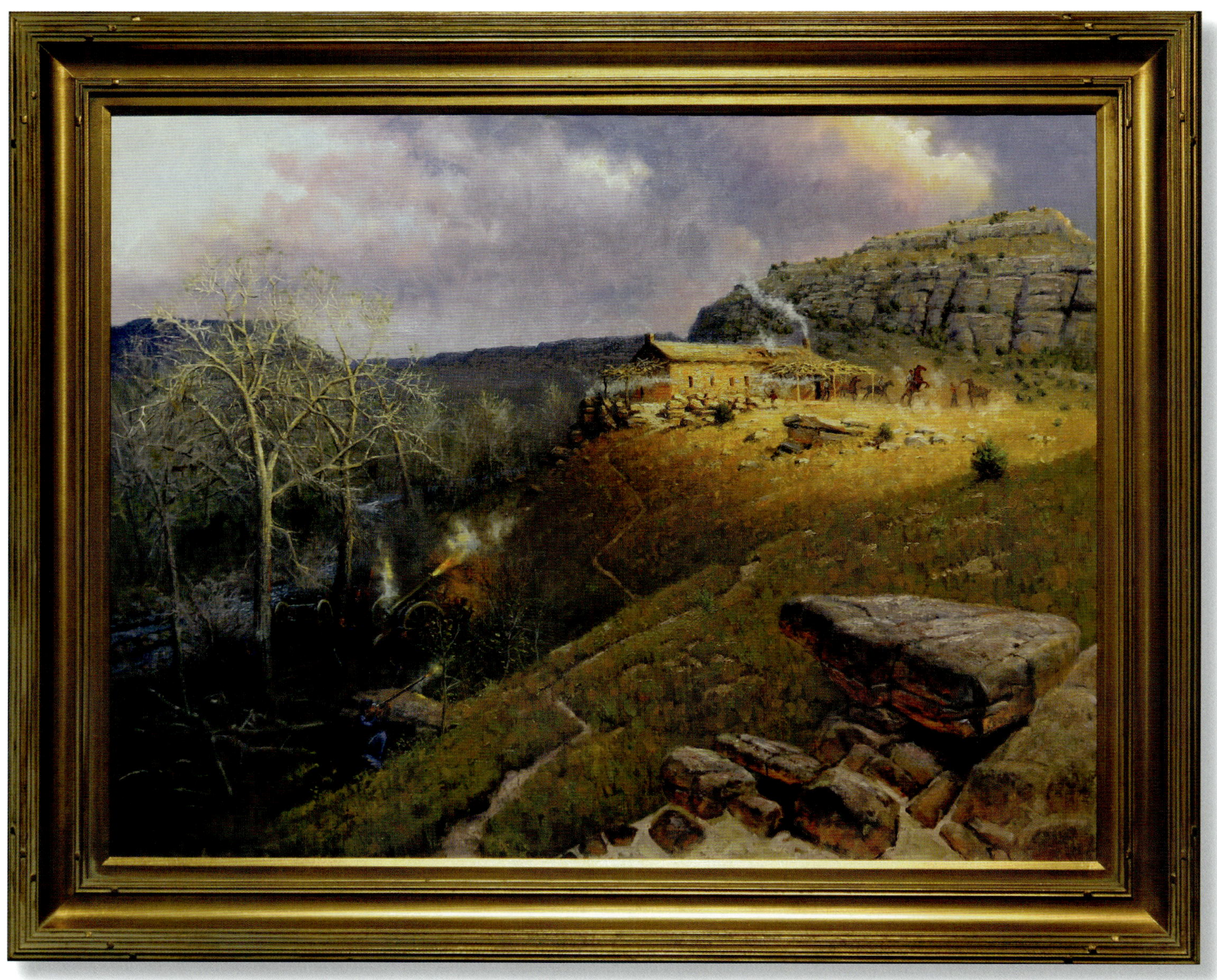

ROBBER'S ROOST

BY WAYNE COOPER

30 x 40, oil/canvas

Outlaws led by Captain William Coe built a rock fortress in No Man's Land, now the Oklahoma Panhandle, in the late 1860s. The structure had 30-inch rock walls with narrow portholes from which to defend it. Coe and his men held the hideout until the U. S. Army attacked it with cannon. Eleven of Coe's men were captured and hung in nearby cottonwood trees. Coe escaped but was captured and hung in Colorado. Today, only the fortress foundation remains. The painting was sponsored by Senator Owen Laughlin and his wife, Charlette.

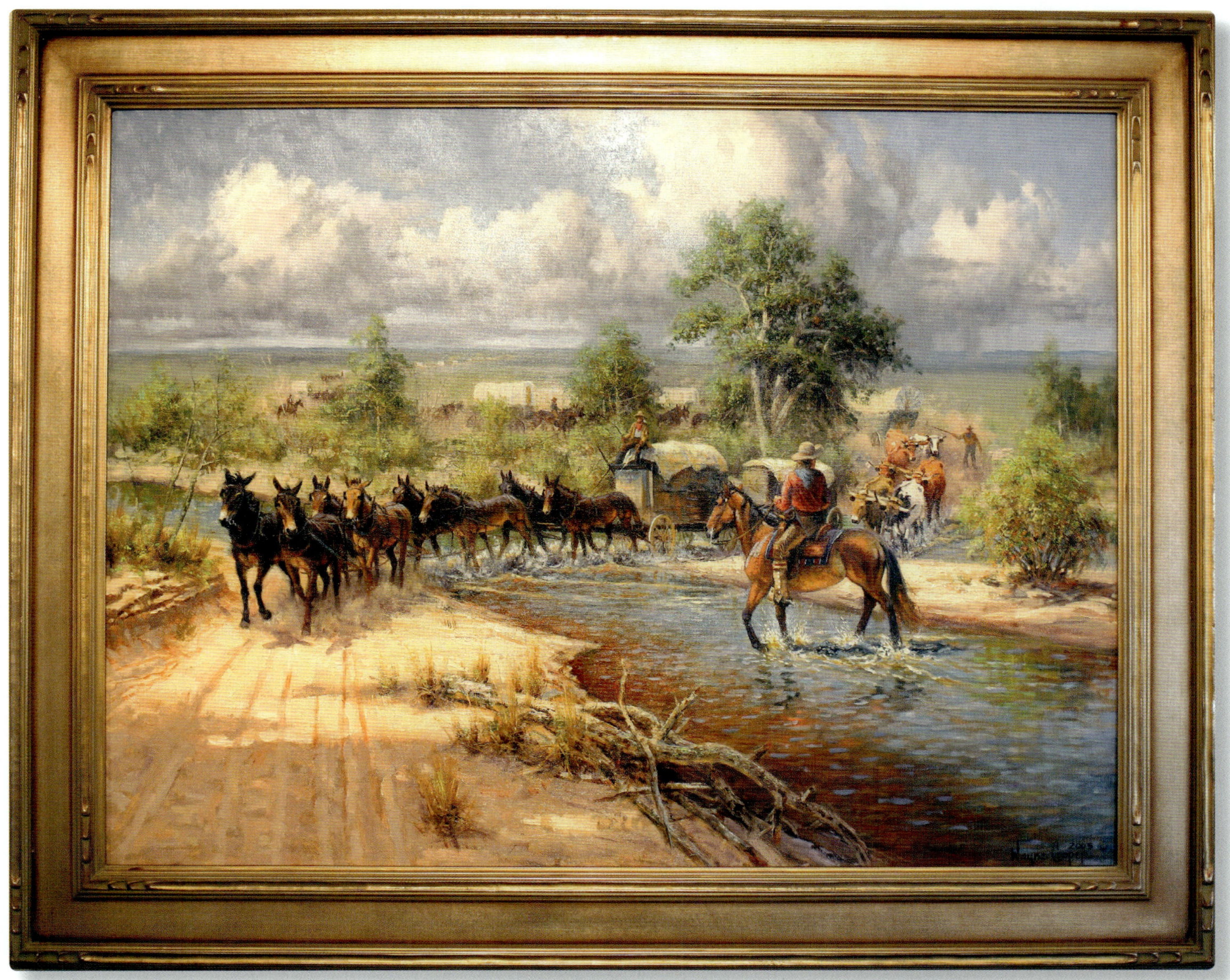

THE SANTA FE TRAIL

BY WAYNE COOPER

30 x 40, oil/canvas

The oldest and longest commercial highway across the Great Plains was the Santa Fe Trail, running from near present-day Kansas City, Missouri, to Santa Fe, New Mexico. The Cimarron Route crossed the Cimarron River in present Cimarron County, Oklahoma, and was a trading route from the sixteenth century. One of the earliest travelers through what would become the Oklahoma Panhandle was the Spanish explorer Don Francisco Vazquez de Coronado, who passed through the area in 1541. The painting was sponsored by Mollie Williford of Tulsa.

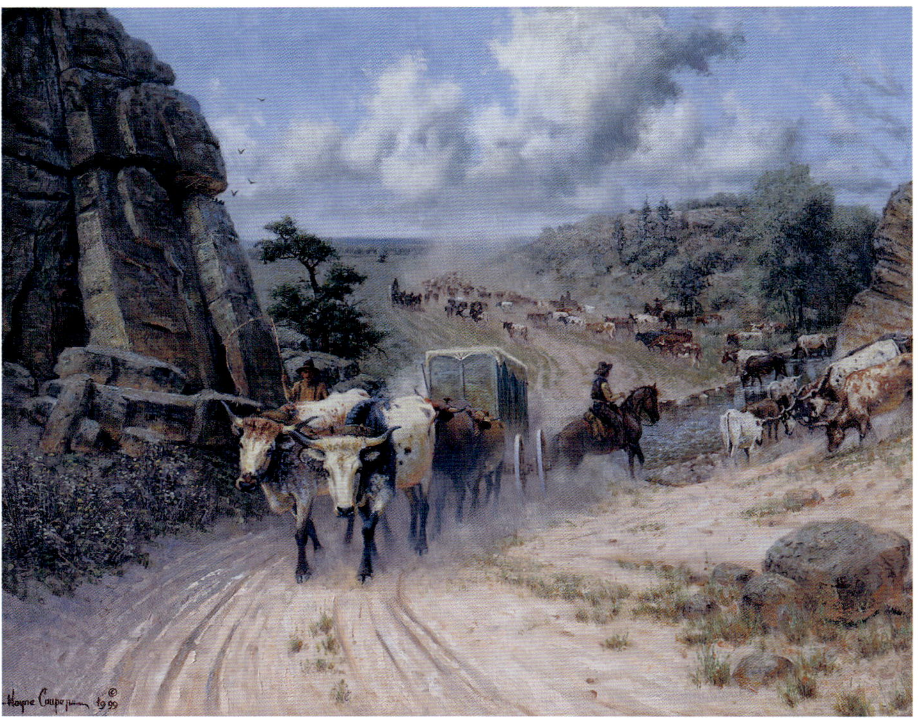

TRAFFIC JAM AT LIMESTONE GAP

BY WAYNE COOPER

48 x 36, oil/canvas

The Texas Road, also called the Osage Trace, carried more cattle and goods than any other trail or road through early Oklahoma. It extended from Baxter Springs, Kansas, to Fort Smith, Arkansas, and eventually to Dallas, Texas. The Choctaws build a bridge across Limestone Creek in northern Atoka County and created the state's first toll bridge. The painting, sponsored by Senator Gene Stipe of McAlester, depicts cattle going north to market through Limestone Gap.

WASHINGTON IRVING MEETING THE OSAGE (AT RIGHT)

BY WAYNE COOPER

36 x 48, oil/canvas

In 1832 Washington Irving visited an Osage village on the banks of the Arkansas River near present-day Tulsa. Around the campfire, the curious Osage no doubt sought a taste of the unfamiliar beverage the visitors were enjoying, coffee. Irving wrote of the visit in his *A Tour of the Prairies,* "Our arrival created quite a sensation. A number of old men came forward and shook hands with us . . . while the women and children huddled together in groups, staring at us wildly." The painting was the first state capitol art project sponsored by Senator Charles Ford.

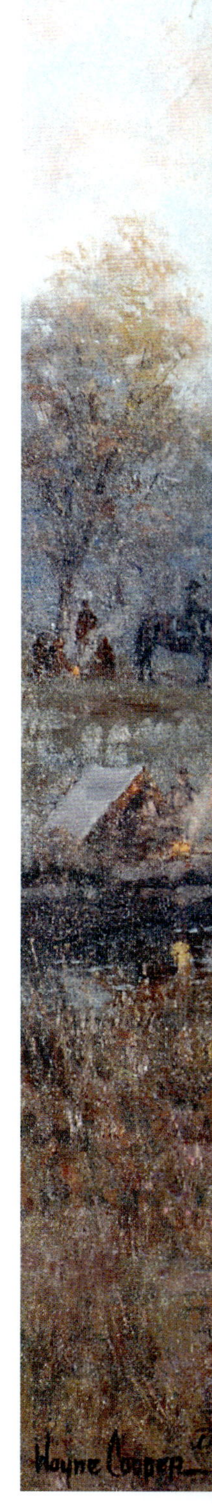

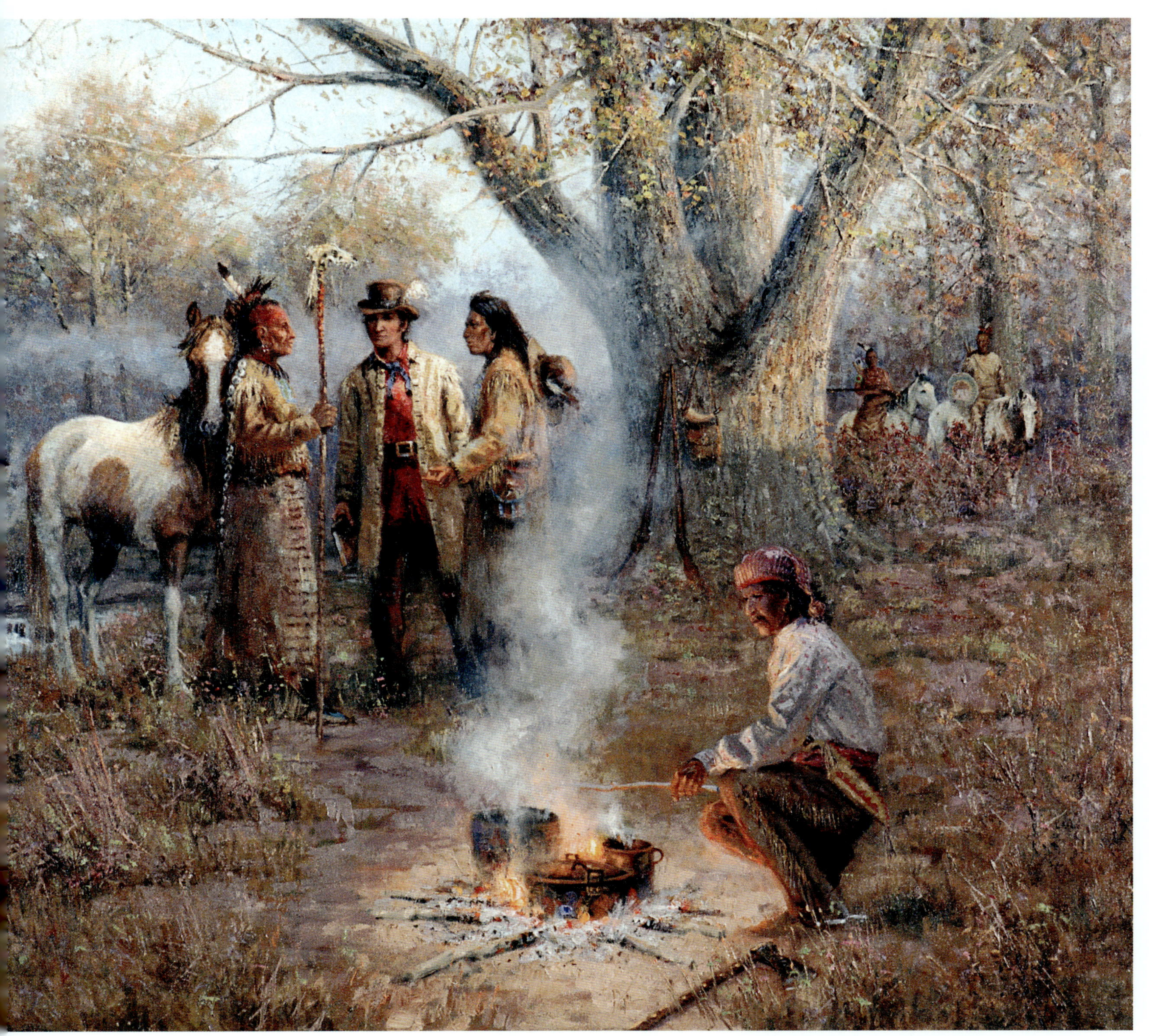

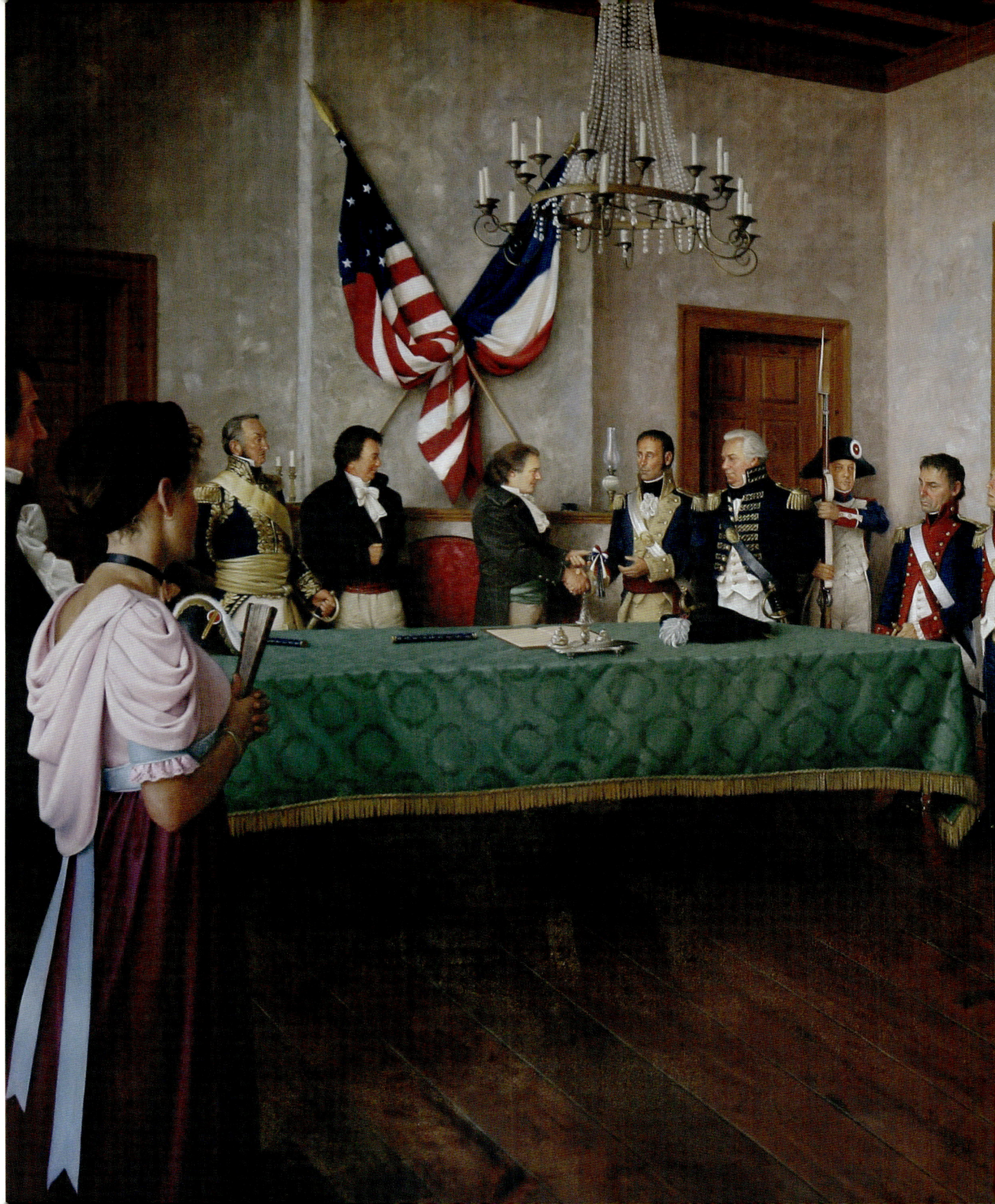

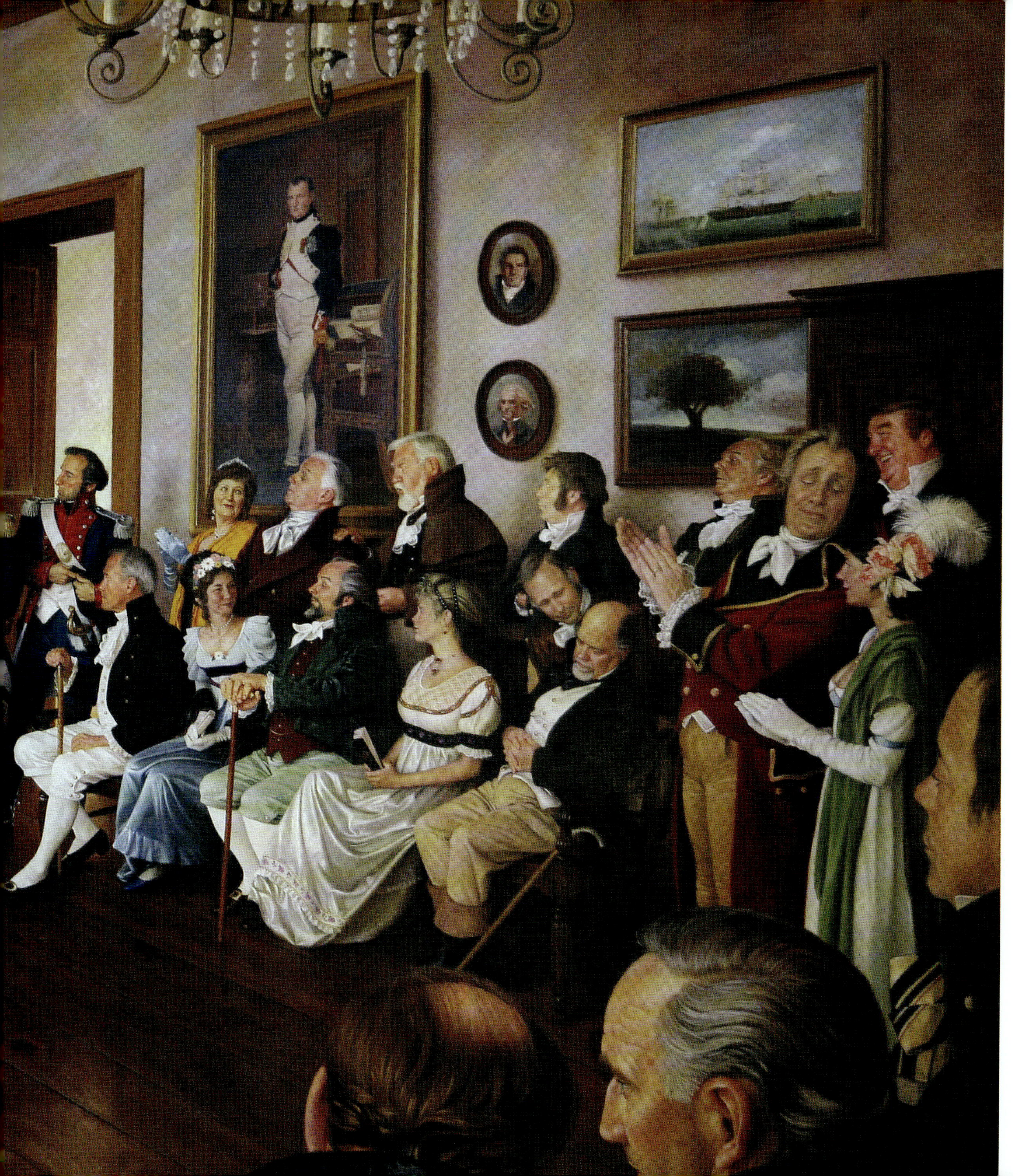

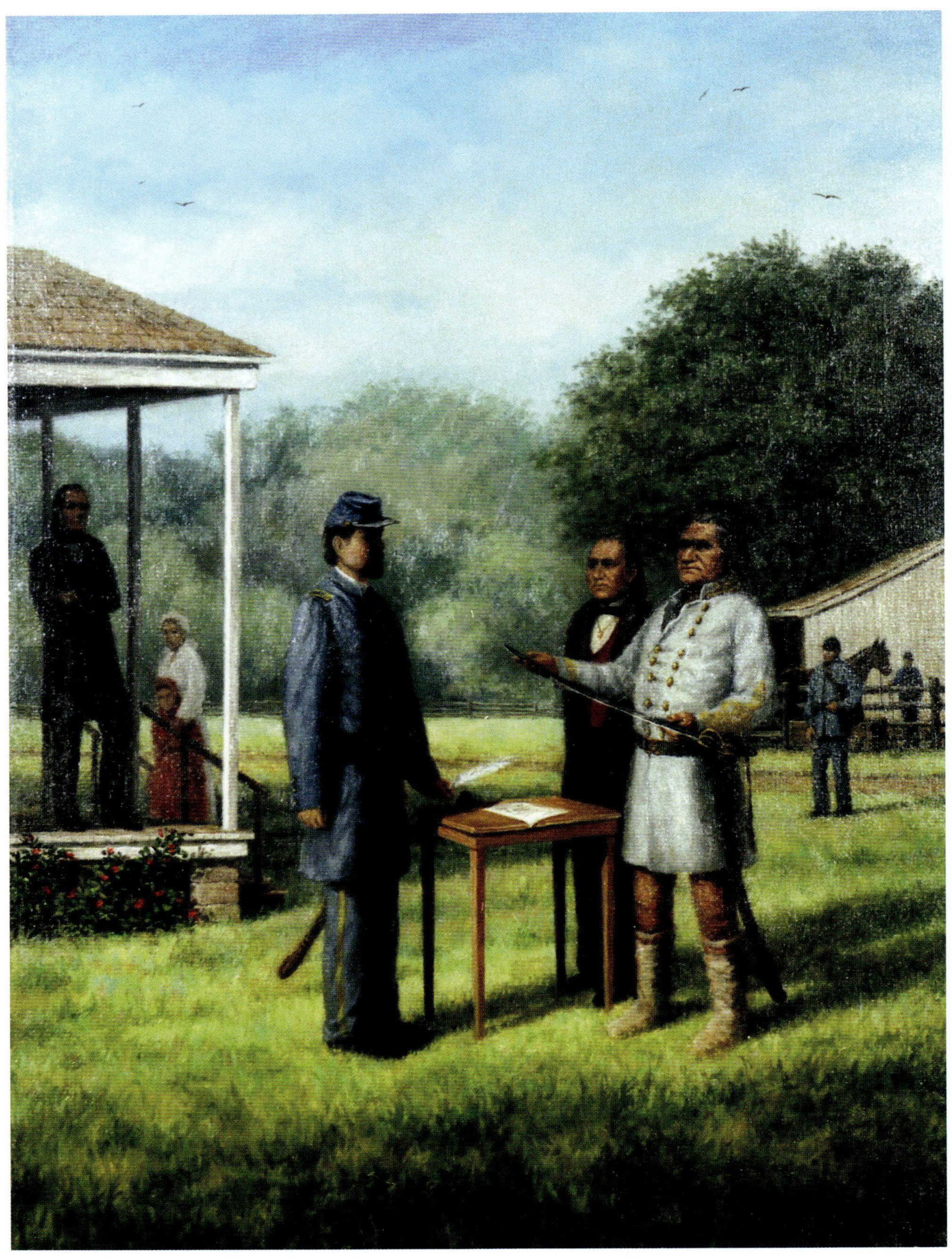

(PREVIOUS PAGES)

CEREMONIAL TRANSFER OF THE LOUISIANA PURCHASE—1803

BY MIKE WIMMER

72 x 120, oil/canvas

Henry and Jane Primeaux of Tulsa sponsored the painting depicting the official transfer of the Louisiana Purchase from France to the United States in 1803. The acquisition of the vast tract of land, including future Oklahoma, nearly doubled the size of the United States. Oklahoma was the last state carved from the purchase. In the painting, Pierre Clement Laussat, the French prefect, presents the documents of transfer to officials of the United States government.

SURRENDER OF GENERAL STAND WATIE

BY DENNIS PARKER

30 x 40, oil/canvas

The only Native American to attain the rank of brigadier general during the Civil War and the last Confederate general to surrender, Stand Watie gave up his command at Doaksville near Fort Towson on June 23, 1865, after General Robert E. Lee had surrendered for the Confederacy in Virginia. The painting was sponsored by Senator Jeff Rabon of Hugo.

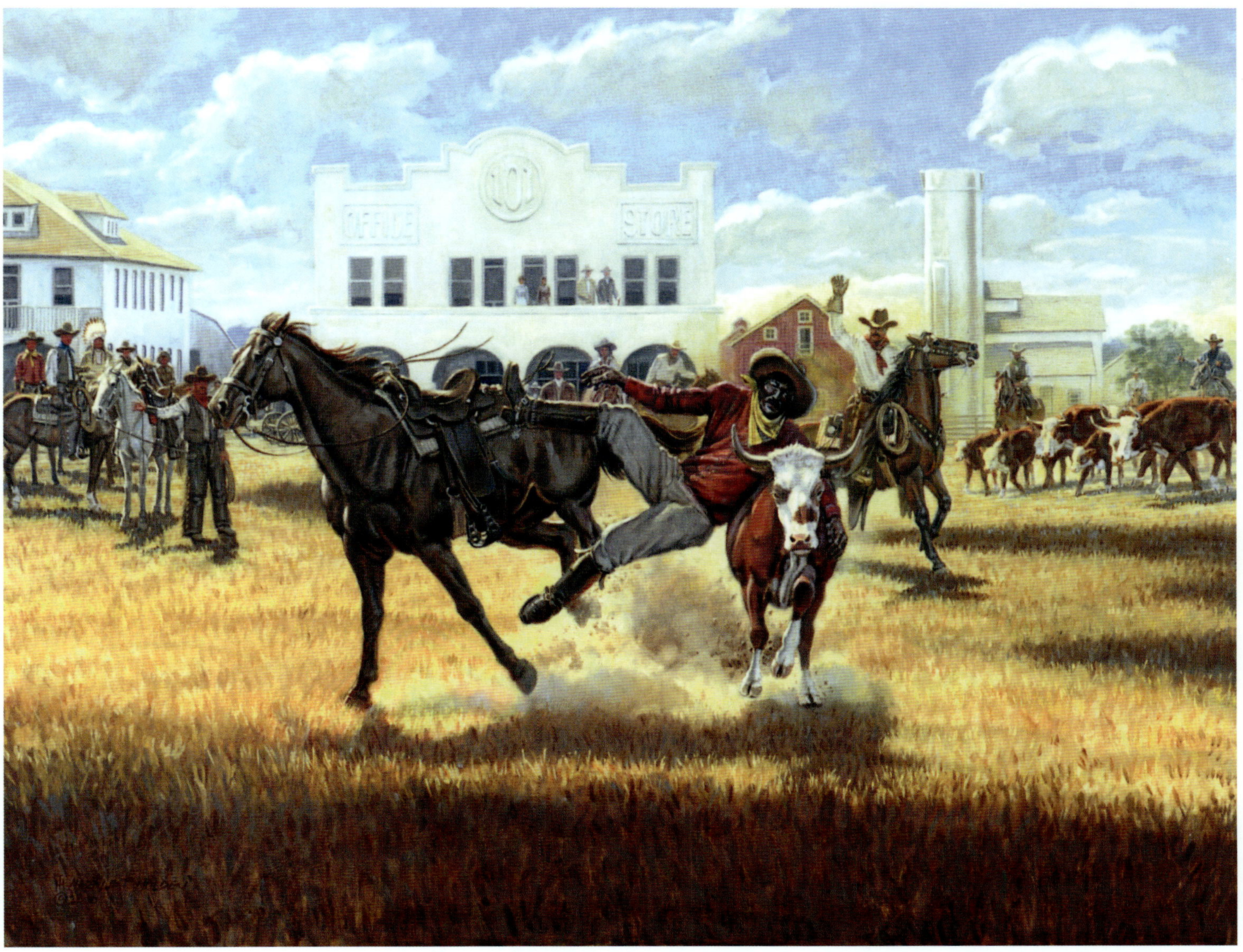

101 RANCH

BY HAROLD T. HOLDEN

30 x 40, oil/board

The world's greatest Wild West Show was featured at the 101 Ranch along the Salt Fork River in the Cherokee Outlet from 1908 to 1932. The ranch was founded in 1879 by Colonel George Washington Miller. The Wild West Show featured cowboys and cowgirls, Geronimo, the leader of the Chiricahua Apaches, and played to large audiences throughout the United States and Europe. In this painting, African American cowboy Bill Pickett practices bulldogging, the rodeo sport he invented. The painting was sponsored by Senator Paul Muegge of Tonkawa.

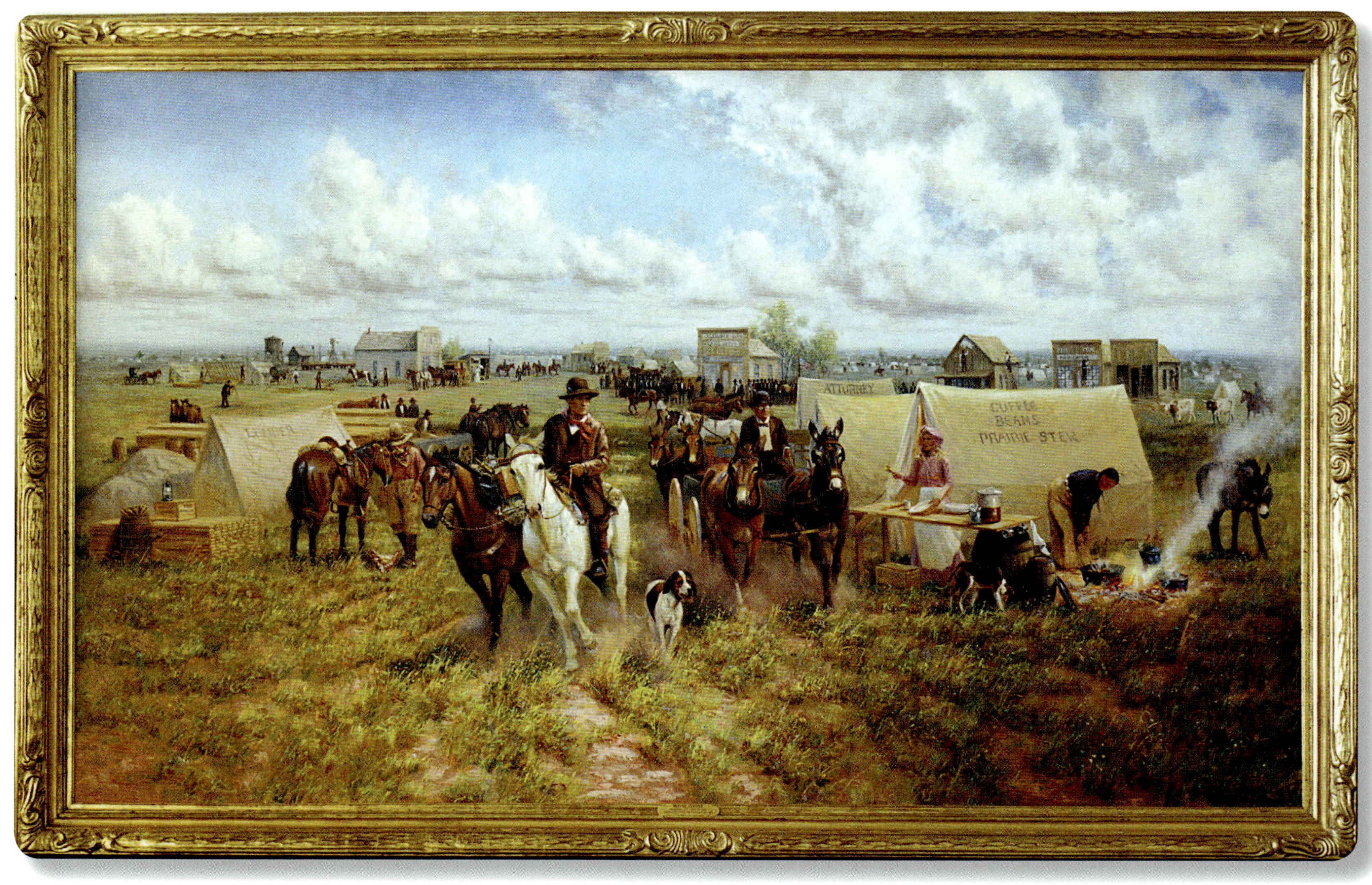

OKLAHOMA CITY—APRIL 29, 1889

BY WAYNE COOPER

72 x 120, oil/canvas

The painting, sponsored by former state representative and attorney general G. T. Blankenship and his wife, Libby, of Oklahoma City, depicts their home town seven days after the Land Run of 1889. Settlers came by railroad, horse, wagon, and foot to settle the new city. Known as Oklahoma Station, the settlement that later became the state's capital city was "born grown." More than 12,000 people arrived at Oklahoma Station within 12 hours of the start of the land run.

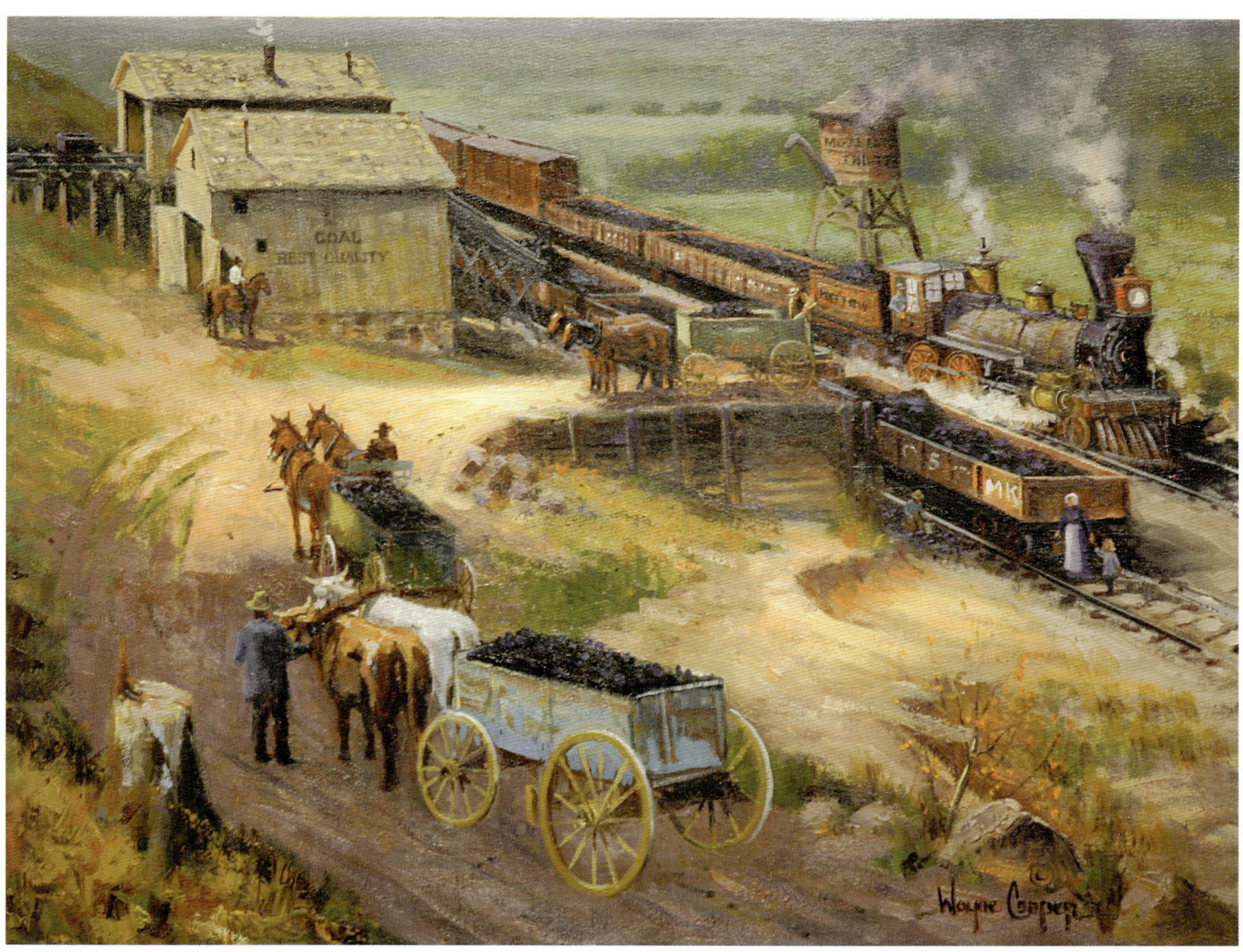

FIRST COAL AND THE KATY RAILROAD AT MCALESTER

BY WAYNE COOPER

72 x 96, oil/canvas

The Missouri, Kansas, and Texas Railroad (the MK&T or "Katy") built tracks into Indian Territory and allowed the coal-mining industry around the new town of McAlester to flourish. In September, 1907, J. G. Puterbaugh established the McAlester Fuel Company to market and transport coal. The painting was sponsored by the J. G. Puterbaugh Foundation.

STEAMBOATS ON RED RIVER

BY MIKE WIMMER

60 x 96, oil/canvas

Steamboats delivered goods to the frontier of Indian Territory and exported cotton and pecans produced by the Five Civilized Tribes. In 1831, the first steamboat traveled on the Upper Red River to deliver supplies to Fort Towson. The ability to ship downstream made cotton production a major industry for Choctaws and Chickasaws. Steamboat operations were suspended with the coming of the railroads. The painting was sponsored by the Stuart Family Foundation.

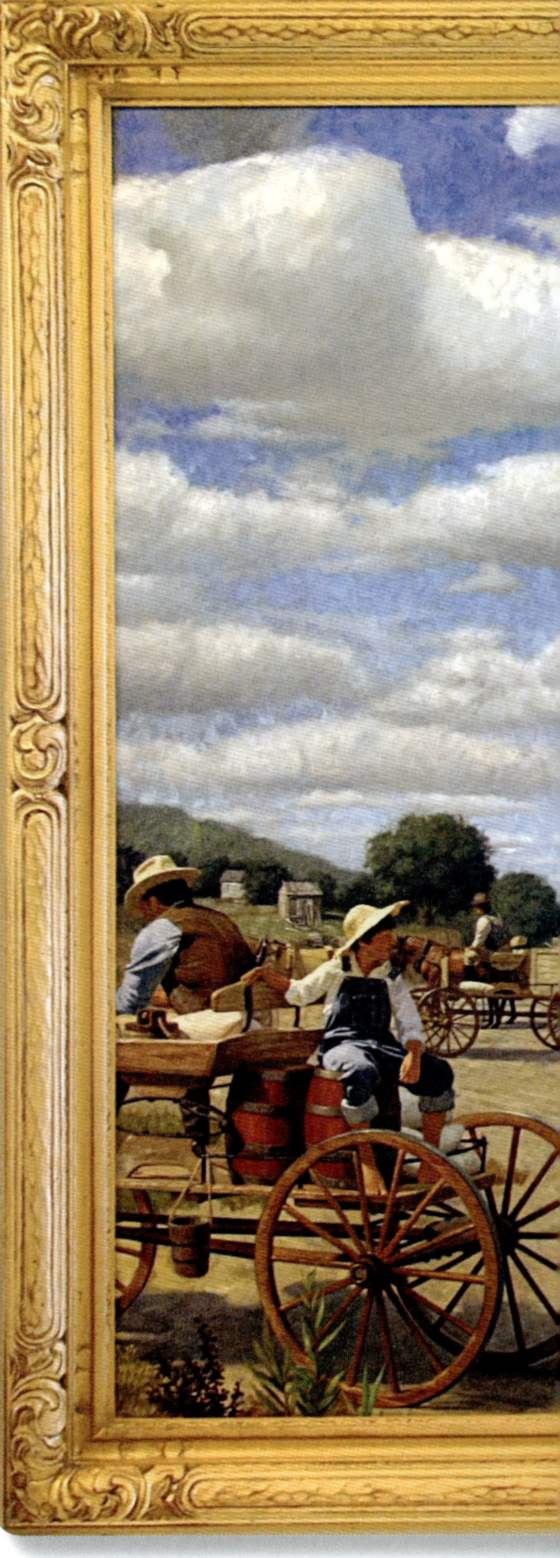

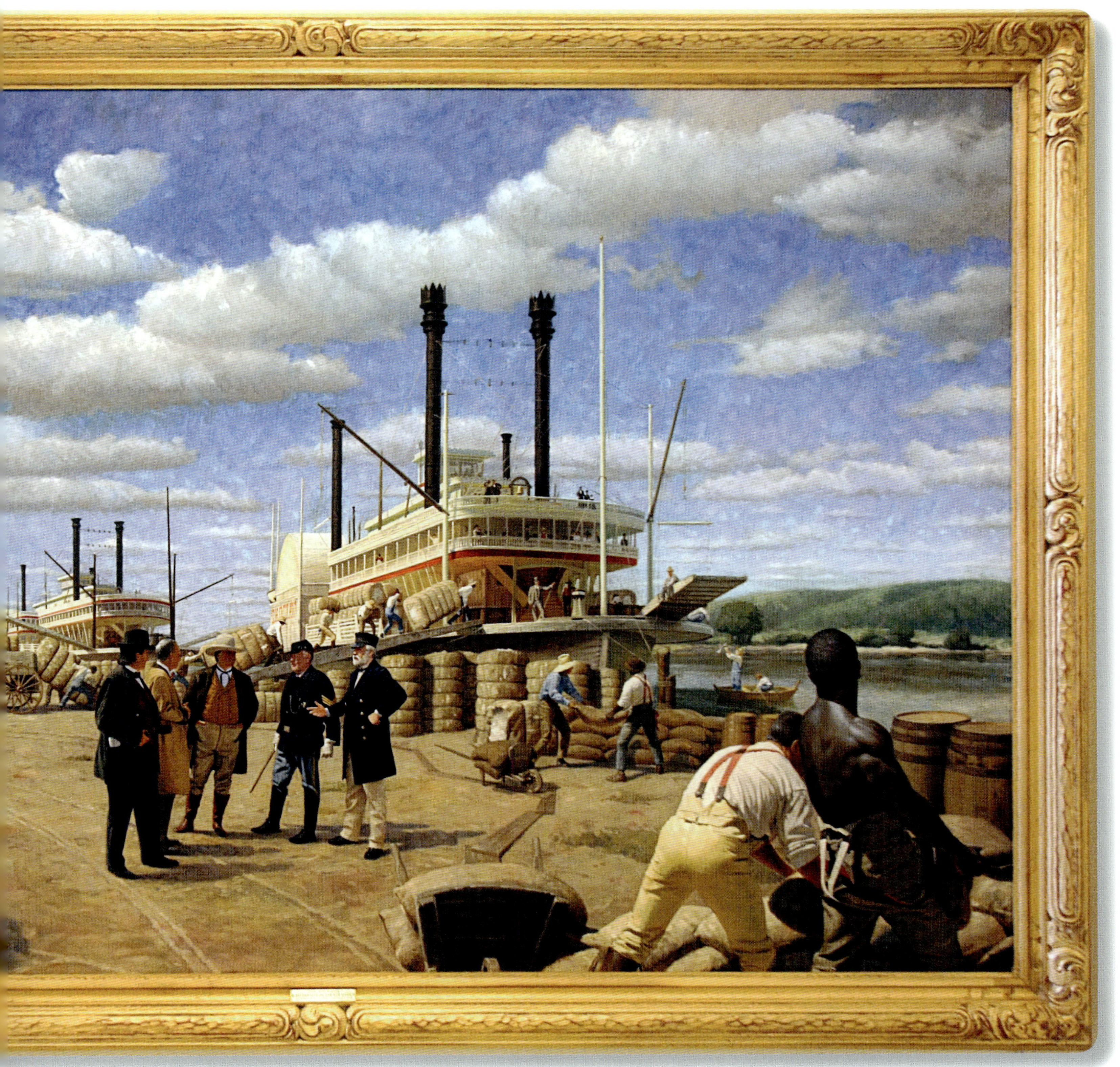

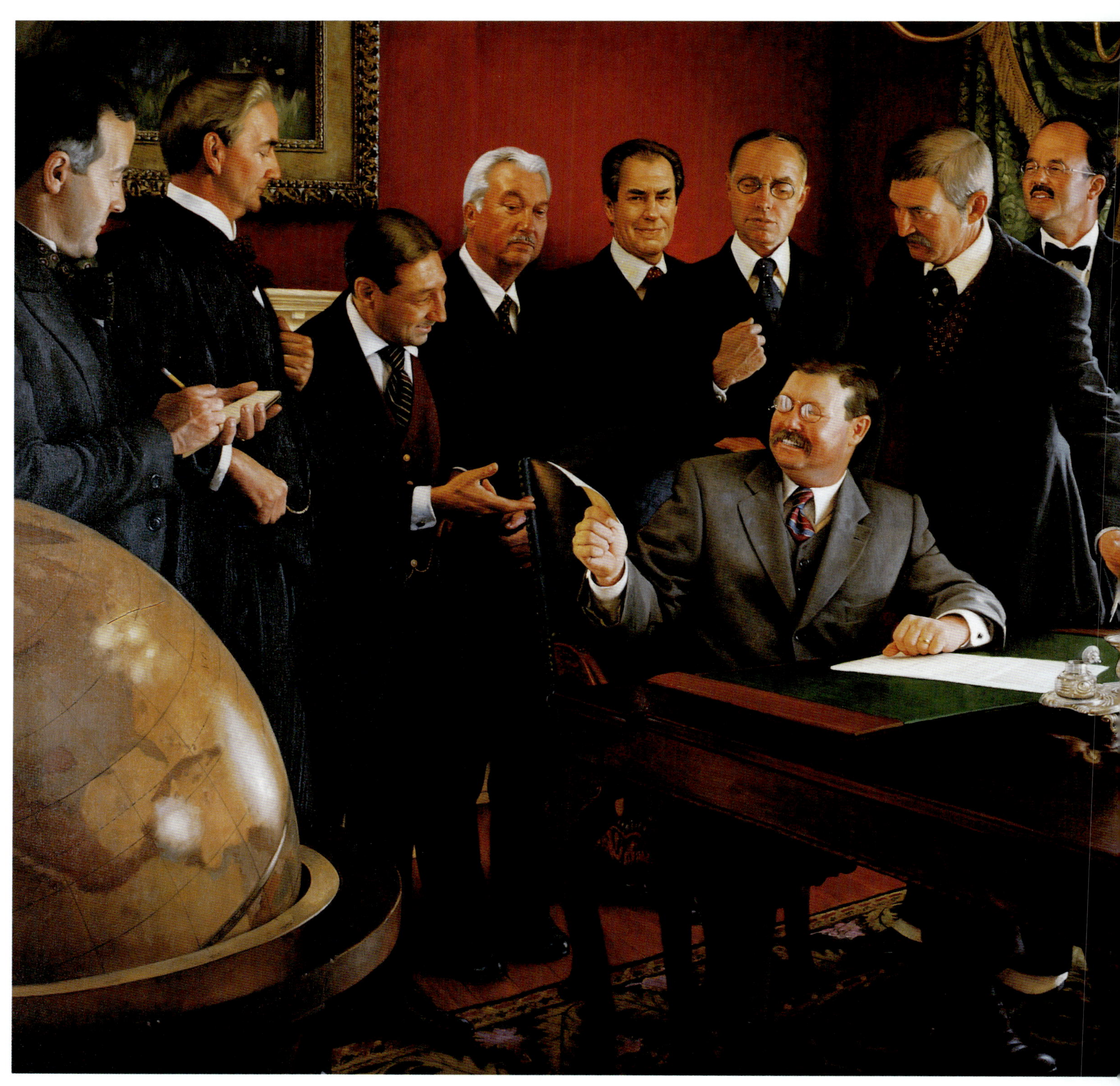

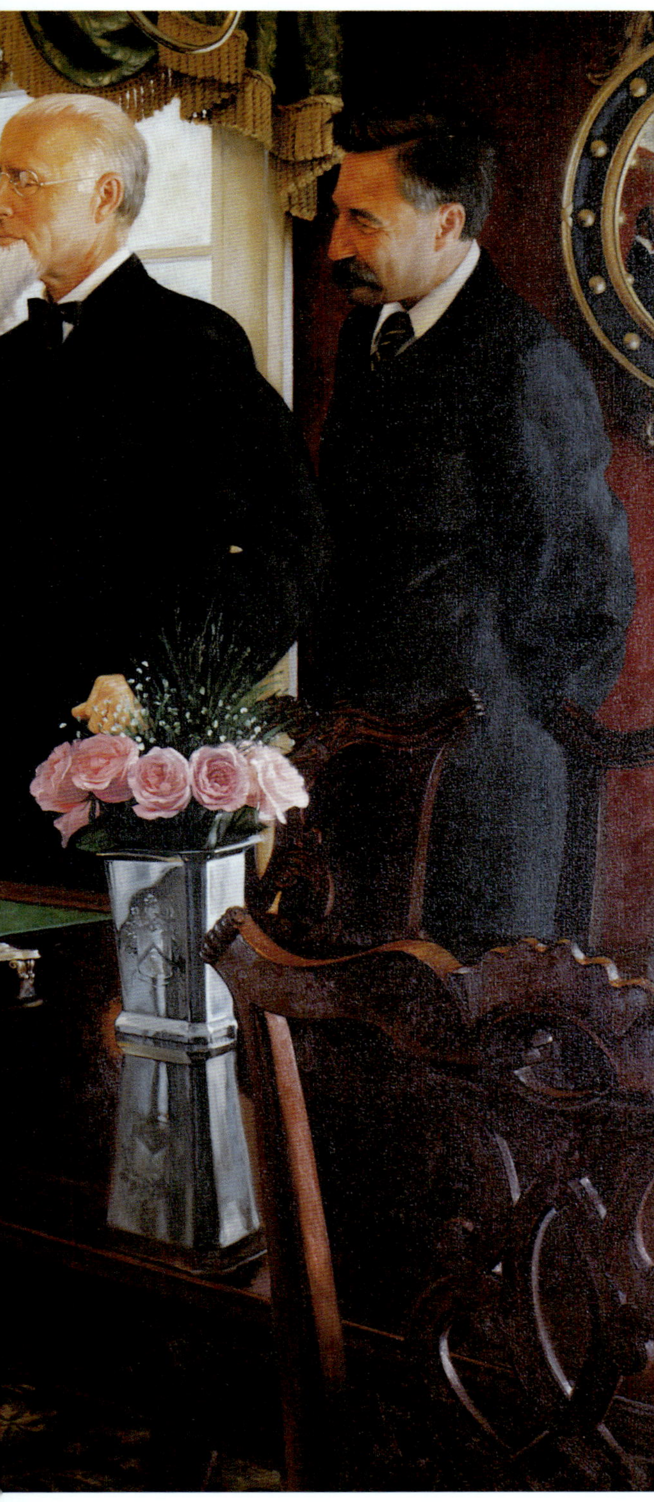

PRESIDENT TEDDY ROOSEVELT SIGNING STATEHOOD PROCLAMATION

BY MIKE WIMMER

56 x 86, oil/canvas

President Theodore Roosevelt signed the proclamation making Oklahoma the 46th state of the Union at 10:16 A.M. on November 16, 1907. There was little ceremony as a small delegation of government clerks from Oklahoma and reporters were witnesses in the cabinet room. Roosevelt used an eagle quill pen to sign the document. The pen promptly was transferred to the Oklahoma Historical Society. With a smile, the president handed the ink blotter to Albert Hammer, a clerk in the land office at Enid. Immediately after Roosevelt signed the proclamation, the news was flashed by telegraph to the new state. The painting was sponsored by Walt and Peggy Helmerich of Tulsa.

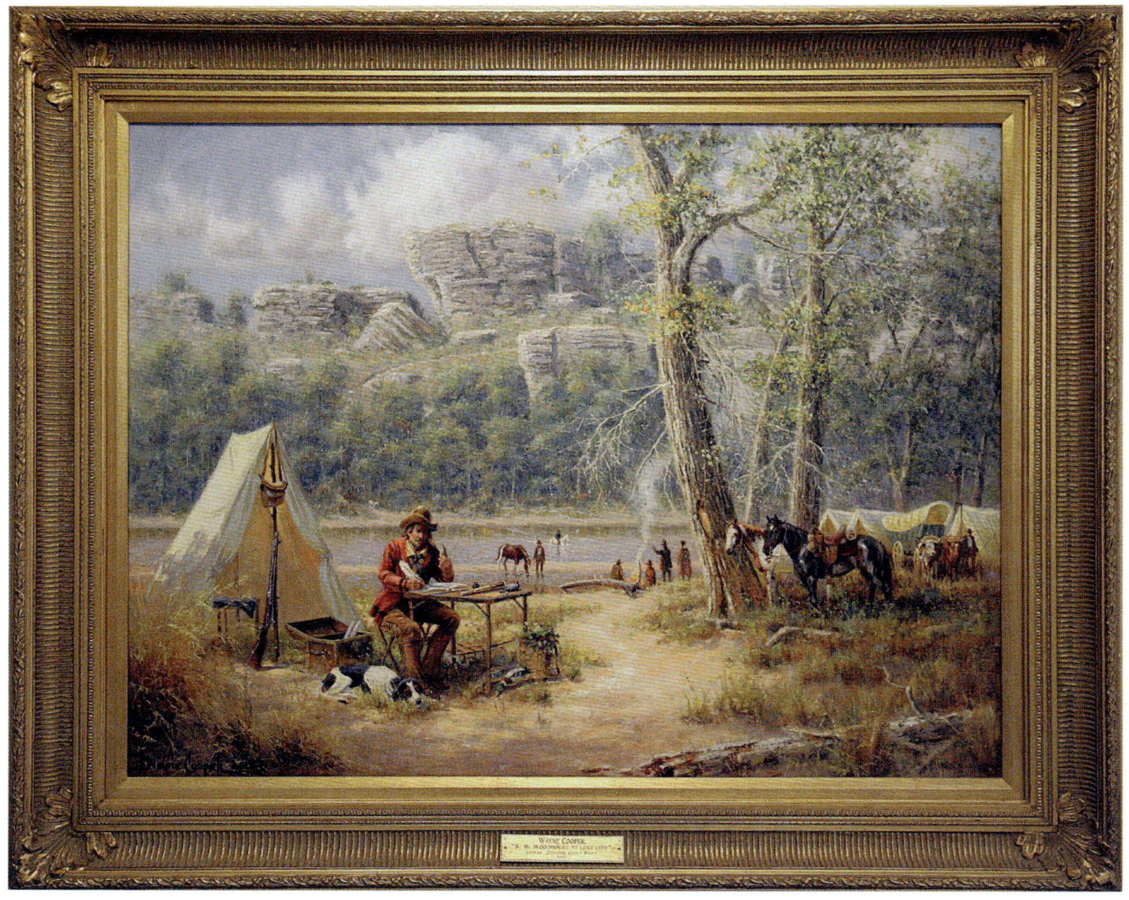

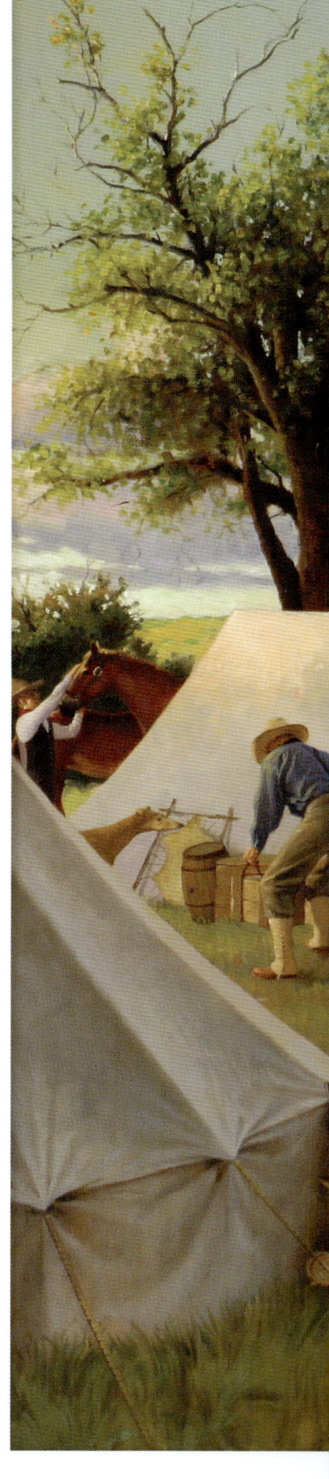

S. W. WOODHOUSE
AT LOST CITY
BY WAYNE COOPER
40 x 30, oil/canvas

Surgeon-naturalist S. W. Woodhouse accompanied a boundary survey team in Indian Territory in 1849–1850 and made one of the first comprehensive natural history studies of future Oklahoma. On September 15, 1849, he camped on the Arkansas River near present Sand Springs and observed huge limestone boulders that resembled a village from a distance. Woodhouse first spotted the scissortail flycatcher that later became the official state bird. The painting was sponsored by Senator Nancy Riley of Tulsa.

PRESIDENT THEODORE ROOSEVELT, FREDERICK, OT (AT RIGHT)
BY MIKE WIMMER
40 x 30, oil/canvas

President Theodore Roosevelt visited Oklahoma Territory in 1905 to hunt wolves and coyotes. The painting, sponsored by Senator Gilmer Capps, depicts a camp scene after a day's hunt. The hunting trip was the idea of rancher Burk Burnett, who wanted the president to consider making the territory a state.

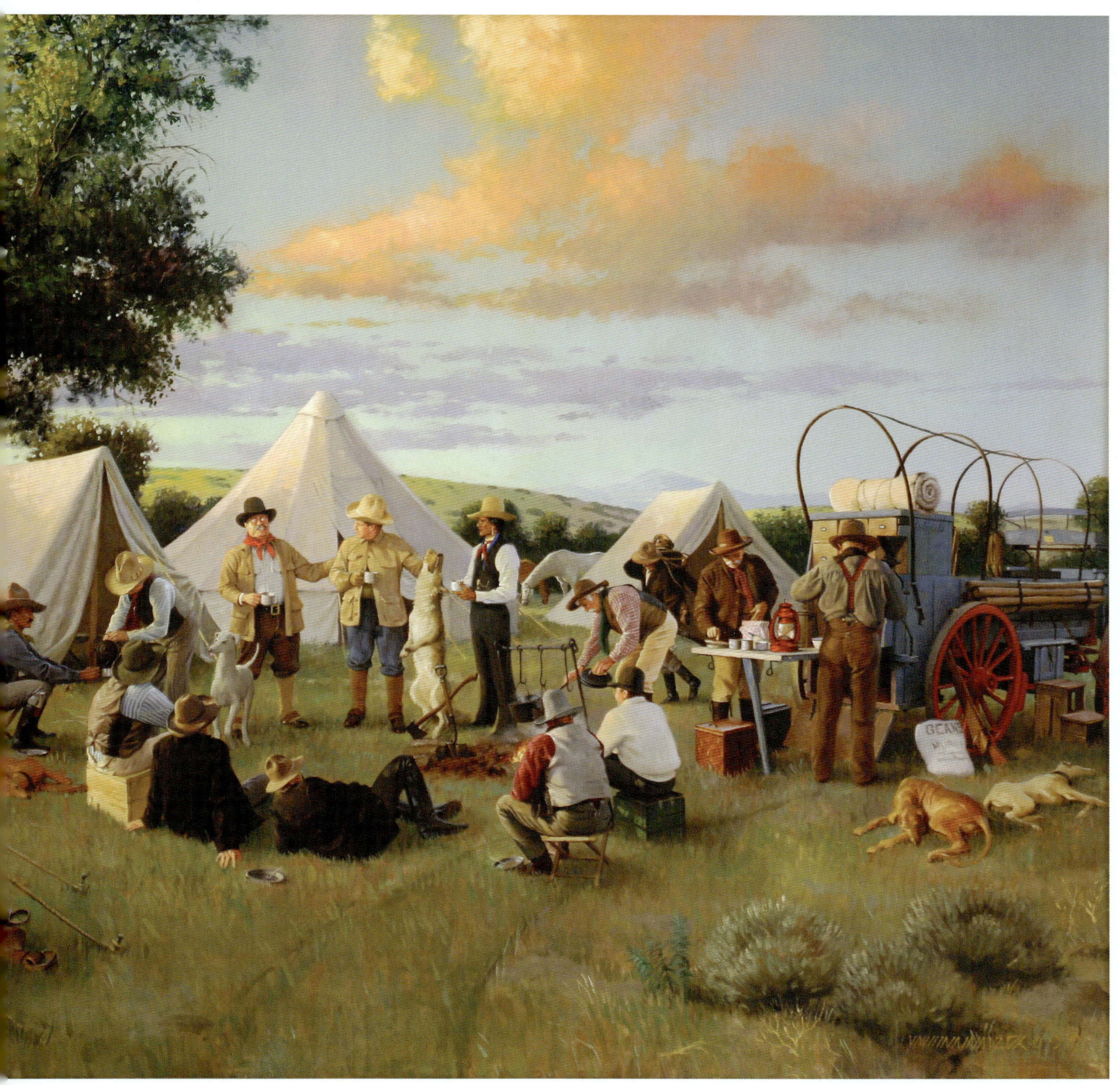

OSAGE TREATY OF 1825

BY MIKE WIMMER

120 x 72, oil/canvas

After the United States purchased land encompassed by the Louisiana Purchase, it was necessary to revise previous treaties with the Osage, basically moving the tribe to Kansas to prevent fighting with the Cherokees. The Osage Treaty of 1825 was signed in St. Louis, Missouri, by William Clark, U. S. indian commissioner, and Clairmont, principal chief of the Osage, and 60 great and little chiefs of the tribe. The ceremony was witnessed by notables such as trader Pierre Chouteau. The painting was sponsored by the Tulsa World and the Lorton family.

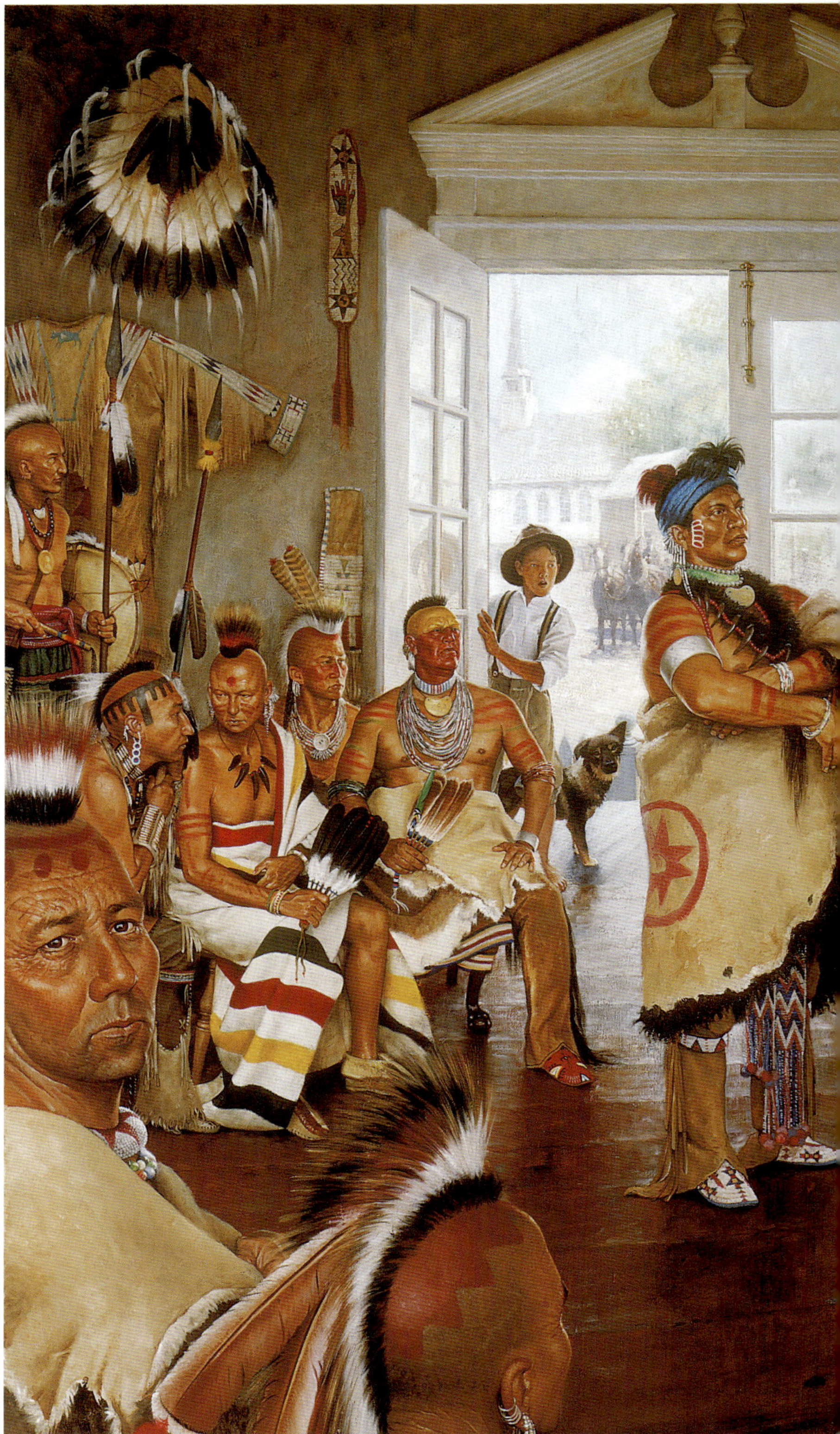

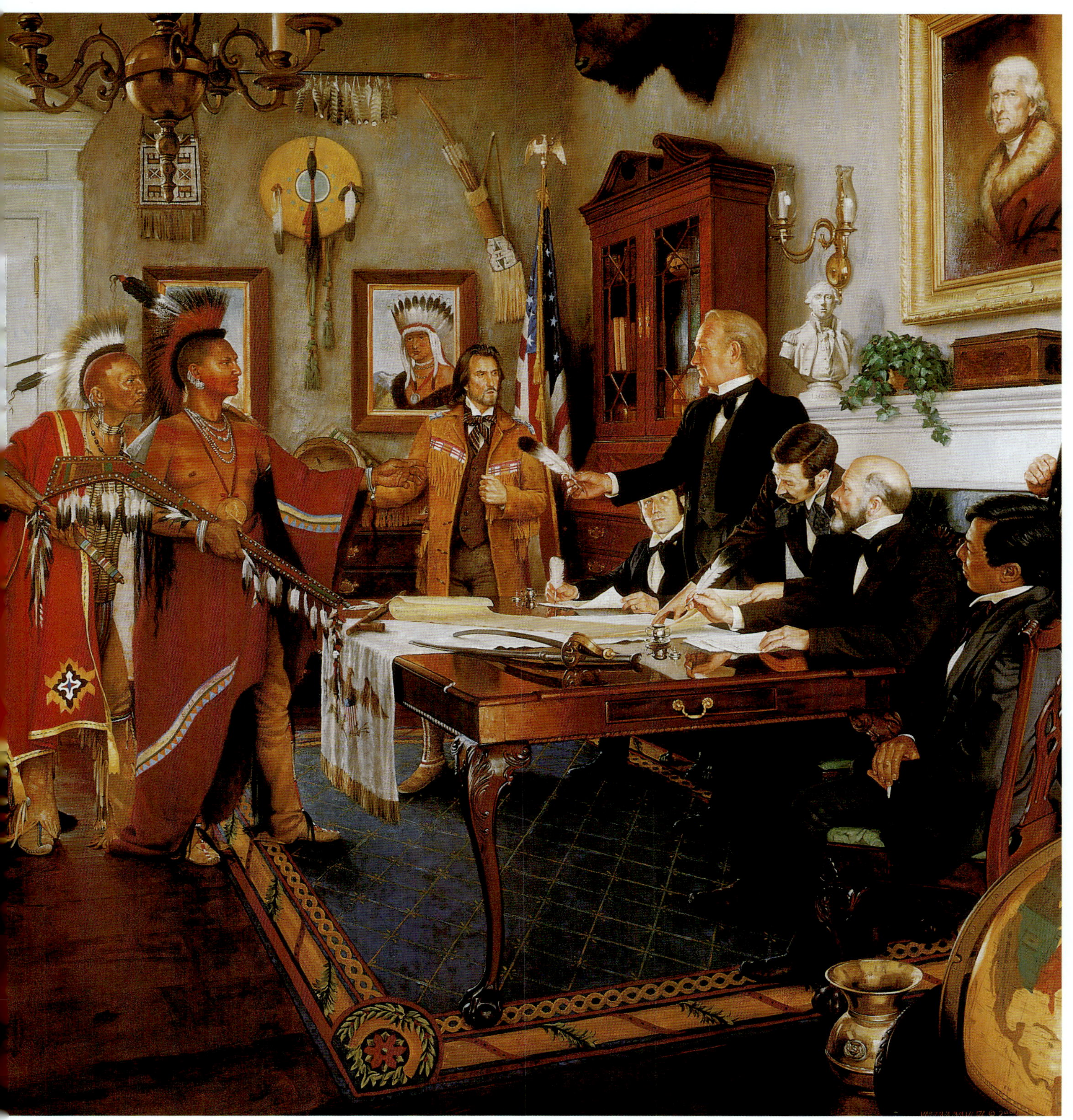

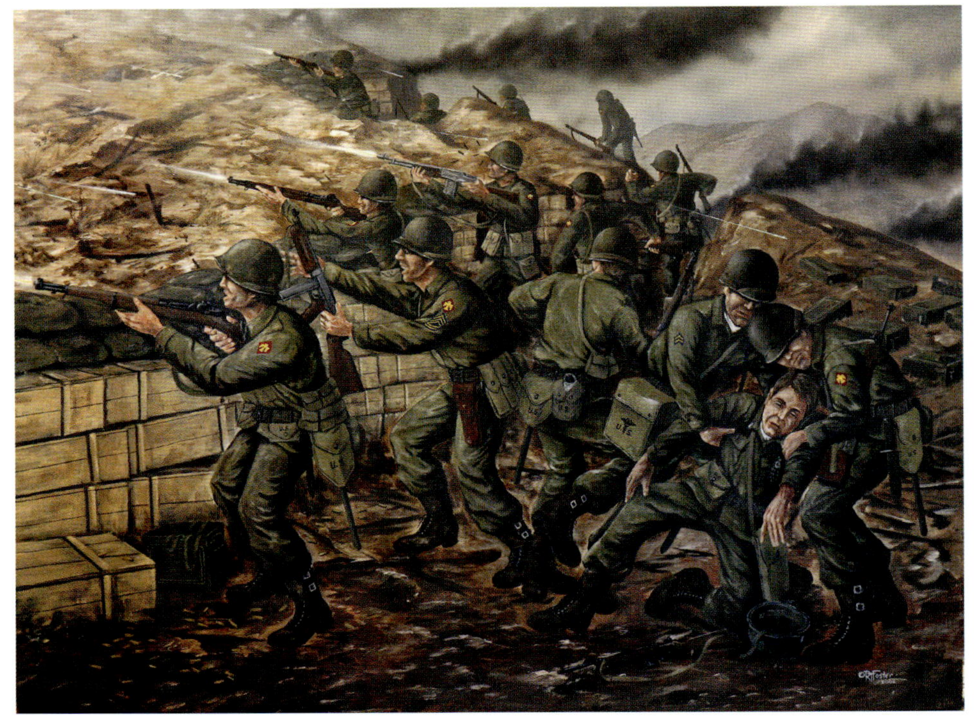

45TH DIVISION AT PORK CHOP HILL, KOREA

BY R.T. FOSTER

36 x 48, acrylic/canvas

The 45th Infantry Division was part of the Oklahoma National Guard and its members valiantly fought in World War II and the Korean Conflict. Known as the Thunderbirds, 45th Division soldiers inflicted heavy casualties on the enemy at Pork Chop Hill in Korea in 1952. The painting was sponsored by the late U. S. District Judge Fred Daugherty, former commanding general of the 45th Infantry Division.

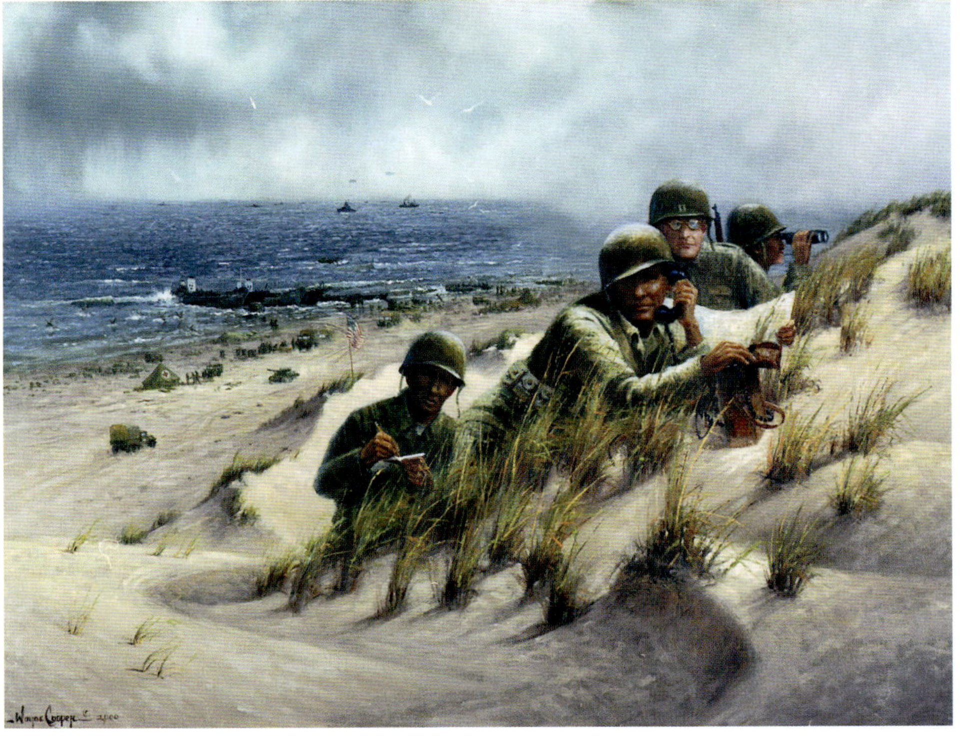

COMANCHE CODE TALKERS AT OMAHA BEACH

BY WAYNE COOPER

36 x 48, oil/canvas

Comanches from southwest Oklahoma used their language to provide an unbreakable code for American military forces in World War II. Phillips Petroleum Company and State Senator Jim Dunlap of Bartlesville sponsored this painting of the final living code talker, Charles Chibitty, communicating with other troops on Omaha Beach in northern France on D-Day.

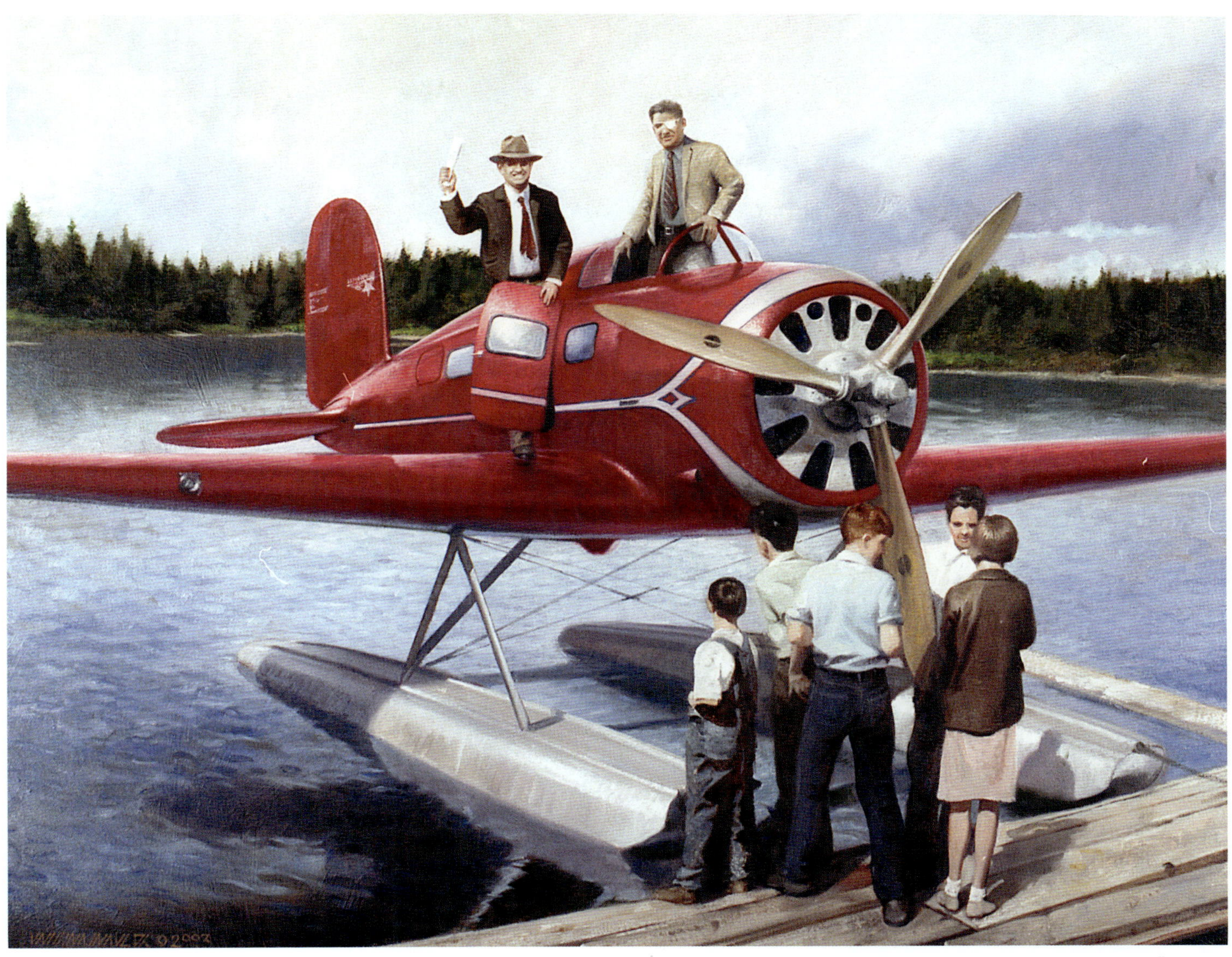

THE LAST FAREWELL OF WILL ROGERS AND WILEY POST

BY MIKE WIMMER

30 x 40, oil/canvas

Oklahoma's two most famous citizens, Will Rogers and Wiley Post, were killed in an airplane crash near Point Barrow, Alaska, on August 15, 1935. The Paul and Helen Sisk Charitable Trust sponsored this painting of Rogers and Post bidding a small group of well-wishers farewell at Fairbanks, Alaska, a few hours before the tragic crash. Their deaths shocked the entire world. When news of the tragedy arrived in Washington, D. C., Congress adjourned for the day.

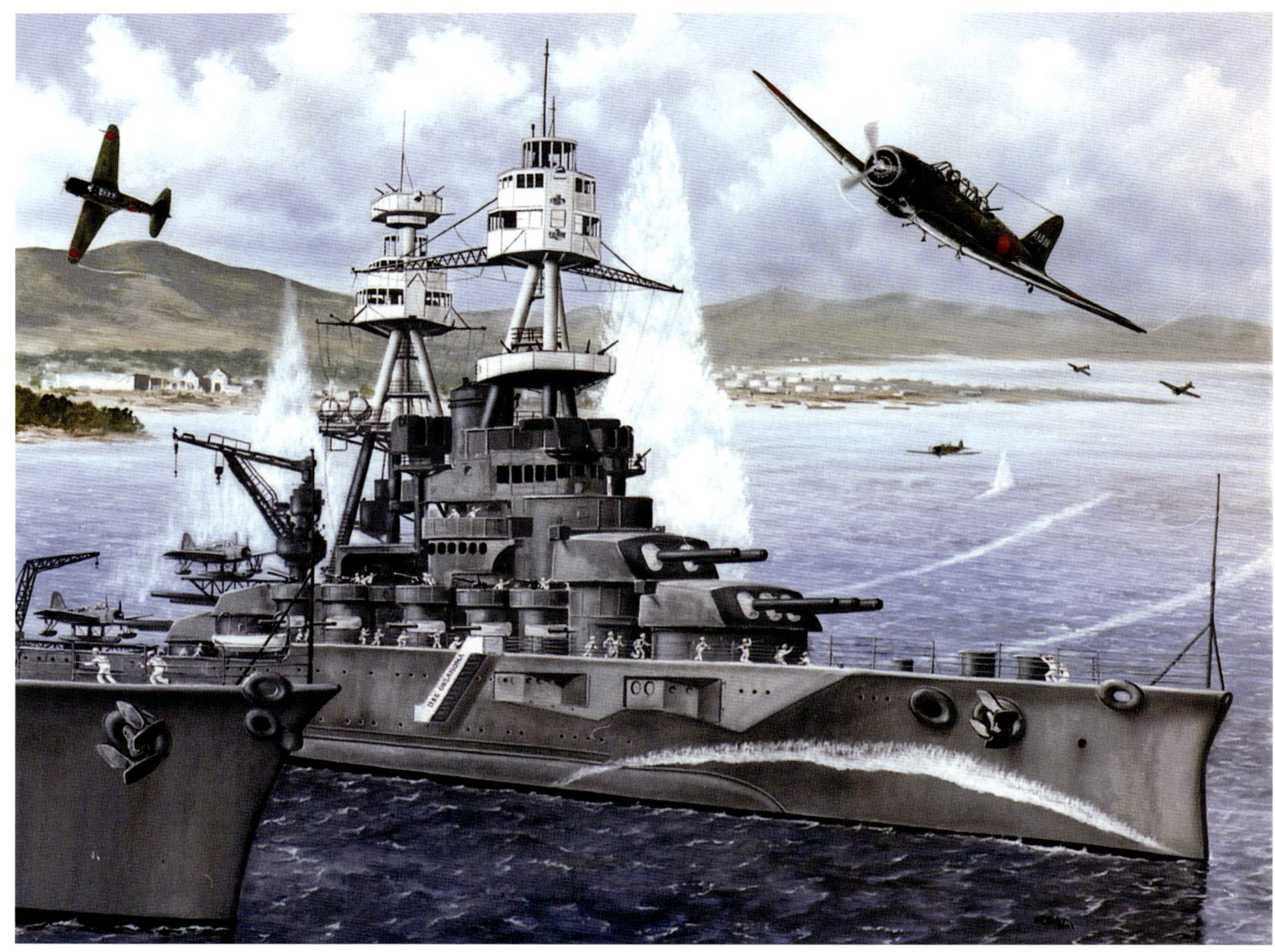

ATTACK OF BATTLESHIP OKLAHOMA AT PEARL HARBOR

BY R.T. FOSTER

48 x 36, acrylic/canvas

The crew of the *U.S.S. Oklahoma* was preparing for an inspection at Pearl Harbor, Hawaii, on the morning of December 7, 1941, when Japanese aircraft attacked the naval base and prompted America's entry into World War II. More than 400 men on the *Oklahoma* were killed, and the proud ship sank. Later, the ship was raised, bodies were removed, and the vessel was sold for scrap. Ironically, the *Oklahoma* developed a list and plunged to the bottom of the Pacific Ocean midway between Pearl Harbor and San Francisco, California. The painting was sponsored by Admiral and Mrs. William Crowe, Jr.

THE U.S.S. OKLAHOMA MEMORIAL AT PEARL HARBOR

BY CHRISTOPHER NICK

30 x 40, oil/canvas

In 2007, a memorial was dedicated at Pearl Harbor, Hawaii, 60 years after the *U.S.S. Oklahoma* capsized there during the Japanese attack of December 7, 1941. The memorial honors the lives lost and includes 429 marble standards, each engraved with the name of a fallen sailor or marine. The painting was sponsored by the Oklahoma Centennial Commission, the Battleship Oklahoma Memorial Commission, Senator Jim Reynolds, and his wife, Diane.

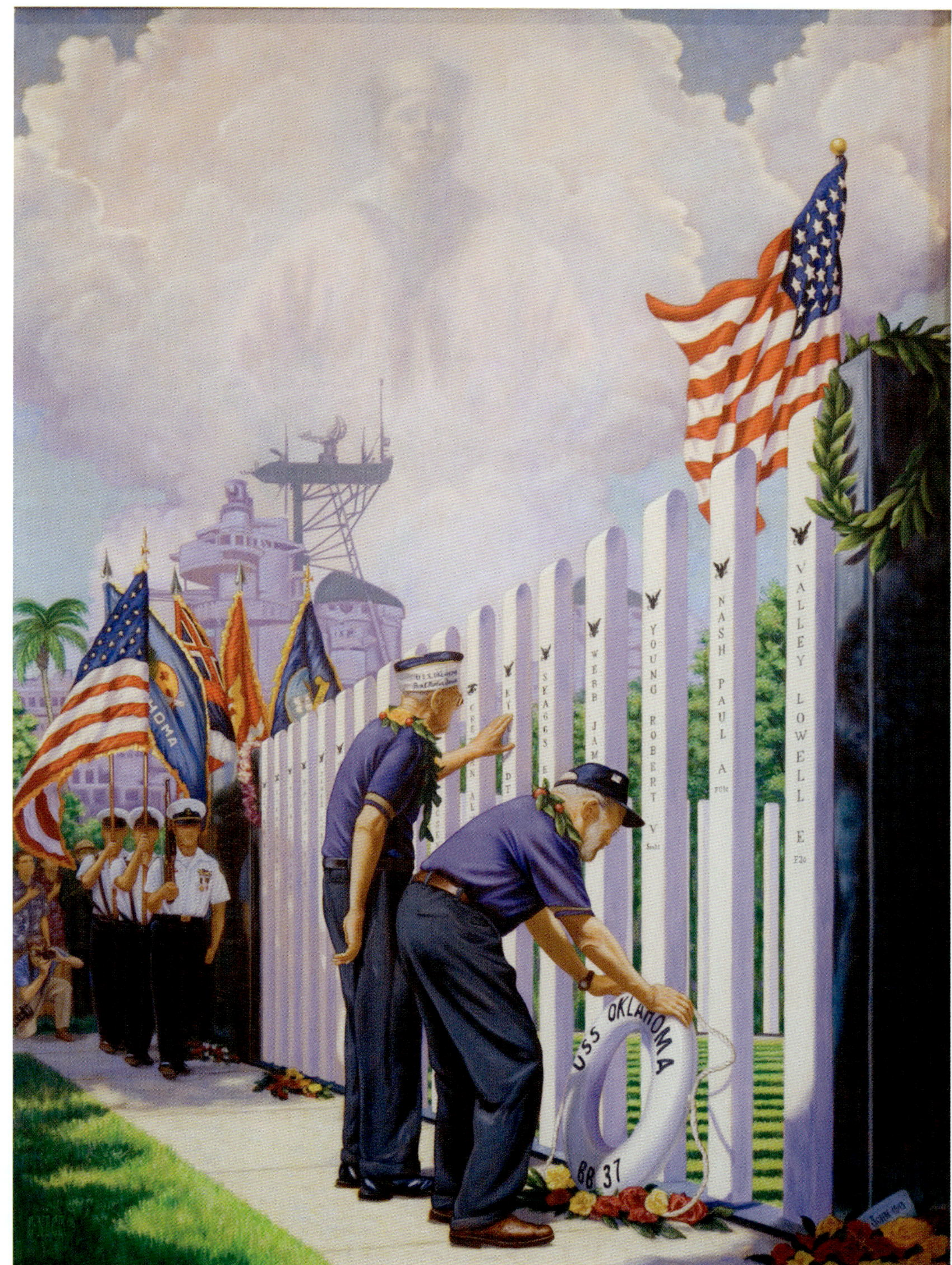

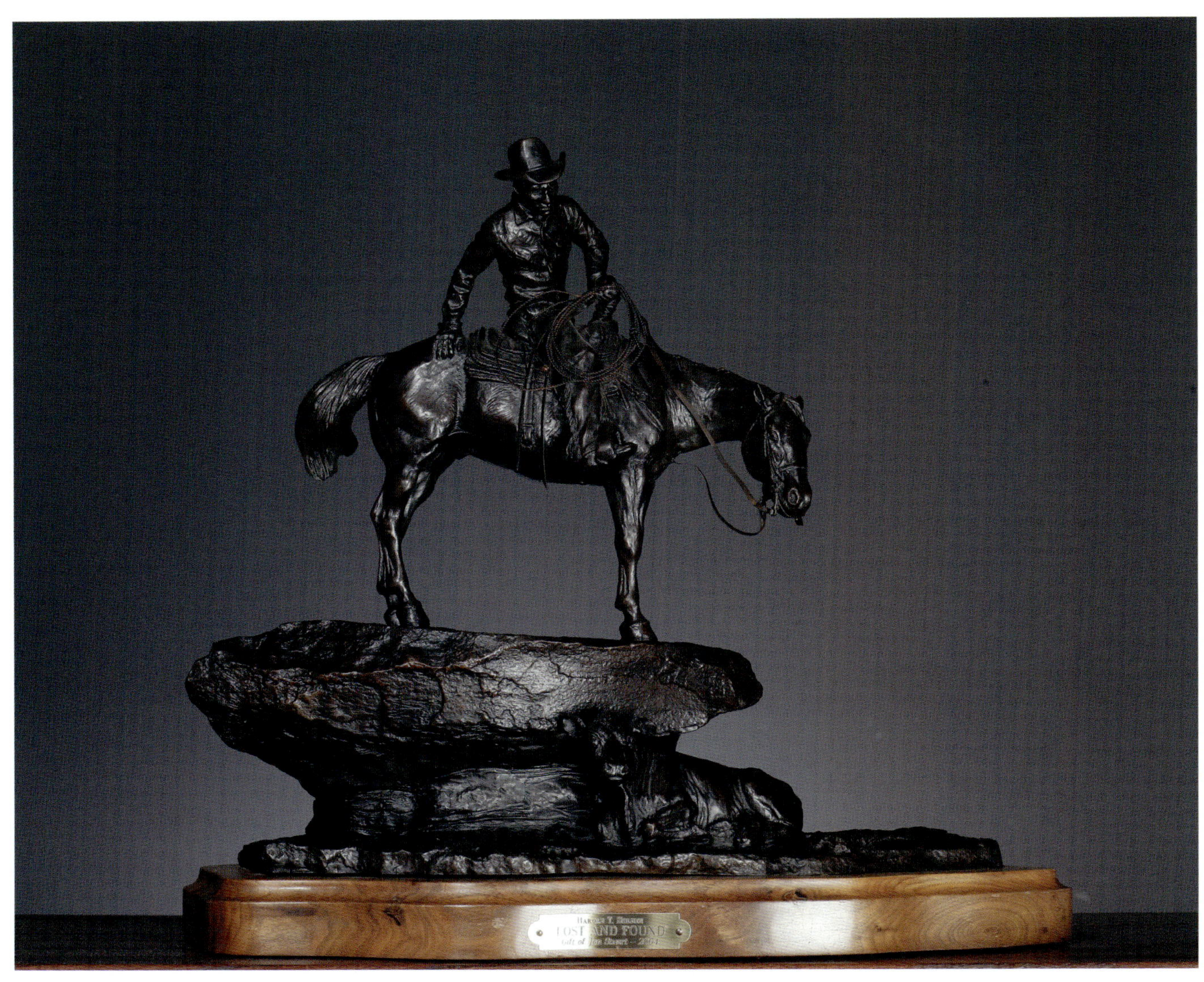

LOST AND FOUND

BY HAROLD T. HOLDEN

17 inches in height

Lost and Found depicts an Oklahoma cowboy who has located a lost calf and is attempting to bring it back to the herd. The sculpture was sponsored by Jon Stuart of Tulsa.

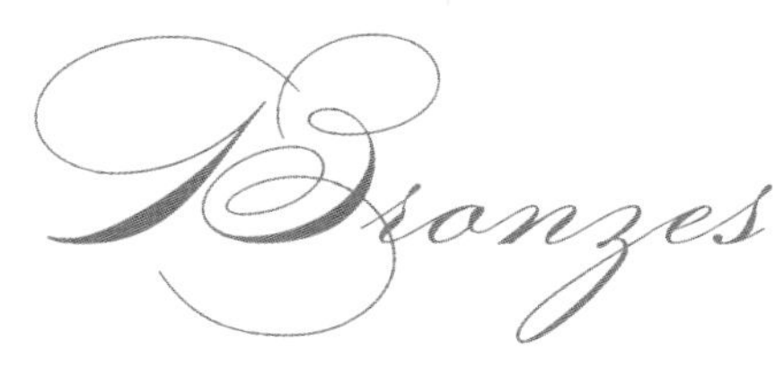

RANDY RAMER, Curator, Gilcrease Museum

As a medium in the creation of sculpture, bronze has maintained an allure for millennia. Its popularity lies in part in its distinctive capacity not only to allow the depiction of intricate three-dimensional detail but also the portrayal of action—nuances of gesture and dynamic movement. This capacity has inspired artists across time and space in their creation of enduring and affective likenesses and abstract forms alike.

Bronze sculptures maintain a luster and texture unlike any other art form. Notably, they instill a sense of permanence well-suited to the commemoration of historic themes. The bronzes in the Oklahoma State Senate Art Collection eloquently depict the interest and power of Oklahoma historical subjects. *Lost and Found* follows in a long tradition of western subjects, particularly horses and riders engaged in the outdoor activities of a cattle-working culture, presented as cast bronze sculptures. Though Charles Banks Wilson's *Sequoyah* pays tribute to an individual and Enoch Kelly Haney's *The Guardian* and his pictorial bronze roundels present iconic images, both artists capture the qualities of dignity and humanity. The scultpural works in the Senate Collection are effective symbols of Oklahoma, with its unique patinas of history and cultural memory.

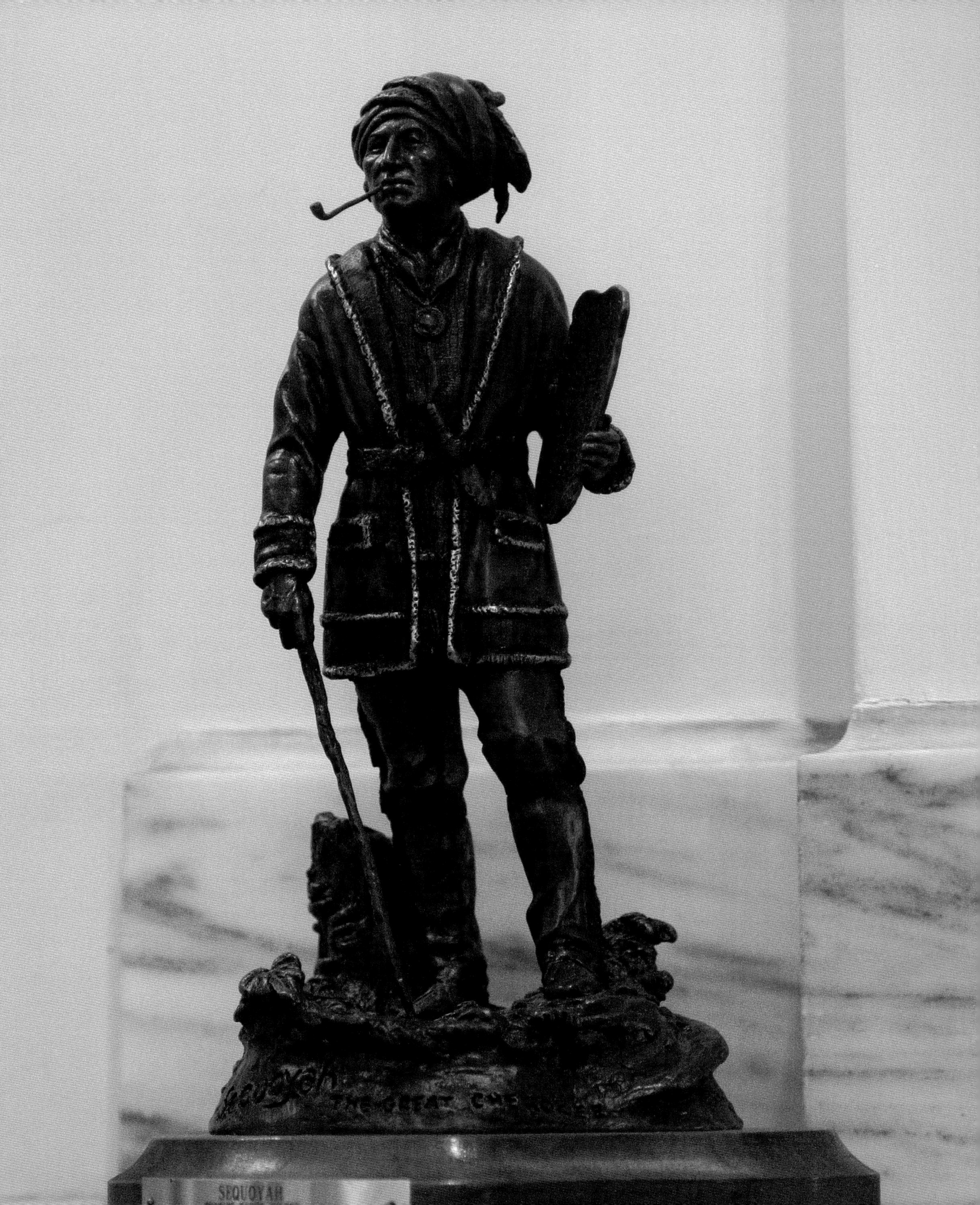
THE GREAT
SEQUOYAH

SEQUOYAH (FACING)

BY CHARLES BANKS WILSON

12 inches in height

Sequoyah, also known as George Guess, was a Cherokee silversmith who created the Cherokee syllabary, making reading and writing in Cherokee possible. He lived in a cabin near Sallisaw, Oklahoma, from 1829 to 1844. He is considered one of America's pioneer educators, having brought his people an effective writing system. The sculpture was sponsored by Senator Charles Ford.

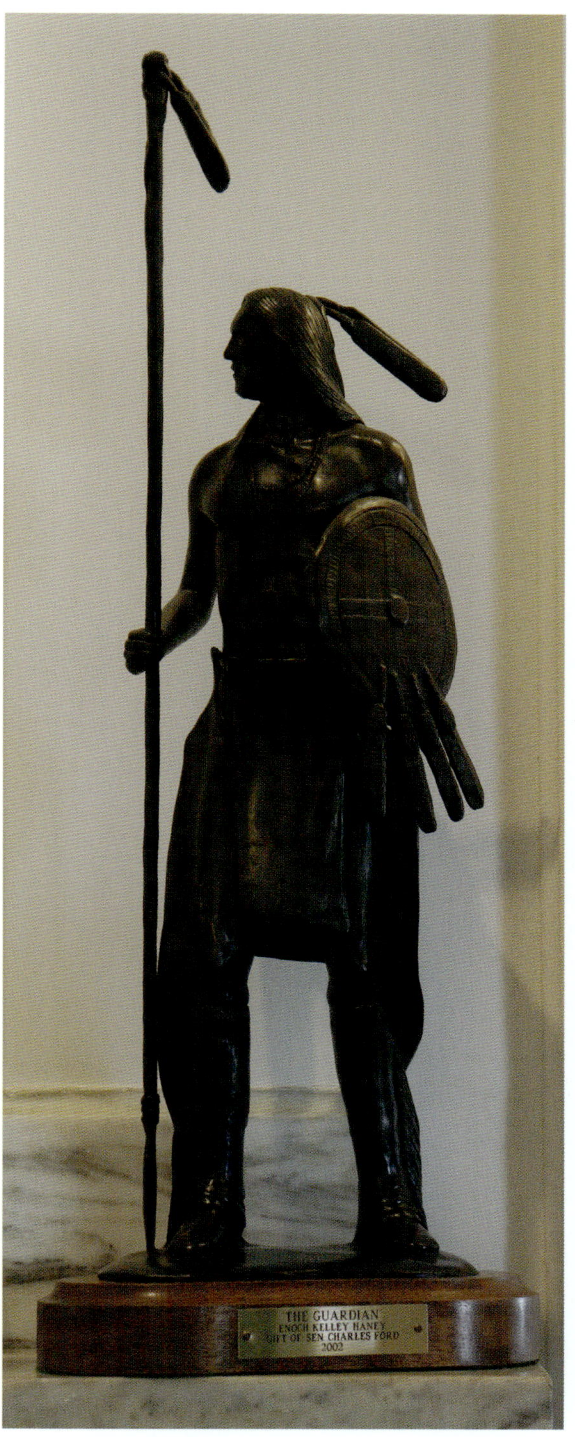

THE GUARDIAN (AT RIGHT)

BY ENOCH KELLY HANEY

27 inches in height

The large sculpture *The Guardian* was selected to adorn the top of the new state capitol dome in 2002. Its sculptor, Enoch Kelly Haney, served as a legislator and is principal chief of the Seminole Nation of Oklahoma. This bronze is a maquette of the 17-feet-tall, 4,000-pound bronze of an American Indian warrior. It was sponsored by Senator Charles Ford.

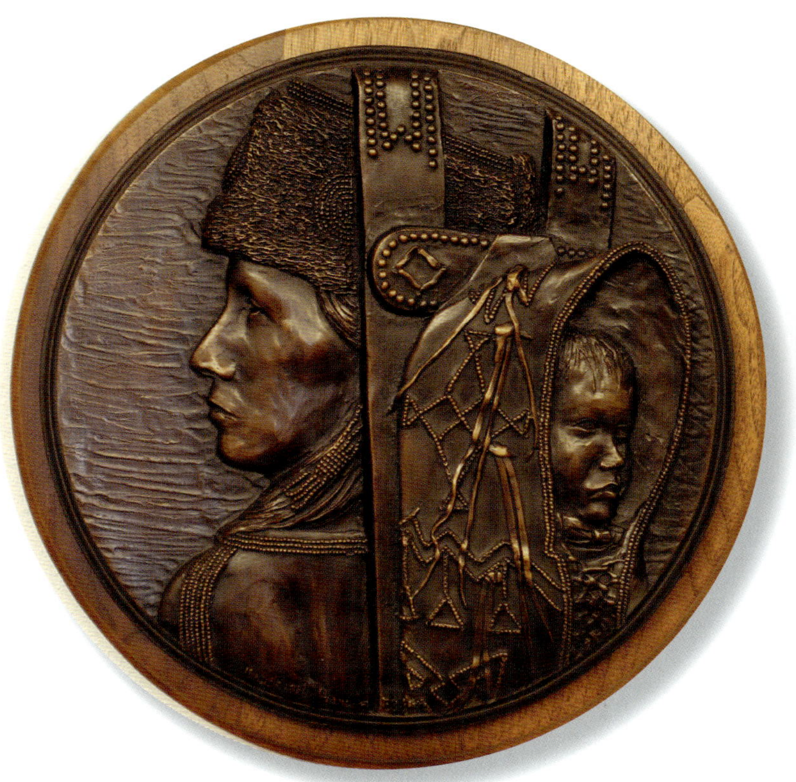

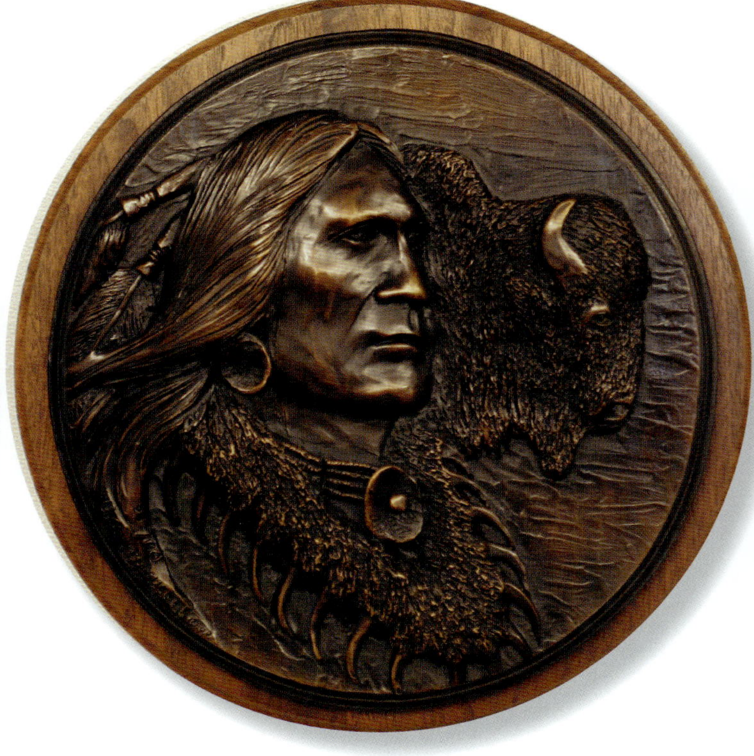

THE SPIRIT OF HERITAGE

BY ENOCH KELLY HANEY

Dimensions in diameter: 11-inch maquette, 33-inch bas-relief

The Spirit of Heritage depicts an Indian mother carrying her infant in a cradleboard, an image that represents traditions that strengthened the western tribes of Oklahoma. It also evokes the generational links and maternal nurturing common to all people. Sponsored by Tulsa Tribune Foundation.

THE WILL TO LIVE

BY ENOCH KELLY HANEY

Dimensions in diameter: 11-inch maquette, 33-inch bas-relief

The Will to Live shows a young warrior against the background of a buffalo, a native symbol of endurance. At one time the buffalo was nearly extinct. Now it not only survives but thrives. Likewise the native people of Oklahoma have faced tragedies and challenges, but have ultimately overcome them all. Sponsored by Tulsa Tribune Foundation.

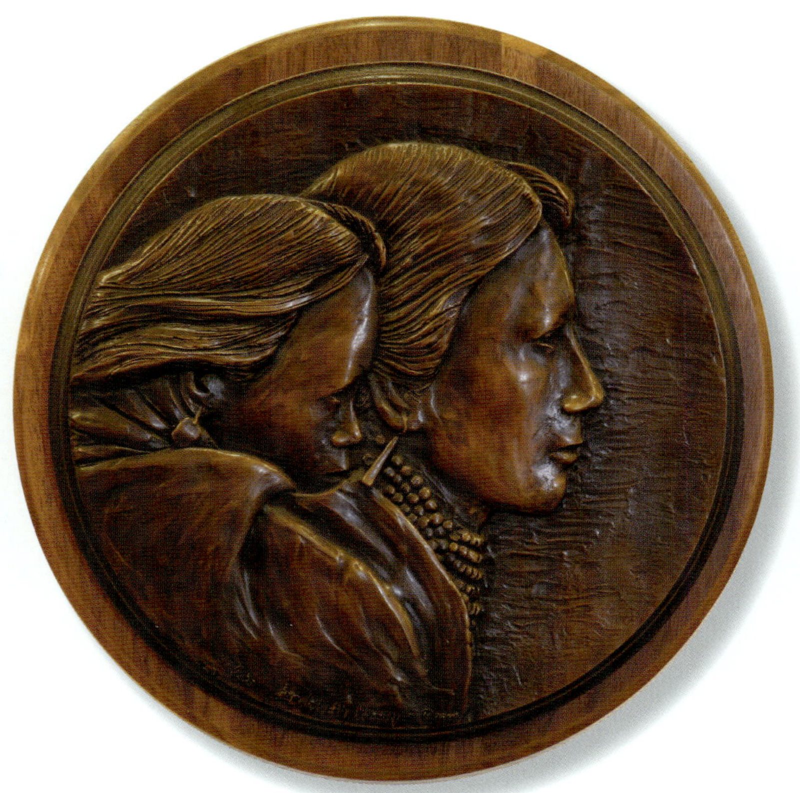

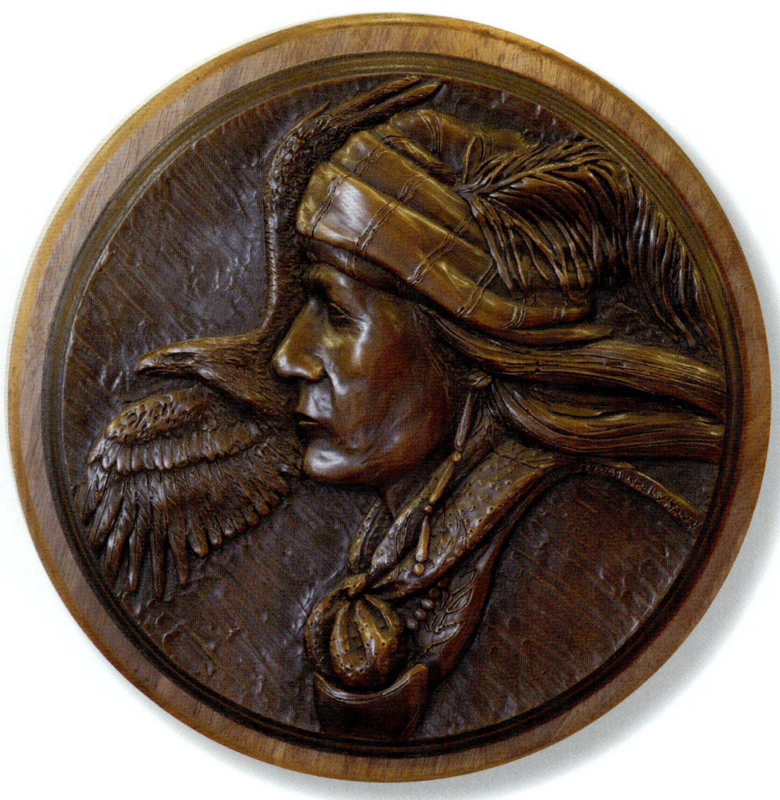

THE POWER OF HOPE

BY ENOCH KELLY HANEY

Dimensions in diameter: 11-inch maquette, 33-inch bas-relief

The Power of Hope shows a mother and child—the mother strong in the face of the adversity that eastern tribes endured during their removal from the southeastern United States to what would become Oklahoma. Protection, dignity, and perseverance suffuse the image. Sponsored by Tulsa Tribune Foundation.

WITH THE VISION OF AN EAGLE

BY ENOCH KELLY HANEY

Dimensions in diameter: 11-inch maquette, 33-inch bas-relief

With the Vision of an Eagle pairs the face of a tribal leader with the image of a creature who symbolizes sharp-eyed observation, strength in motion, boldness, and dignity. Sponsored by Tulsa Tribune Foundation.

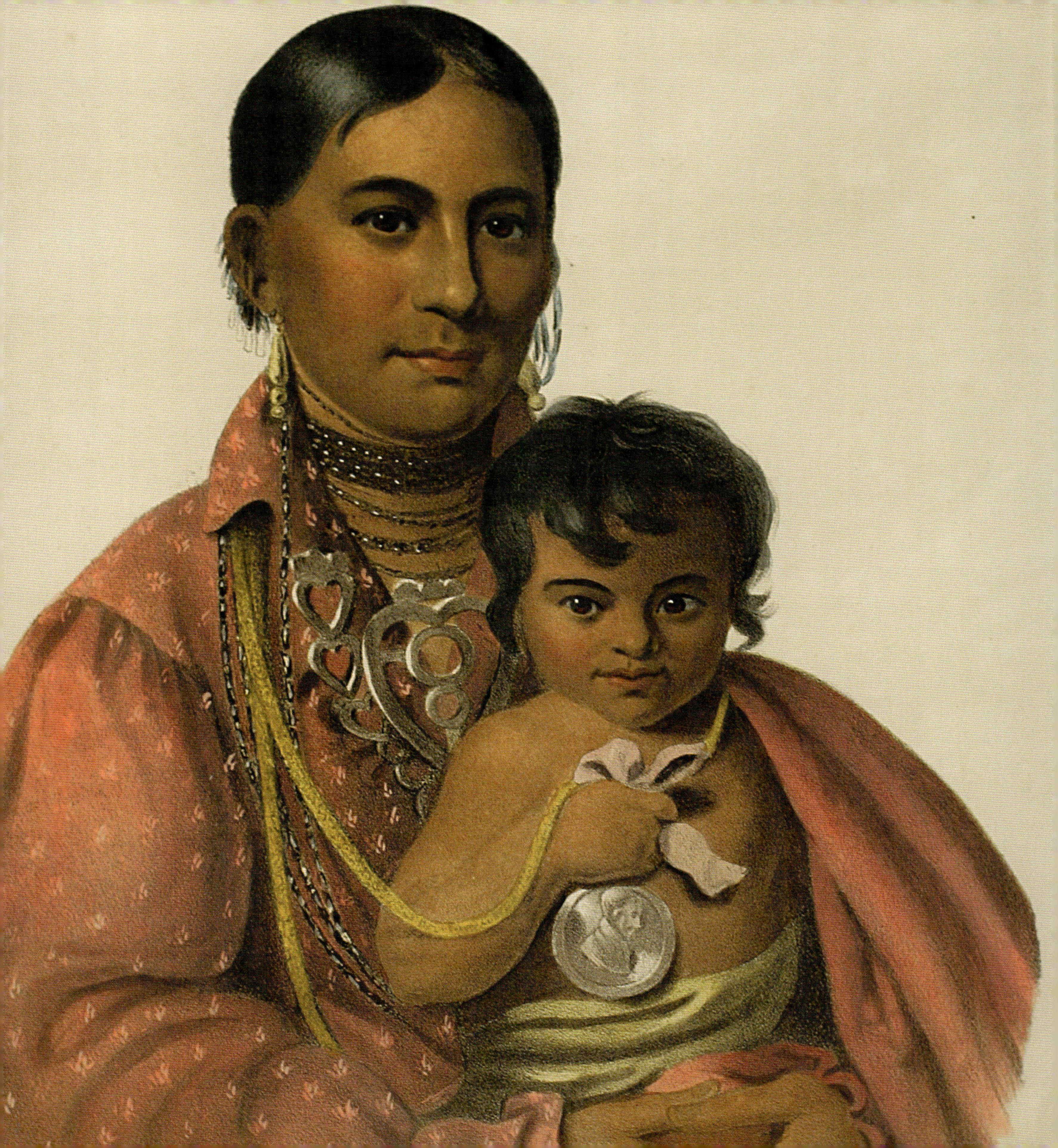

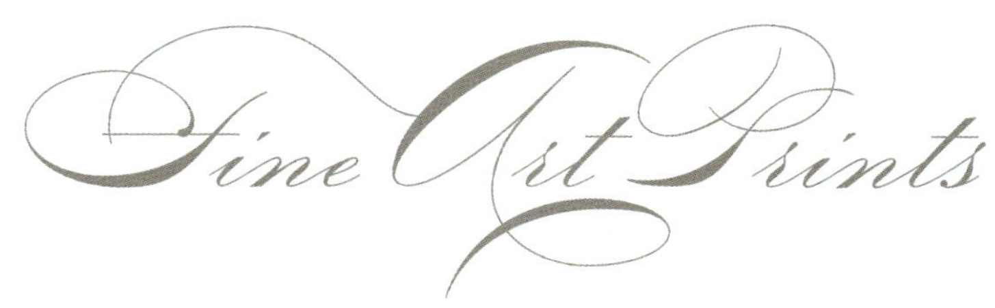

McKENNY AND HALL AND J. O. LEWIS LITHOGRAPHS

The State Senate Collection contains 94 octavo-size and 55 folio-size hand-painted lithographs from the McKenney-Hall Portrait Gallery of American Indians. The original color portraits of the most famous Indians in American history were painted by Charles Bird King and other important American artists. The collection was the work of Thomas Loraine McKenny, superintendent of Indian trade under several presidents of the United States, and James Hall, a frontier lawyer, judge, and newspaper editor. The lithographs are important because the original paintings were destroyed in a fire while on display at the Smithsonian Institution in Washington, D. C., in 1865. State Senator Charles Ford traveled across the North American continent in search of McKenny-Hall portraits. The Senate Collection also contains 12 folio-size lithographs of North American Indians by J. O. Lewis.

Not shown here but on view in the 2009 Gilcrease exhibition are McKenny and Hall portraits of Cherokees Se-Qua-Yah (George Guess), Major Ridge, John Ridge, John Ross, and Tah-Chee; Creeks McIntosh and Me-Na-Wa; the Choctaw Push-Ma-Ta-Ha; Seminoles Miscanopy and Mistippee; the Seneca Red Jacket; and Chippewas Squaw and Child, Hayne-Hudjihini (Eagle of Delight), and Rant-Che-Wai-Me (Female Flying Pigeon). Not shown here but on view at Gilcrease from the J. O. Lewis collection are Tens-Qua-Ta-Wa (Shawnee), Pach-E-po (Pottawattomie), Cha-Co-To (Pottawattomie), Tshu-Gue-Ga (Winnebago), Kee-O-Tuck-Kee (Pottawattomie), and Richardville (Miami).

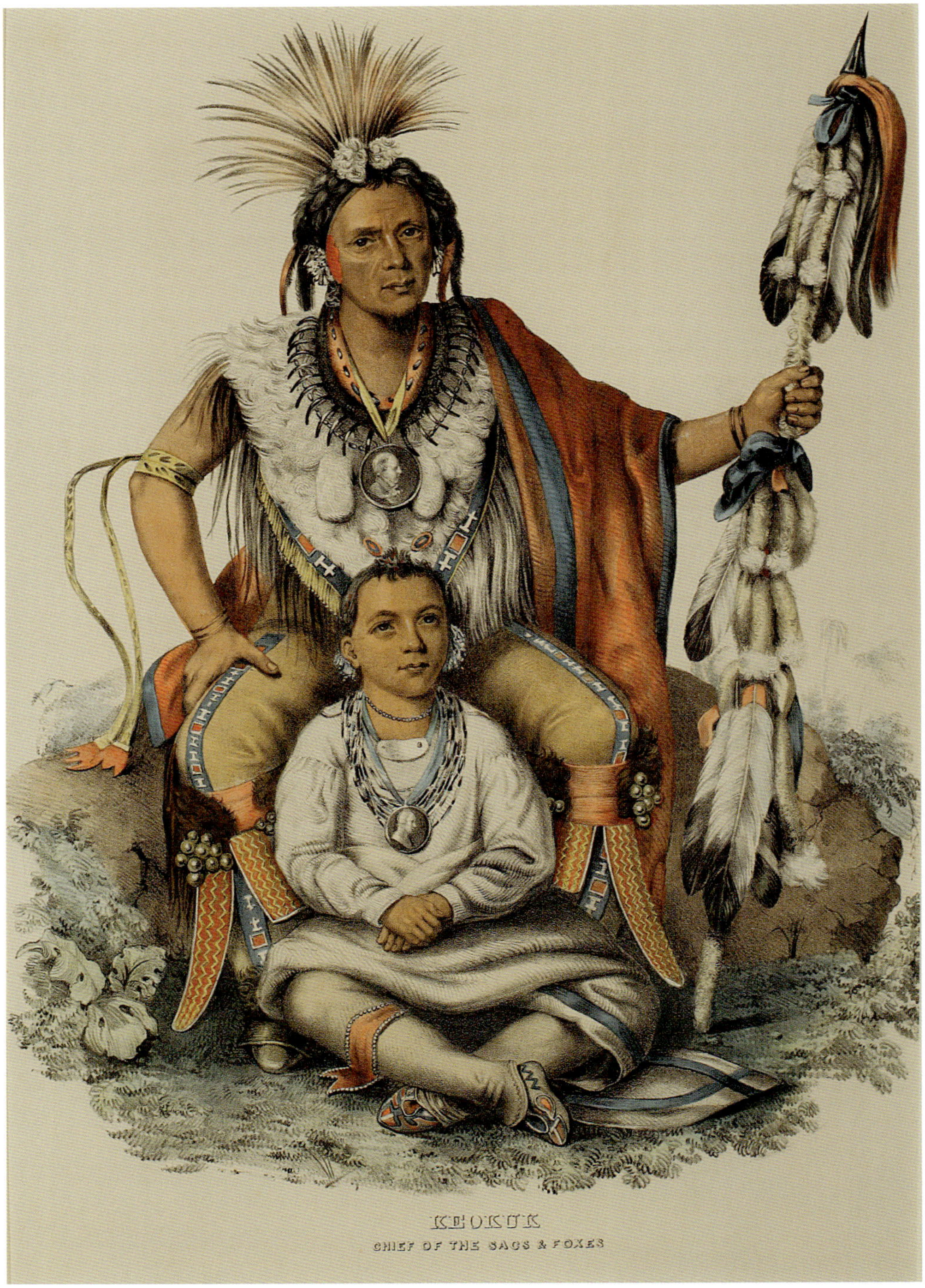

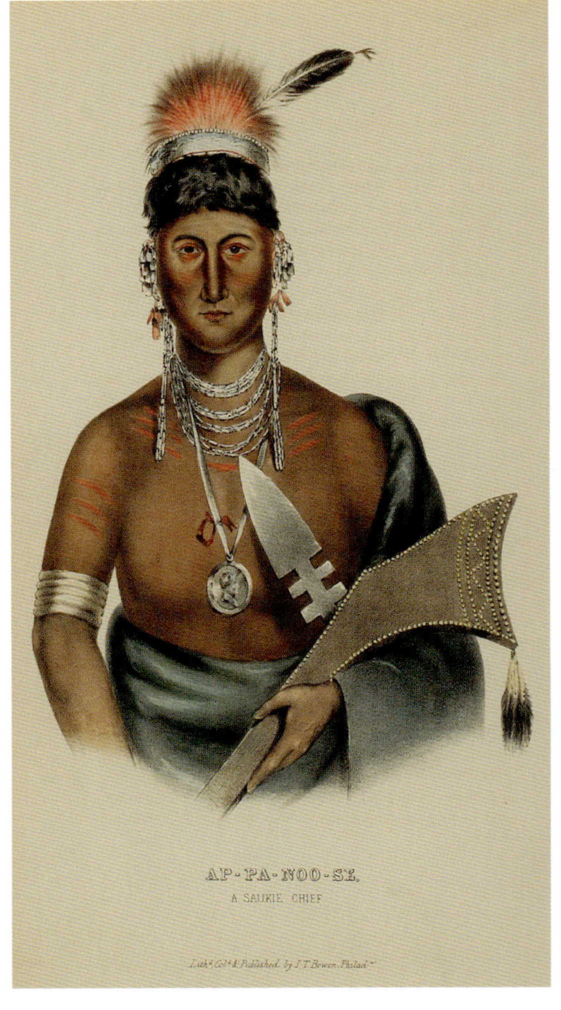

AP-PA-NOO-SE, A SAUKIE CHIEF (ABOVE), MCKENNEY AND HALL

KEOKUK, CHIEF OF THE SACS AND FOXES (LEFT), MCKENNEY AND HALL

CLOCKWISE FROM UPPER LEFT:

MAUCK-COO-MAUN, A CELEBRATED IOWAY CHIEF
J. O. LEWIS

MEN-DOW-MAIN, OR THE CORN, A CHIPPEWA DWARF
J. O. LEWIS

PETALESHARRO, A PAWNEE BRAVE
MCKENNEY AND HALL

MO-HON-GO — OSAGE WOMAN
MCKENNEY AND HALL

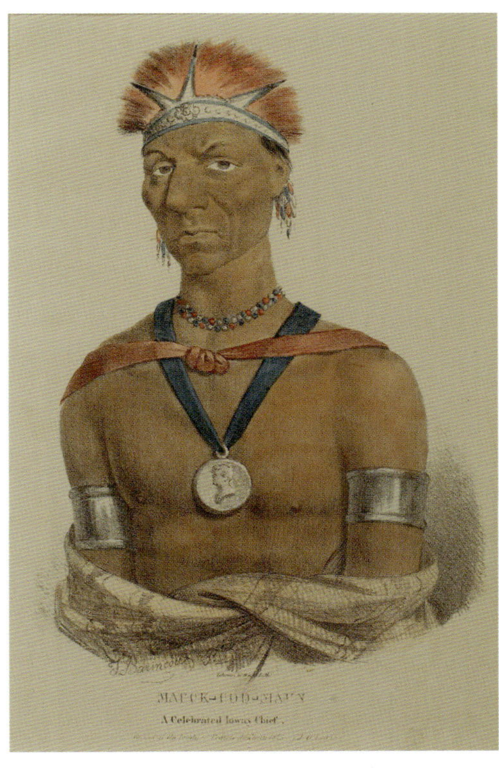

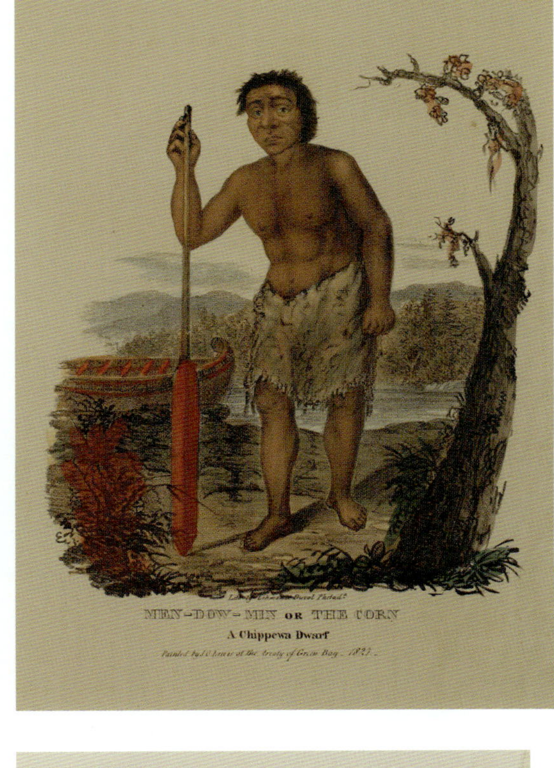

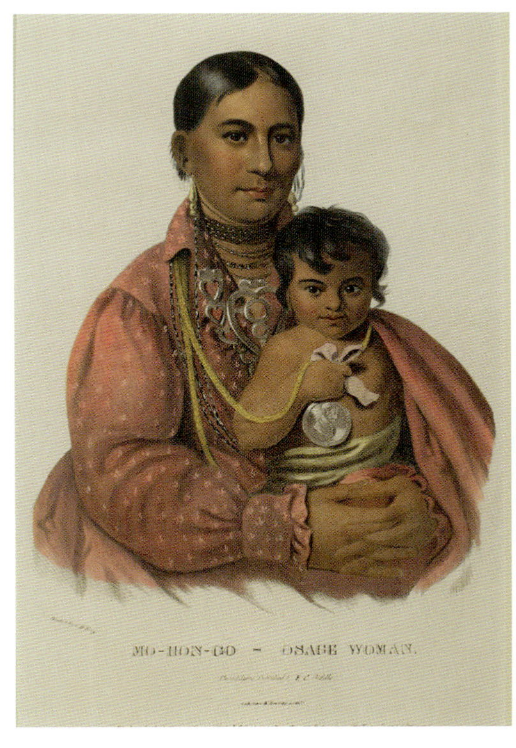

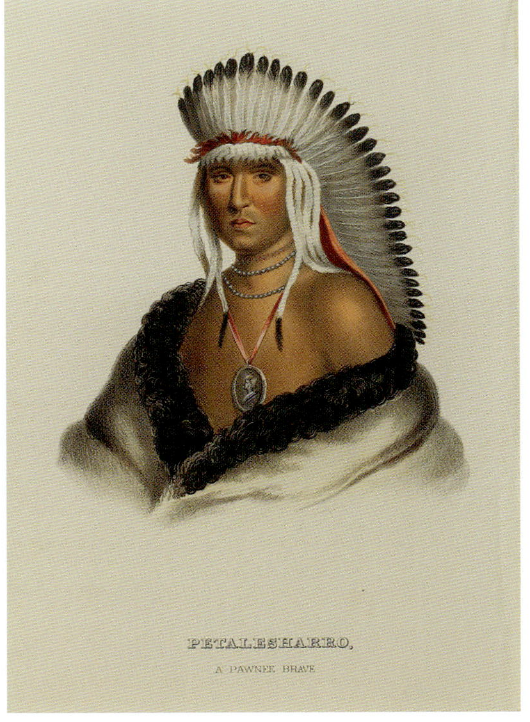

ADDITIONAL WORKS IN THE SENATE COLLECTION

ANTIQUE TALL CASE CLOCK

Sponsored by Senator Charles Ford

ANTIQUE TALL CASE CLOCK

Sponsored by Senator Charles Ford

46-STAR FLAG

A gift from the Woolaroc Museum

OKLAHOMA'S FIRST FLAG

Sponsored by Senator David Meyers

EIGHT ANTIQUE BRONZE LIGHT FIXTURES

WORKS IN OTHER VENUES

Most of the Oklahoma State Senate Art Collection is on permanent display in the State Capitol. The following works are displayed in other venues.

SAM HOUSTON MAYES

TIMOTHY TYLER

Oil/canvas, 24 x 30, on view at Mayes County Courthouse. Sponsored by Grand River Dam Authority.

EARLY DAY PILOT

DAVID GARDNER

Life-size bronze, on view at Tulsa Riverside Airport. Sponsored by Friends of Riverside Airport.

REACHING FOR EXCELLENCE

SANDRA VAN ZANDT

One-and-a-quarter life-scale bronze, on view at Oklahoma School of Science and Mathematics, Oklahoma City. Sponsored by Dollar Thrifty Auto Group.

THE GUARDIAN

ENOCH KELLY HANEY

Bronze, 15 inches in height, on view at Gilcrease Museum. Sponsored by Senator Charles Ford.

HISTORIAN BERYL D. FORD

BARBARA HENSHAW

Life-size bronze, on view at Tulsa Historical Society. Sponsored by Senator Charles Ford.

THREE COCK PHEASANTS

BRUCE KILLEN

48" bronze at Oklahoma Wildlife Department Sponsored by the Stuart Family Foundation.

ONE GOOSE

BRUCE KILLEN

36" bronze at Oklahoma Wildlife Department Sponsored by the Stuart Family Foundation.

Reaching for Excellence, Sandra Van Zandt

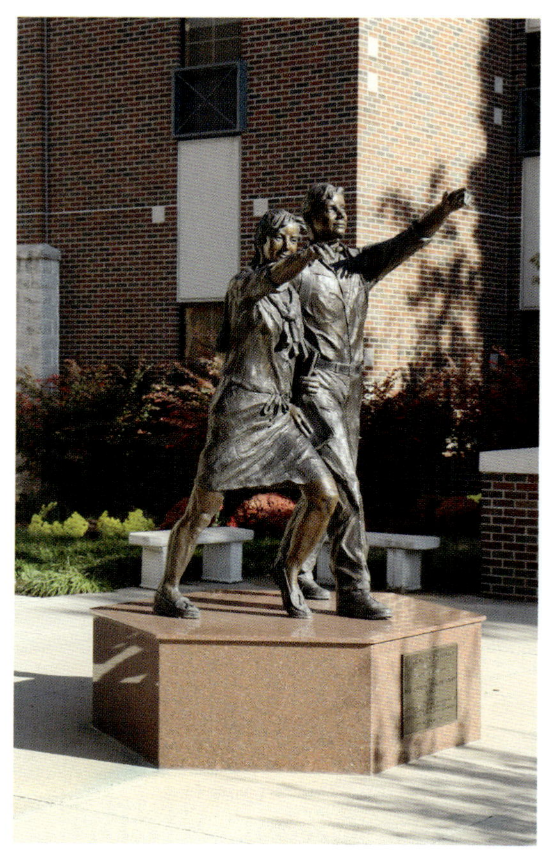

ARTISTS REPRESENTED IN THE COLLECTION

JOE BEELER spent much of his time as a youth studying the techniques of Charles Banks Wilson. Trained at The University of Tulsa and recognized as a pioneer in the field of Western art, Beeler began his career as an illustrator for the University of Oklahoma Press. Of Cherokee blood, he has had one-man shows in every major Western museum in the United States. His work is represented in numerous collections including Gilcrease and Woolaroc Museums in Oklahoma and the Cody Museum in Wyoming. In 1965, Beeler helped found the Cowboy Artists of America. He lived until his death in 2006 in Sedona, Arizona, where the town has honored him by erecting a statue of him in the downtown area.

WAYNE COOPER has used his Native American heritage to portray Western and Native American subjects. His experiences of being raised on a small ranch give him first-hand knowledge of Oklahoma ranch life. Cooper's oils, water colors, charcoals, pencil, sculpture, and lithographs are contained in many private and public collections worldwide. He calls Depew, Oklahoma, home.

R.T. FOSTER of Oklahoma City is known for acrylic, pencil, and watercolor paintings. He won Oklahoma's 1987 and 1991 Waterfowl stamp competition and has painted a variety of subjects from historical aviation to Civil War battle scenes and from portraits to wildlife. A veteran of Marine service in Vietnam, Foster's tribute to President George Bush's Air Group 51 is displayed in several museums, including the National Air and Space Museum in Washington, D. C.

JOHN FREE, a recognized Western sculptor and animal painter, was raised on his grandfather's ranch near McAlester, Oklahoma, and learned the life of a cowboy. He began sketching scenes from his life as a child and drew from his Osage and Cherokee heritage. He studied to be a veterinarian, but turned to art to express the life of a cowboy. After studying privately in Taos, New Mexico, he opened his own foundry in Pawhuska, Oklahoma.

BORIS GORDON was born in Russia and studied at the Royal Academy in London and Academy of Art in Munich. He arrived in California in 1906 and began painting. He painted portraits of Presidents Herbert Hoover, Dwight Eisenhower, and Harry Truman. Gordon was selected by Oklahoma actor and humorist Will Rogers to paint his portrait in 1931. Gordon died in 1976.

ENOCH KELLY HANEY of Seminole has served Oklahoma in many ways as a member of the Oklahoma House of Representatives, the State Senate, and as Principal Chief of the Seminole Nation. He was the first fullblood Native American to serve in the Oklahoma legislature. He was named Master Artist of the Five Civilized Tribes and has been honored for his work in education. He is widely heralded as an artist. His most significant contribution to art in Oklahoma is *The Guardian,* a sculpture of a Native American warrior chosen to adorn the new State Capitol dome in 2002.

BARBARA HENSHAW of Tulsa studied at The University of Tulsa and Philbrook Museum and privately in Colorado. Her bronzes are on display in private homes, corporate offices, the Tulsa Historical Society, the Donald W. Reynolds Center, Tulsa Opera, and Tulsa Ballet.

HAROLD HOLDEN graduated from high school in Enid, but calls Kremlin, Oklahoma, home. He was trained at Oklahoma State University and the Texas Academy of Art in Houston. An accomplished painter and sculptor, Holden has major works on display throughout the world, including the National Cowboy and Western Heritage Museum and the Whitney Gallery of the Buffalo Bill Historical Center. In 1993, his art work was chosen for the Cherokee Strip Commemorative Postage Stamp. His public monuments include *Boomer* in Enid, *Crossing the Red* in Altus, and *Headin' to Market* at the Oklahoma City Stockyards.

MIKE LARSEN of Perkins, Oklahoma, began painting landscapes at age 19. He studied at Amarillo Junior College and the University of Houston. Of Chickasaw heritage, Larsen attempts to produce paintings that are very expressive but historically accurate. The focus and purpose of his painting are shamans, healers, brave warriors, earth mothers, and ballerinas. His tribute to Oklahoma's famous Native American ballet dancers is a permanent mural in the Oklahoma State Capitol. Larsen draws from his experiences of growing up on the plains of Oklahoma and Texas.

ROSS MYERS began his professional art career at age 15 in Tulsa. He graduated with a fine arts degree from the University of Tulsa and owned his own art school for 25 years. He is best known for his expansive landscapes of the southwestern United States and his native Oklahoma. Myers' works have been featured in galleries and museums in several states and can be found in private and corporate collections nationwide.

CHRISTOPHER NICK of Oklahoma City grew up in rural Oklahoma and began as a small child rendering pencil sketches of his observations of nature. Encouraged by his teachers to pursue art, he continued to draw and paint until he was accepted into the Atelier LeSuer in Minneapolis, Minnesota. There he received formal training in the tradition of the Old Masters.

DENNIS PARKER apprenticed to artist Richard Goetz and was trained at the New York Art Student's League and the New York Academy of Art where he spent time with Daniel Green, David Laffel, and Ted Jacobs. From his studio in Oklahoma City, Parker has won honors for pastels and oils. He teaches and demonstrates throughout the state.

KATHRYN WALKER RICHARDSON trained at Oklahoma State University and studied independently with Dennis Parker, Daniel Greene, Bettina Steinke, Harley Brown, and Morgan Weistling. She also attended the New York Art Student's League and the Cape Cod School of Art. She lives in Choctaw, Oklahoma, and has served as a board member of the Oklahoma Arts Council.

LINDA TUMA ROBERTSON of Edmond studied with John Shelby Metcalf at age nine and was introduced to oils which have remained her lifetime focus. Trips with her parents around Oklahoma and the West opened her eyes to the natural beauty of the land. By the time she was 20, her works were displayed at the Kennedy Center in Washington, D. C., and the Oklahoma Museum of Art. Robertson desires to reflect her love for nature and to communicate to the the emotion that led her to paint the scene.

GORDON SNIDOW of Ruidoso, New Mexico, discovered Gilcrease Museum while in elementary school and decided to become a cowboy artist. He was a leader of the development of the American Western Art Movement and is known as the foremost chronicler of the contemporary cowboy. He grew up in Missouri, Texas, and Oklahoma and graduated from Webster High School in Tulsa. He studied at the Art Center College of Design in Los Angeles, California, and is a charter member of the Cowboy Artists of America.

SONYA TERPENING graduated from Oklahoma State University and now paints from her home in Grapevine, Texas. She was won many awards for her painting in transparent water colors. Terpening's works have been shown in the Gilcrease Museum, the National Cowboy and Western Heritage Museum, the Oklahoma Museum of Art, the C. M. Russell Museum, and many other venues. She painted the cover art for histories of Pawnee and Washington counties.

TIMOTHY TYLER began his career as an artist at age 14 in Stratford, Oklahoma. By age 16, his paintings were exhibited at a private gallery. He has exhibited in many American cities and at Gilcrease Museum. His paintings appear in public and private collections worldwide. He lives in Fayetteville, Arkansas.

SANDRA VAN ZANDT of Talala, Oklahoma, studied art at Cottey College in Missouri. She established her reputation with bald eagle sculptures now seen in city, museum, private, and corporate collections throughout the nation. Her *The Spirit of Naval Aviation* stands at the entrance of the National Museum of Naval Aviation in Pensacola, Florida. She has been commissioned to sculpt a series of life-size monuments of Will Rogers for Claremore, Oklahoma, the hometown of both Rogers and Van Zandt.

BARBARA VAUPEL of Henryetta, Oklahoma, taught herself to draw. She left her native California for Oklahoma with the dream of painting horses. Her first commissioned paintings were horse portraits and rodeo scenes, including a portrait of Sam Walton with his hunting dogs and pheasant. In the years preceding her death in 2006, her work turned to landscapes, reflecting her love of the Oklahoma countryside.

CHARLES BANKS WILSON spent much of his career painting documentary portraits of famous Oklahomans. Born in Arkansas, but raised in Miami, Oklahoma, he studied art at the Art Institute of Chicago. With the help of Thomas Hart Benton, Wilson went to New York where he began a career as a book illustrator. He returned to Oklahoma during World War II and taught at Northeastern Oklahoma A & M College. Among his most heralded works are his paintings of Robert S. Kerr, Sequoyah, Jim Thorpe, and Will Rogers that highlight the fourth floor rotunda of the Oklahoma State Capitol.

MIKE WIMMER was born in Muskogee, Oklahoma, where he began painting in the seventh grade. He studied at the University of Oklahoma in Norman where he now lives and works. After painting a portrait of Oklahoma aviator Wiley Post for display in the State Capitol in 1998, Wimmer has added many paintings to the halls of the Oklahoma State Capitol. More of his works are displayed there than those of any other artist. He has illustrated books for most major American publishers and has produced artwork for some of the nation's largest corporations.

JEREMIAH BAKER of Edmond has hand-carved and gilded numerous custom frames for works in the collection.

INDEX TO WORKS BY ARTIST

GENERAL SUBJECT INDEX

G

H

I

J

K

L

M

N

O

P

R

S

T

U